# A MEASURE
# SHORT OF WAR

# A MEASURE SHORT OF WAR

*A BRIEF HISTORY OF GREAT POWER SUBVERSION*

JILL KASTNER
AND
WILLIAM C. WOHLFORTH

**OXFORD**
UNIVERSITY PRESS

Oxford University Press is a department of the University of Oxford.
It furthers the University's objective of excellence in research, scholarship,
and education by publishing worldwide. Oxford is a registered trade mark of
Oxford University Press in the UK and certain other countries.

Published in the United States of America by Oxford University Press
198 Madison Avenue, New York, NY 10016, United States of America.

CIP data is on file at the Library of Congress

ISBN 978–0–19–768316–3

DOI: 10.1093/oso/9780197683163.001.0001

Printed by Sheridan Books, Inc., United States of America

# CONTENTS

# FIGURES

—◦◦◦—

ix

# PREFACE

THE RUSSIAN MEDDLING in the 2016 U.S. presidential campaign took the world by surprise. The affronts were audacious, encompassing lies on social media, the wooing of Trump campaign staffers, hack and leak "doxxing" of Democratic operatives, and alarming probes of election infrastructure. It seemed the very bedrock of American democracy was under attack, subjected to an assault of malign, mischievous fiddling by a familiar old foe from a different era.

Warnings from national security officials between 2014 and 2016 went unheeded. A spy in the Kremlin sent a message that Moscow was beefing up its disinformation capabilities and was hell-bent on interfering in Western democracies. But similar to the lead-up to Pearl Harbor in 1941, the alarm bells were not loud and specific enough to generate anticipation and preparedness. What's more, the novelty of the situation in light of America's quarter-century of geopolitical dominance led to a degree of inertia. China was the new focus, and Russia was a distraction. Intelligence officials struggled to get the go-ahead to push back. "The truth is," one official said, "nobody wanted to piss off the Russians."[1] Those clamoring for a closer look were merely so many Cassandras, doomed to prophesy and remain ignored.

No longer. What 2016 revealed, after parsing the cacophony of pundits and headlines, was that one great power was subverting another, and no one really knew how to deal with it. Indeed, the level of agitation colored the response to the attack. It's easy to forget how the Obama administration was deterred from even publicizing the Russian operation for fear that doing so might elicit retaliation from Moscow that could derail the entire election. That paralysis was in equal measure a result of the apparent novelty of the meddling and the fact that the meddler in this instance was a major power with a reserve capacity to exert a lot more leverage and inflict more pain should things get out of hand.

For those trying to make sense of fast-moving events, finding context proved challenging. "There was no playbook for this," said former Central Intelligence Agency Director John Brennan.[2] There existed little analysis of subversion as a topic, along the lines of the literature on conflict, war, or nuclear escalation. There was no shortage of studies of covert action, but these were overwhelmingly weighted toward great powers acting against weak targets, particularly in the twentieth century. What about peers or near peers? On that subject, there was a dearth of scholarship and understanding. It was clear that there was no agreed taxonomy; subversion was a phrase bandied about but inelegantly applied. And it was frequently used in discussions about a new age of subversion in which we supposedly found ourselves.

But if we were in a new age of subversion, what did that imply? Was there an old age of subversion? Did we think subversion had disappeared and was now resurgent? And how could we know whether we were in a new age of subversion if we didn't have a clear understanding of its overall history? Although an overview of subversion literature readily highlighted subversion's seductive lure, none of it gave us what we wanted, which was a concise but sweeping history that both illustrated subversion's pervasiveness and offered a way to think about its behavior applicable across both geography and time. Such a study would allow us to understand why states choose subversion, why they don't, when they might, against whom, and with what degree of violence. It would place subversion in its proper context in the field of international relations, where it has fallen through the cracks for so long, and examine the sometimes surprising political and strategic barriers to successful subversion. Coming back to our initial focus, it might help us understand the events of 2016 and give us a context for crafting responses to future subversion.

We decided to write this book in hopes of providing a better way to think about great power subversion. We turn the subversion lens onto historical events to see if they take on new meaning. Our aim is to come away smarter, with a roadmap to subversion's role in great power politics. We want to demystify measures short of war.

# ACKNOWLEDGMENTS

THE ORIGINS OF this book lie in our collaboration on a paper that eventually appeared as "A Measure Short of War: The Return of Great Power Subversion" in *Foreign Affairs* in 2021. We are grateful to the magazine's Daniel Kurtz-Phelan and Stuart Reid for taking an interest in our topic, for not giving up on us after our halting early efforts, and for shepherding that essay to publication. In turn, some of the arguments in that article can be traced back to "Realism and Great Power Subversion," the 2019 E. H. Carr Memorial Lecture at the Department of International Politics, University of Aberystwyth. Wohlforth is indebted to Professor Ken Booth and his Aber colleagues for the invitation and for the critical comments they offered along the way to that lecture's publication in the journal *International Relations* in 2020. Wohlforth is also grateful to the Dartmouth students who took his seminar on subversion in great power politics as part of the foreign study programs in London during the fall of 2019 and 2021: Your sharp minds helped hone the arguments that follow.

We've traveled a long road from our early efforts to the writing of the book you hold in your hands. We could never have made it had friends and colleagues not offered their time and wisdom through numerous COVID–era Zoom interviews. Special thanks are due to Dan Fried, Fiona Hill, John Lenczowski, Eric Rubin, Thomas Simons, and Jake

Sullivan. Our thanks for further expertise and moral support go to Doug Brinkley, Paul Feenan, David Gioe, Thea Gioe, William Imboden, Igor Istomin, Loch Johnson, Lachlan Nieboer, Marc Trachtenberg, Gavin Wilde, and James Graham Wilson. We must single out James Stone for his generous assistance in disentangling the intricacies of Otto von Bismarck's diplomatic moves. David Blackbourn, Hugh Bowden, Jeff Freidman, Tom Otte, and Gavin Wilde read all or parts of the manuscript and provided comments that challenged us to raise the bar analytically (and correct some oversights and mistakes). Alex Joel provided truly invaluable research assistance. Thanks to Dave McBride and Mary Funchion at Oxford University Press for taking this on and waiting patiently for the finished product. With all that help along the way, mistakes that remain in the finished product can only be the results of our own shortcomings.

# I

## Subversion 101

THIS BOOK IS an exploration of a very specific tool that states use to advance their interests: targeted, hostile action within another state to weaken it or cause it to alter its policy. We call this *subversion* because that word best conveys the idea of undermining accepted authority, in this case the authority of a state's leaders to set its course or, more generally, the lines of authority that give a state the capacity for purposive action.

We talk of states for convenience, but the concept of subversion applies more broadly to any group in a competitive setting with enough of a social hierarchy to have a recognized leader (or government) who grasps the benefit of in-group cohesion and loyalty. This applies not only to states but also to sprawling colonial empires, city-states, kingdoms, and so on. An outside rival trying to surreptitiously influence events within the polity is inherently hostile. Subversive statecraft thus has this special quality of being aggressive, bad, and dangerous— something the subverter knows the target will regard as untoward, underhanded, sketchy, or dicey. That's why subversion is usually covert or deceptive and why, when it is overt, it is generally resented and resisted by the target.

Our definition emphasizes action that operates *within* the borders of the targeted state. This distinguishes subversion from all the other tools short of war that states may use to affect things going on within other states. To see why this matters, take a step back and ask what states are trying to do with their foreign policy. The answer is clear: influence other states' foreign policies. Getting what you want in international politics entails exerting influence on what other states do. States choose from a large array of tools to achieve such influence: diplomacy, war, alliances, economic blandishments or punishments, and so on. What makes each different is the particular means it employs. Diplomacy is negotiation between governments. War is organized violence. Coercion is a conditional threat to use violence. Alliances are formalized promises to act under certain circumstances. Sanctions are interruptions in normal commerce conditioned on changes in the target's behavior. And so on.

All these tools can operate in two ways: by altering the external environment the target state's leaders face or by affecting the mix of constraints and incentives they confront at home. Although scholars sometimes choose to ignore it, what leaders *want* to do in international relations and what they are actually *capable* of doing are powerfully affected by politics on the home front. Leaders want to stay in power, so they keep an eye on domestic opponents. Leaders need to extract resources domestically to pursue international aims, so they care about domestic cohesion and the functioning of the institutions they use to manage politics and economics at home. Many policy tools are thus aimed at affecting things within the target state. Sanctions, for example, harm the target's domestic economy and weaken its capability to act. They might also cause disarray, disaffection, pressure to change policy, and even attempts at regime change. But almost all policy tools can work on the target leaders' domestic front. Even diplomacy can work this way: A state may couch a formal diplomatic proposal to a target government with an eye toward appealing to domestic factions.

What distinguishes subversion thus cannot be its domestic focus, which is a routine feature of many policy tools. Rather, it is *where* this tool operates that marks it as distinct: directly inside the target. Although diplomacy, economic statecraft, alliances, and so on all can work by influencing what happens within the target, they operate externally, and usually indirectly. The idea is, "If we can create the right external pressures or inducements, people inside the target will get the message and try to change policy, or change leaders, or the country will be too weak to act against us." In contrast, the subverter also wants to make things happen within the target but does so by *acting directly within it.*

We define subversion as *hostile* to the current rulers within the target state and *seeking effects* by direct action inside it. Recall that subversion undermines authority. If a foreign power acts inside a state by invitation, if the state's current leaders welcome it, it does not qualify as subversion. Covert action in support of the incumbent government is not subversion. When President Franklin Roosevelt welcomed the activities of British intelligence on American soil to help bring the United States into the war against Nazi Germany, for example, this did not count as subversion by our definition.[1] Covert yes, but not subversive.

It is important to stress how distinctive this definition is. Under it, behaviors that many people might not consider subversive—such as human rights promotion—may count as such because our focus is on the perspective of the people running the foreign policy of the target state. From this viewpoint, actions on their territory by foreign governments that undermine their policy are by definition subversive, and actions in support of their policy are not. Our focus is on subversion's place in interactions *between* governments, and this means we have to foreground the perspective of incumbent rulers even if we object to those rulers' purposes. We seek to understand the strategic dynamics that occur when a government meddles against another, and that entails considering how targets respond to hostile external interference. The strategic desiderata that emerge when a foreign meddler acts with an incumbent ruler against other domestic forces are also important, to be sure, but they are a different kettle of fish.

Cases of closely divided governments admittedly place stress on this definition. If, for example, President Donald Trump had accepted Russian help against Joe Biden in the 2020 U.S. presidential election, it would have been distasteful, shocking, and a sad day for American democracy, but it would not have been subversion by our definition, strictly applied. Still, in that case, the subverter would have had to consider the possibility that its interference would fail; that the person responsible for U.S. foreign policy might soon be named Biden; and thus that its meddling would indeed be met with a punitive response, even if delayed. In that case, some of the constraints on subversion that arise from the target's potential responses (discussed below) would still apply.

Finally, if external action inside a target state is hostile but does not seek to produce effects inside the target, it also does not fit our definition. Gathering intelligence via espionage or stealing secrets and bringing them back home for use is hostile and constitutes direct action within the target, but it does not directly produce effects inside the target. Spying and theft are not subversion by our definition. Yet if information acquired via espionage is subsequently disseminated within the target to undermine authority, it is subversion. The hacking and leaking of information from the Democratic National Committee in 2016 was a case of subversion, not just theft.

Note, finally, that we focus on subversion as a measure *short* of war, not a measure undertaken in war. Subversion can be an aim or tactic of belligerent states at war, but for reasons that will become clear presently, the logic governing subversion among non-belligerents (or not-yet-belligerents) is sufficiently different to warrant its own study. To be sure, the bright line between peace and war can be blurred in some periods and some cases. But overall, the distinction is clear enough to be useful for our analysis.

Subversion is worth the time and trouble to define and analyze because it has a particular effect upon the target that other forms of statecraft do not (aside from war). It constitutes a form of micro-invasion, a violation, creating the psychological state of fear that the enemy is or might be inside the tent. To borrow from Hollywood, it's the point in the horror movie when the protagonist realizes the call is coming from inside the house. Subversion causes this consternation when discovered because it has on occasion been very successful. Usually, those cases of decisive subversion occur when a great power targets a smaller power, but there are the occasional decisive moments between great powers as well. Proof of subversion's fearsome reputation is to be found in governments' reaction to it. As cases we discuss below show, democracies can be pretty brutal against it, and autocracies can be much worse.

## Looking at Subversion in a New Way

Most writing on international politics focuses on standard tools of policy such as diplomacy, balancing, and war, without explicitly thinking through how they are related to subversive statecraft. Yet to understand this above-board realm of international politics, we argue, you need to grapple with its subversive undercurrent. And to appreciate the role subversion plays, we need to look at it in a new way, elevating it to its rightful position in the pantheon of foreign policy tools, right alongside diplomacy, balancing, and war. Thus viewed, subversion transcends the way it is typically perceived—as manipulative, disruptive, and skulduggerous behavior that "bad" actors employ for nefarious purposes—and becomes a subject of serious study and thought.

But we are faced with an obstacle: how to organize a bewildering array of behavior that is united chiefly by its subversive, authority-undermining nature. Previous studies have taken a variety of approaches to this challenge. A half century ago, the amateur historian (and close friend of Ronald Reagan) Laurence W. Beilenson published a sweeping history of subversion portraying Lenin as a master strategist who transformed the practice utterly—and making a plea for the United States to follow suit.[2] Lenin-obsessed though it was, the book's approach to its subject is the closest to ours. Yet perhaps because of its quirky (although admirably learned) qualities, Beilenson's approach never gained traction among intelligence professionals, analysts, and scholars. For the most part, the tactic since then has been to lump subversion, espionage, and covert action together under the general heading of "intelligence studies." That is understandable: Subversion is one of the things intelligence agencies do. Governments call upon their intelligence services for subversion because those are the agencies that specialize in covert action.[3] But subversion existed long before intelligence agencies were conceived, and those agencies also engage in activities such as intelligence collection that function under a completely different political logic.

Recognizing that different logics apply to different activities within that broad category, scholars more recently have begun to break it down into specific activities, such as election meddling, propaganda, disinformation, proxy wars, or regime change operations.[4] Others highlight the experience of a particular country or a particular historical period—usually the Cold War.[5] Some organize their subject by level of subversiveness as defined by specific interests or ideologies. Political scientist Loch Johnson created an influential "ladder" of covert action with rungs defined by reference to international law as it stood in the

1990s: The more blatantly an operation violated those norms, the more escalatory it was deemed to be.[6] But as mentioned above, not all covert action is subversive. And 1990s understandings of the rights and wrongs of cross-border covert action do not apply to other eras (nor even to all states at the time). Other writers organize covert or "gray zone" action according to anticipated escalation, which depends on the precise interests and stakes in a specific setting.[7] What constitutes escalation in a given rivalry thus hinges entirely on its specific details and history.[8]

Then there is the possibility of judging subversive activity by the scale of the effort or the outcome, by its "severity" or its "success."[9] But to classify and explore subversion in this way, one must unpack the subverter's intent or the subversion's impact, something easier to do within a specific case than across a large number of cases. Subversion can be aimed at two general kinds of effects: a change in policy or a general weakening of the target state (either of which, in extremis, might entail a change of its regime). And although these different subversive aims may generally track severity, they will not always be readily distinguishable. Sometimes, forcing a target to change its policy is a way to weaken it, and sometimes imposing costs via subversion to weaken a target is intended as a bargaining tool to get it to change its policy.

None of these approaches works for us. Studies that focus on specific tools, periods, and actors have the luxury of precise definitions that can take a lot for granted. And they rarely explore the nuance of how subversion varies depending on whether it occurs between great power peers or between strong and weak states. In practice, this means that most of what we know about subversion has to do with the powerful subverting the weak, and it fails to highlight distinctions between great power–weak power subversion and peer-on-peer subversion. In addition, our store of knowledge is heavily stocked with evidence from the Cold War.

In contrast, this book casts a very wide net, considering subversion across a broad variety of actors and historical periods. Although we touch on all kinds of subversion to provide context, we want to narrow our focus to its role among competing great powers, states that possess the lion's share of resources in international politics, because that's where we can best see the constraints on subversion. As we show below, there are persuasive reasons to expect that subversion will operate differently between the Goliaths than between the Goliaths and the Davids. After all, these states are called great powers for a reason: Since 1815, the top five or six countries have controlled 60–80% of the resources—military and economic—in the world. Subverting one of them—even a little bit—promises potentially huge gains, but it also poses especially large risks, casting a special shadow over subversive statecraft among these behemoths.

Although rare cases of overt subversion are easier for us to explore, the bulk of our material deals with covert subversive operations, and like all works on covert statecraft, ours faces the challenges of missing pieces of the historical record. But precisely because we cast such a wide net, covering so many cases in so many historical periods, we can have some confidence that we are capturing the overall nature of the phenomenon.

There are big payoffs to our capacious but great power–focused approach: It allows us to see the threads that connect diplomacy, rivalry, and war among history's most consequential states. These are threads that you can't see if you ignore subversion or define it too narrowly. And it allows us to appreciate all the subversion that great powers might undertake but choose not to. That opens a window to understanding the ways in which the above-board foreign policy we *do* see might be influenced by potential subversion we do *not* see.

## Types of Subversion

Trying to dissect subversion, to impose a taxonomy of types and tools, is not just an intellectual exercise. It is crucial because the very quality that lends subversion its power—confusion and its attendant anxieties and paranoias—is the thing that must be addressed in order to counter it. And countering it has taken on new importance since 2016. The explosion in the number of government agencies designed to deal with subversive activity since the Russian election meddling is a reminder that in order to tackle a problem, you must first define and understand it.

The point of subversion is simple: to weaken a target state or induce it to change its policy. Yet there is a seemingly endless variety of ways to bring this about. Subversive activities can be used to weaken a target state by providing logistical, organizational, or financial support for a divisive domestic movement, thus distracting the government from pursuing its interest on some other front. They can be deployed to change another country's foreign policy by supporting one side of a domestic debate. Interference in local referenda might be used to sow doubt about long-standing alliances with neighboring countries, or even about the institutions of the target country itself. And then there is the apex predator of subversive action, regime change. If the subverter cannot overcome the existing government's policy or commitments by other means, or if a different ruler might prove a weaker rival, regime change might be in the offing. Coups and assassination are obvious tools for such pursuits. But a subverter could also employ any of the tactics we have mentioned, from propaganda for the overthrow of a regime to financial support of opposition political parties, to achieve the same goal. If the people rise up, if the subverter's favored candidate wins, the subverter will have achieved its goal at a cost far cheaper than war.

But how to tame such complexity? To organize our broad approach to subversion as a tool of foreign policy, we focus on its variation along two dimensions: violence and covertness. A subversive operation may be entirely nonviolent, or it may entail the use of force, from dispatching a lone assassin to deploying a large insurgency. And it might be completely covert, implausibly deniable, or even overt.

Overt subversion might include public statements; attributed news stories; or "white propaganda," where the source of information is acknowledged and the target population is aware of the information's provenance. Overt activities might include transparent material assistance to groups or forces within the target country, such as open funding of opposition political groups or attributed public information campaigns promoting a goal antithetical to the existing regime.

Overt subversion may seem like an oxymoron at first, and its inclusion here may raise an eyebrow. After all, subversion is hostile and transgressive, and those undertaking it will normally want to obscure their agency. But there are two principal reasons for including overt subversive activity. The first is that, as we will show, sometimes an action can have greater impact *because* it is overt. Suppose, for example, there are masses of people in the target state that are strongly attached to the subverter and opposed to their own government. In such a case, subversive actions such as propaganda or electoral interference gain strength by identification with the subverter. There was a time, for example, when communist parties' connection to Moscow was a selling point. The Communist International's headquarters was in Moscow, and party leaders from countries throughout the world overtly traveled there to receive instructions from Stalin. Some deniability was maintained with the putative separation between the party and the Soviet government, but that was widely seen for the fig leaf it was. The whole arrangement was close to the overt end of the spectrum.

The second is to allow for ideological myopia. States conceal their role in subversion in part because it is seen as bad and underhanded. But we need to allow for the possibility that some overt activities on a rival's territory may seem subversive despite a lack of truly subversive intent on the part of the perpetrator, which thus makes no effort to hide its agency. One state's exuberant proselytizing may be another state's subversion. The goal is still to effect changes within the target state, but the subverter may adhere to an ideology that justifies or legitimates it. In professing mere fealty to the higher principle justifying its involvement in the target's domestic politics, the intervening state may well abjure any subversive intent. That is, when a state can legitimate meddling in another's domestic affairs by citing some principle or ideology, the action may be overt but the subversive *intent* may be concealed. Indeed, leaders may even believe that they are somehow "helping" the target state. We see this, for example, with medieval popes and Catholic monarchs seeking to return Protestant rebels to the fold, with states using human rights principles to justify actions that defy other states' sovereignty, or even with well-meaning democracy promotion in the 1990s and beyond.

Although overt action sometimes has a role to play, the fact remains that subversion usually falls toward the covert end of the spectrum. In most cases, most of the time, states try to obscure their role in subversive action.[10] The psychological shift, the sense of heightened danger or affront or aggression, from overt to covert is undeniable. One can imagine that it works on an inter-state level in a way similar to that between individuals, where deception is perceived as a major transgression in the relationship, usually with dire consequences.

What causes a subverter to move from overt to covert activity? Separately or together, four incentives push the subverter to make an underhanded thing—subversion—even more underhanded by adding deception—lying—to the mix. The first incentive would be to conceal the activity from the subverter's own domestic political audience. There are many reasons for that, including the public's moral qualms and a leader's desire to avoid oversight and judgment if the operation fails or backfires. This is of course mostly a problem in democracies. The second incentive is to avoid a situation in which overtness works against success because association with a foreign power undermines the project. Propaganda may lose its persuasive power if it is viewed as clearly serving the interests of a foreign state. Election interference may backfire in any setting in which nationalism or patriotism matters to voters. An insurgency's appeal might fade if it is perceived as the tool of an external actor with its own agenda. The third incentive is to avoid the reputational costs of violating norms against subversive action. To the degree that states operate under mutual understandings of appropriate behavior that proscribe meddling in domestic affairs, they will wish to deny doing so, if possible.[11] The fourth incentive for covertness is to control escalation. As we've stressed, subversion is transgressive, hostile, and threatening. It seeks to undermine the authority of the target. It is unwelcome, to say the least. It thus always risks retaliation. If the target is genuinely unsure of the identity of the subverter, however, it cannot retaliate.

Covert subversion is much better known and understood in the popular mind than its overt cousin. The events of 2016 burned the topic into the American public consciousness, although such recognition came much earlier for Estonians, Ukrainians, Georgians, and other Moscow targets. The power of covert information warfare on a target population has been well known since ancient times; even Thucydides understood the ease with which an audience can be swayed. "Most people," he wrote, "will not take trouble in finding out the truth, but are much more inclined to accept the first story they hear."[12] Gray and black propaganda, in which the source of the information is disguised or denied, plays a starring role in covert subversion, as does disinformation, defined as outright lies disguised as truth—an increasing problem in the age of artificial intelligence and the internet. Unlike rhetoric, propaganda, disinformation, and forgeries shy away from skilled argument and rigorous testing. They seek to persuade without consent.

Further covert activities encompass the full range of malign behavior commonly associated with subversion, including economic sabotage and secret financial and material support for opposition groups, such as cash for political campaigns, bribes, radio transmitters, printing gear or Xerox machines, and so on. A subverter can covertly manipulate public information, such as through the theft or hack and release of sensitive data, for the benefit of an opposition actor or to weaken the existing regime and its institutions. And then there are the really big kinetic tools used in the most widely known cases, again usually of great power on small power subversion: sabotage, assassination, coups, and regime change.

One convoluted aspect of covert subversion revolves around the concept of deniability. "Covert" implies that an operation aims to be deniable if discovered. This helps mitigate the costs of loss of trust associated with a target realizing it has already been attacked. Yet there is also a liminal in-between category of implausibly denied subversion. The subverter clearly still wishes to be able to deny responsibility, but we acknowledge special dynamics in play when covertness is truly just a fig leaf. Implausibly deniable statecraft became especially salient to analysts in the 1980s in response to the "Reagan Doctrine" of major support for anti-communist insurgencies in Nicaragua and Afghanistan.[13] But it's hardly a new phenomenon. As noted, the Soviet government's support of the Comintern in the 1920s and 1930s, for example, was common knowledge even as Moscow implausibly denied it. In both cases, the "open secret" suspicion of the adversary at work helped amplify the effect of the subversion itself. If a government wants to send a signal through covert action, it must make it less than perfectly covert. Why was polonium used to kill Russian defector Alexander Litvinenko in London in 2007 and the Russian nerve agent Novichok used in an attempted assassination of Sergei Skripal in Salisbury in 2018? Although these are not instances of subversion per se, they illustrate the appeal of strategic ambiguity surrounding a government's agency.

In some cases, the logic of implausible denial can govern both the subverter and the target. Both may desire to avoid escalation and so may implicitly collude in implausibly denying the intervening state's responsibility. For example, the Soviet leadership knew that the United States was supporting the Afghan mujahideen in the 1980s. U.S. leaders maintained the fiction of denying responsibility—in the face of overwhelming evidence to the contrary—to reduce pressure on Soviet leaders to retaliate. If the target wants to keep its option for cooperation open, it may choose to play along with the implausible deniability script.[14]

Finally, the distinction between nonviolent and violent action is a serious one, but there are also gradations. Subverters know that the physical destruction of life or property represents a distinct kind of action. Violent subversion includes not only the old weapons of sabotage, assassination, and funding of armed insurgencies but also cyber activities that result in damage to infrastructure or endangerment of human life. Violent subversion can be either overt or covert, but above a certain threshold, overt violence would blur the line between measures short of war and war itself. There are many steps up to that threshold, ranging from inserting a tiny number of saboteurs in a rubber dinghy on a beach to creating and arming a full-blown insurgency on the target's territory.

### The Pros and Cons of Subversion

Understanding how subversion is used requires a clear vision of its pros and cons. On the pro side, subversion is above all cheap. That's the reason states have turned to it so often throughout history: It can be much less costly than conventional statecraft. To strengthen its position vis-à-vis a rival, a state need not resort to balancing and war if subversion might promise the same results for a fraction of the investment. To change a rival's policy, a state need not engage in coercion, deterrence, expensive economic blandishments, or entangling diplomacy if subversion offers a cheaper option. Why bother raising an army and invading an adversary if you can use the subtler tools of spreading propaganda, paying politicians, or dispatching internet trolls to achieve similar ends? Why ensnare yourself in complicated alliances or break the bank building up your military to contain a rival if you can simply join forces with a faction on the inside? Even if subversion is not potent enough to substitute for traditional statecraft, it can still serve as a surreptitious handmaiden. A gain is a gain. And if the target is a great power with potent capabilities and a wide web of influence, even a nudge can matter a lot.

In addition to being cheap, subversion is flexible. A state can target a variety of pressure points to induce an adversary to change its behavior without having to lob artillery across the border or agree to expensive commitments, inducements, or concessions. If the situation heats up, subversion can be denied, or subversive actions dialed down, allowing the subverter an escape route in a rapidly escalating environment. The general who starts a war just to see how far he can get is a fool; the subverter who subverts for the same reason is simply being rational.

That flexibility extends to victims as well. With subversion, a target state has breathing room to practice restraint and consider its options, a luxury not present when tanks are driving across the border in a war. Ironically, states may decide not to retaliate too hard against subversion because they want to retain the right to use it themselves. They might tacitly collude with each other to tolerate some measure of subversion, each thinking that now or in the future the meddling game might work to their own advantage.

Together, these potential benefits suggest that subversion can also act as a safety valve to prevent war. If a state has a big enough stake in an issue, war might be the unhappy outcome without subversion to provide other options. The subverting state has an alternative method of advancing its position without resorting to force in the first instance. Ukraine was a salient and recent case in point, until the Ukrainians became so skilled at fighting back in the gray zone that Vladimir Putin made the fateful decision to invade. Kicking the can down the road is sometimes an attractive option for all parties concerned.

With all those benefits, why don't we see subversion more often? The answer lies in the hefty list of drawbacks attached to it. There are prosaic but important operational challenges at all levels. Making propaganda credible to a foreign audience, finding and manipulating political operatives in the target, or supporting local insurgents are not easy tasks, especially in distant targets. And subversion tends to run into tough trade-offs among conflicting goals. It is difficult simultaneously to achieve a major impact while maintaining secrecy and control over the operation, especially if large numbers of local operatives are involved.[15]

Retaliation is always a danger, and the more powerful the target, the more dangerous the retaliation might be. A target may retaliate in kind, subverting the subverter, but it might choose other means, including sanctions or war. And that may push the subverter to raise the stakes in reply. Escalation, in short, is a risk whenever subversion is attempted. This may occur in a carefully calculated series of moves and countermoves, with the option for leaders to dial back at any stage, or it could escape leaders' control. This is especially true with violent action, when actors on the ground may exceed their brief or, in the age of cyber-attacks, when physical damage may travel in unintended directions and the list of victims may extend far beyond the target.

The risk of escalation is connected to a second downside of subversion: its clunkiness as a tool for signaling intentions, one of the most important aspects of international statecraft. When one state seeks to alter another's behavior, it has a range of options. Diplomacy is the starting point, followed by wielding other traditional carrots and sticks, including, in extreme cases, a building up of military forces. These actions are used to send messages to the target state, something to the tune of "change your behavior, and we'll offer you carrots—or, if you refuse, we'll use the stick." The message is that the state seeking change is not unalterably hostile to its rival but is merely searching for a way to achieve its goals, and it only intends to impose costs if the target state does not acquiesce in some way. It is a dance designed to induce the desired behavior without actually using the stick.

Subversion—direct and unwelcome action on the target's territory—lacks much of the adroit contingency of above-board foreign policy. Its attractive flexibility comes with considerable risk. If discovered, its directness risks conveying the message that the subverter has given up on persuading the target government and simply wants to weaken or change it. The fact that it occurs against the target's wishes also conveys hostility. If the target rulers had their druthers, foreign powers would not be messing about in their domestic affairs. The subverter is consciously violating that preference. To be sure, the subverter may wish to send the message that its meddling is contingent upon some change in the target's policy. But it is much more difficult to convey that signal when you are directly undermining the authority of your target. This awkward situation is exacerbated by the fact that perpetrators usually deny subversion. Tacit signaling in that shady setting is a fraught game. It is challenging, to say the least, for a state to pretend it isn't doing something while also offering to stop.

The signaling challenge is about intentions, what a state plans to do to realize its aims. It blends into another, even deeper problem: the subverter's motives, the deep sources driving those aims. Intentions are about what a state plans to do; motives are about why it wants to do it.[16] The Ur-question of foreign policy is, "What is driving that state to do what it does"? Or, "Whom am I dealing with, a Hitler, a Stalin, a Brezhnev, a Gorbachev"? What all leaders want to avoid is misplaced trust, taking the role of Chamberlain at Munich, mistaking Hitler for a more limited-aims revisionist. With all leaders on the lookout for misplaced trust, if you are actually *not* a leader with massively malign motives, the last thing you want to do is to be misperceived as such. If subversion is detected, the risk is you'll move the needle on the target's estimate of your motives toward the malign end of the scale. You face the danger of being taken for a Stalin or Hitler, even if you're actually a Brezhnev or a Gorbachev.

This potential to erode trust, the lifeblood of international relations, is a major downside of subversion. After all, subversion is an affront, aggressive, not a declaration of war but undeniably an escalation of rivalry. Even the wariest of rivals frequently need to cooperate, if only to avoid unwanted escalation. And cooperation requires some confidence that the other side is trustworthy, that it will reciprocate cooperation. Even if the rivalry is intense, a small measure of trust can provide hope for cooperation and de-escalation in the future. Such trust can be sustained even in the face of traditional military build-ups, threatening alliances or hostile signaling, because those are indirect actions that only have direct effect in some future contingency.

But once direct action has been undertaken to undermine the target government's authority, it may conclude that the subverter is irredeemably hostile and can't be trusted. In other words, subversion might push the target to reclassify you from an actor driven by motives that allow some trust in cooperation to one who will greedily accept any concession and then stab you in the back—from a Gorbachev to a Stalin or a

Hitler. If you don't actually have those greedy and hostile motives and want to cooperate on some things, subversion can be a risky move.

## How to Think About Subversion

To recap, subversion offers a load of potential benefits to a state trying to achieve a gain. It promises big payoffs at a small cost; it's scalable, (mostly) deniable, and can offer new or complementary options for action when other tools of statecraft come up short. These pros are balanced by some serious downsides. At some hard-to-define threshold, subversion runs the risk of punishing retaliation and escalation. And even if the subverter means to use it as a cheap and flexible tool of statecraft, it might send an unwanted signal of hostile intent and malign motives that undermine trust.

This cost–benefit trade-off means that subversion can play out in complicated ways. A regime might conclude that the situation between rival states is so bad, or the level of hostility has grown so high, that trust no longer matters and subversion is worth a try. It may regard its rival as so much weaker that a subversive operation is undertaken with a measure of impunity. It may be out of other good options, lacking the political heft for diplomatic success, lacking allies for balancing, or lacking economic weight for effective blandishments or sanctions. It may determine that its diplomacy needs a boost and opt to stir up domestic politics in its peer rival to give its diplomatic agenda more traction. It may simply choose to be a thorn in its rival's side, weakening the target through a harassment operation of disinformation or violence. A weaker power may use just such a campaign to distract its rival, buy time, or force itself onto the agenda: Russia in 2016 was arguably in this position.

In thinking about all these possibilities, which factors might we expect to play the most salient role in subversion's story? What enables or constrains subversion? Five factors stand out in the vast relevant literature on international politics and intelligence: power, norms, operational challenges, target vulnerability and technology.

If we were to poll scholars of international relations, they would emphasize the importance of power.[17] Power can refer to many things: military capabilities, economic resources, diplomatic influence, and leverage. It acts as both an enabler and a constraint. From the subverter's perspective, power considerations affect the calculus in deciding whether to act. Can the subverter afford to jeopardize trust that might be needed on some other front? Is it confident in its ability to defend against possible military or economic retaliation? For the target, power helps deter unwelcome subversion in the first place. Can the target credibly threaten the hostile subverter with retaliation? Can it rally allies against the subverter? Can it issue sanctions that damage the subverter's economy?

Power can affect the type of subversion and its level of violence. If two states are roughly equal in power, the constraints—fear of escalation or retaliation and fear of losing opportunities through the destruction of trust or reputation—are high, and one great power would think twice before having a subversive go at its great power rival. Even if it does decide to subvert, we would expect it to stay in the shadows, focusing on information operations or political meddling rather than sabotage, assassination, or other more kinetic avenues. On the other hand, power disparities lie behind some of the more spectacular instances of decisive subversion throughout history. This is only logical: All else being equal, a big and powerful state is more likely to try subversion against a weaker adversary because it's not that worried about its weaker victim's ability to strike back. In addition, although the downside risks of signaling hostile intent and eroding trust still matter, they generally matter less when dealing with a much weaker target. The upshot is that we are likely to see more—and bigger—subversion of small powers by big powers than among great power peers. This is what gives us the greatest hits list of subversive activity, most recently in the Cold War. Great powers tried stuff on smaller powers that they would never dream of trying with a stronger rival. This dynamic informs one of our findings: Among great powers, the gloves generally stay on, and subversion, when it happens, is usually limited to nonviolent options, such as propaganda and disinformation.

On a more granular level, we also need to consider the special power of great powers. In general, the more robust institutions and wealth of great powers make them more expensive to take on. They are tougher targets on the home front, with stronger counter-subversive capabilities across the board: domestic police and intelligence bureaucracies, communications, public education systems, and so on. In addition, their huge material capability gives them greater opportunities to act far from their own shores. They can contemplate retaliation in faraway and inconvenient locations for the subverter. They also can influence allies and other partners. Of course, not all great powers are perfect peers: Even in a great power dyad, power imbalances may occur that can incentivize subversion. But it's clear that subversion between peer great powers will play out differently than similar subversive efforts between equally matched states lower in the power hierarchy. A great power would need a powerful incentive to attempt subversion against a tough great power foe.

Cases in which stronger powers are constrained or weaker powers try their hand at subverting a stronger rival tell us that there is much more going on than just sheer power dynamics. If we were to return to those same international relations scholars polled earlier, many would talk about the importance of norms: shared beliefs about right and wrong. In international politics, one of the most important of these norms is sovereignty. Our own definition of subversion centers on this idea: that a state has ultimate authority within its territory, and other states must not interfere in it without permission. There exists a rich literature about this, often said to have been enshrined in the much-heralded Peace of Westphalia, inked in 1648 at the end of the Thirty Years' War.[18] In the ensuing centuries, sovereignty became a cherished norm in the international relations pantheon. For many pundits and scholars, it is axiomatic that the impropriety and consequences of violating this norm act as a deterrent to subversion. And in the first instance, this may be true. States know that they are not supposed to meddle in another's territory, and so it requires a conflict important enough to risk reputation and loss of trust before a rival will contemplate it.

But this is a malleable constraint. After all, we know that the norm of sovereignty is routinely honored in the breach when big powers decide to meddle in small ones. There has never been a time when the world witnessed perfect sovereignty, perfectly respected for its own sake. Other norms that allow or even demand violations of sovereignty are always present. Transnational ideas around religion, identity, or ideology, for example, have been used at various points to justify the violation of sovereignty itself. Protecting oppressed co-religionists has frequently been the battle cry of the subverter. So too is the advocacy of an ideology antithetical to that of a rival power. The most glaringly obvious example of this in recent history is the public rhetoric surrounding the promotion of communism or democracy. These norms may be invoked to provide a moral or ideological fig leaf for aggressive subversion.

It turns out that norms, like power, can act as either a constraint upon or an enabler of subversion. The upshot? Norms do not prevent subversive behavior. Sometimes they encourage a subverter to give it a righteous try. At other times, the opprobrium attached to the idea of violating the norm of sovereignty merely tends to drive subversive behavior underground. Although ideas about sovereignty will doubtless influence strategic choice, over the long haul what matters is the ability of the state to enforce its sovereignty, not the norm of sovereignty itself.

If you were to poll intelligence practitioners and scholars, they would highlight a third factor: operational obstacles. In contrast to power and norms, which can both incentivize and deter subversion, operational obstacles act as a straightforward constraint. Subverting a state generally imposes requirements that work against each other. Speed, secrecy, impact/scale, and control are all desirable but difficult to achieve simultaneously. For example, when the target hardens its defenses, if you want effects, the operation needs to scale up, which tends to compromise secrecy or control or both. Big operations become noisy and easier to detect; small, stealthy operations struggle to achieve speed and impact.[19] The end result is that, on the ground, subversion is often self-limiting.

Logistical obstacles constrain subversion, but the two final factors are pure enablers. The first is the set of conditions within the target state itself. Vulnerabilities can present opportunities a rival may not be able to resist. Domestic factions, social and political polarization, or the presence of fifth columns or fellow travelers provide cracks in the social and political foundations that an adversary can exploit. Natural disasters, the aftermath of war, and other exogenous shocks also can provide temporary openings for an opportunistic subverter. The second enabler of subversion is the advent of new technologies, which may be imagined as another example of an exogenous shock, particularly in communications. The printing press, the radio, and the internet have all transformed the battlefield of subversion, forcing victim states to scramble to counter their effects. They usually succeed, but the initial phase following a new technology's appearance can prompt an opportunistic adversary to give subversion a try.

These are the main factors whose interplay either encourages subversion or holds it at bay. But what causes a shift in a rivalry from other forms of statecraft to subversion? Where does *intent* come from? One source is frustration. When other tools of statecraft aren't delivering, subversion begins to look increasingly attractive. When diplomacy isn't working, when hostility is high, or when a state lacks the military or economic punch to force an issue it cannot afford to abandon, subversion is a rational addition to the mix. Another source is having less and less to lose. Escalation as a constraint loses its impact as relations deteriorate and rivalry ramps up. Likewise, signaling and trust matter only to the degree that the subverter cares about its reputation and perceives a benefit from cooperation, bargaining, or negotiation. As we move from total amity to total enmity, the constraints of trust and signaling weaken, and subversion becomes more likely.

Thinking about constraints and enablers of subversion in this way helps us in our quest to understand great power subversion. The constraints we've listed operate most strongly among great power peers that have a lot to lose if cooperation breaks down, and less strongly when we deal with power imbalances or existential conflicts. This affirms a pattern that scholars have already established: The most, and most intense, subversion (regime change, violence) tends to involve strong versus weak targets or peers at war.[20] We are curious to take that a step further and look for larger trends. How has great power subversion changed over time? How does the Russian meddling of 2016 fit into this framework? And what does this lead us to expect from great power subversion in the future?

### Moving Forward

We have defined subversion as a distinct tool of statecraft short of war, drawn upon the most relevant stock of expert knowledge about international politics to identify opportunities for subversion, and highlighted the ways in which we expect great power subversion to be special or different. The next step is to expose our rough and ready framework to the real experience of great powers through time. This will allow us to explore subversion's costs and benefits in more detail before we zero in on its twenty-first-century manifestation.

What follows is a series of historical cases, a sampling of great power on great power subversion from antiquity to the present day, surveyed in Chapters 2–5. Because it would be impossible to investigate every case of subversive activity through every society and epoch, we narrow our historical focus to four periods: classical antiquity, early modern Europe, and the nineteenth and twentieth centuries. Our cases may be limited compared to the universe of possibilities, but they encompass massive variation. We examine subversive episodes that are ancient, early modern, and modern. We chronicle subversion among city-states, sprawling contiguous empires, classic overseas colonial empires, modern nation states, monarchies, democracies, oligarchies, fascist states, and communist dictatorships. We shine light on subversion in multipolar and bipolar international systems.

Examining these episodes of great power politics through the lens of subversion will help us refine our understanding. Once we've explored subversion's history, we'll use Chapters 6–8 to put 2016 in context. We begin by telling the story of great power subversion's brief exit from the world stage after the end of the Cold War and then chronicle its subsequent roaring return, showing both the immediate origins of Russia's 2016 operations and their relation to subversion's long history.

Finally, we take a moment to look back and look forward. Chapter 9 reviews and refines the framework we developed here in light of our extended historical journey. Chapter 10 then offers an assessment of what the future holds for subversion in great power politics.

# 2

## Classical Antiquity
### Greece and Rome

IF WE'RE GOING to examine subversion across time, we must start at the beginning. The ancient world is rife with examples of one "power," whether it's a group of exiles, a tribe, a clan, or a city-state, trying to get its way in a dispute with another by using the tools of subversion we've laid out. Read Sun Tzu's *The Art of War* and see the emphasis on deception in the Warring States period of China. Victoria Hui shows how the rise of one state to dominance reached a critical point when all the other states could see the writing on the wall. "In mapping out a grand strategy for the final wars of unification," Hui writes, Qin's leader "Li Si understood that other states, facing imminent death, would fiercely resist Qin. To preempt last-minute balancing efforts, Qin complemented military campaigns with handsome bribes." She notes that "it is unlikely that Qin could have achieved domination without such tactics."[1] Bribe is the operative word here: Money talks.

Read Kautilya's *Arthashastra*, the classic early Indian manual of statecraft, and you'll note the same emphasis prevailing in the state system of India in the fourth century BC, before its consolidation into the Mauryan Empire. Again, you'll see a focus on covert influence as a means to weaken the internal coherence of rivals.[2] "Miraculous results," it claims, "can be achieved by practicing the methods of subversion."[3]

Repeatedly, the same theme emerges: Before you attack, it helps to have inside help, invidiously cultivated.

We see this in spades in the rivalries of the ancient Mediterranean, first in classical Greece, that period between the Persian Wars at the beginning of the fifth century BC and the death of Alexander the Great in 323 BC, and then in Rome during both the Republic and the Empire. Although we cannot expect the same degree of granular detail as we encounter in later periods, we can rely on Herodotus, Thucydides, Plutarch, and their contemporaries to give us valuable insight into the politics of the great power states (or equivalent thereof) during this time. They paint a portrait of a war-prone Mediterranean world teeming with fractious city-states of various sizes, continually forming and shifting alliances in the quest for power, wealth, and protection.

Modern scholars might argue that imposing our ideas about subversion upon the ancient world is anachronistic because the ancients had no idea of our modern concept of sovereignty. This is linked to those discussions of the norm of sovereignty—in which one state should not meddle on the territory of another—supposedly laid out in the Treaties of Westphalia that ended the Thirty Years' War in 1648. Yet there is ample evidence that the sovereign concept was alive and well in the old days, despite the lack of international relations theorists to elucidate it. Scholars point to three things the ancients did have that add up to something that looks an awful lot like sovereignty. First was the idea of "autonomy," rooted in the Greek word *autonomia* and referring in fifth-century Greece to the resistance against Athens' increasing power and attempts to control smaller states. A similar concept, *eleutheria* or "freedom," also reflected smaller powers seeking to be free from the control or influence of larger, stronger powers. Second was the notion of territory, jealously guarded. The political scientist Dan Reiter notes that

> several Athenian actions of non restraint directly violated smaller power territoriality, including seizing economic assets like mines and ports, demanding that smaller power lands be granted to Athenian settlers, tearing down fortifications of smaller powers such as city walls, or sending garrison troops. These violations of territoriality often facilitated the violation of smaller powers' autonomy, especially

if such actions made the smaller power weaker in relation to Athens, thereby facilitating Athenian coercion.[4]

Finally, the history of this period is full of treaties agreed by states in which the first two concepts were recognized, and the violation of which was treated with deadly seriousness. Examples include the Thirty Years' Peace, signed between Athens and Sparta in 446/445 BC, and the Peace of Philocrates concluded in 346 BC between Athens and Macedon under Philip II. All of these factors give us the wherewithal to speak of subversion in this period.

Our discussion of measures short of war in the ancient world is distinct from later periods because in that setting the line between war and peace was especially blurry. The reality is that the world of the ancient Mediterranean was one of nearly constant conflict. Warfare was expected on an annual basis, making it almost impossible to delineate life neatly into wartime and peacetime.[5] Parts of what follows must of necessity treat evidence of subversion in war.

**Figure 2.1**  A memorial to the Battle of Thermopylae, 480 BC. War was a constant in classical antiquity, creating an especially fertile ground for subversive activities.
*Source*: Joaquin Ossorio Castillo/Shutterstock.com.

With this in mind, let's first home in on Classical Greece to explore our ancestors' way of using subversive influence to best advantage. We quickly see plenty of evidence of internal meddling, disinformation, and bribery. For example, Sparta was allegedly the first Greek state to design a secret service, the *Krypteia*, to keep an eye on its potentially rebellious helot population (a group somewhat akin to slaves; see below), a tempting target for rivals seeking to weaken Spartan power. From Herodotus, we learn that disinformation played a key role in the Greek victory over the Persian fleet at Salamis in 480 BC. For their part, the Persians did their best to undermine the Greek alliance against them by shipping gold into the Peloponnese to be distributed as bribes to shift Greek loyalties.[6] Again, money talks.

What's more, contemporary diplomacy had subversive agents baked in. Within the Greek city-states, political exiles often attempted to subvert the government of the cities from which they had been banished. In so doing, they tended to look for support from the dominant powers of the day: Sparta, Athens, or Persia. Political competition thus fostered the constant danger of exiles colluding with factions within the city, supported by one of the great powers of the region, to overthrow the government and shift alliances.[7] Within the Athenian alliance, for example, allies revolted when anti-Athenian factions seized control from pro-Athenians. Thucydides gives us examples from Epidamnus, Boeotia, Lesbos, Samos, and others. Regime changes meant a shift of allegiance. In one example, an Athenian-supported pro-Athenian coup was followed by a Persian-supported anti-Athenian coup, with exiles playing a major role in both.[8]

At the same time, there existed within the cities the position of *proxenos*, typically a prominent member of society who was designated by a foreign state to look after its interests in his own city, whether commercial, religious, or political. The proxenos would have been somewhat the opposite of a modern-day diplomatic representative, who represents their own country in another state. A proxenos hosted foreign ambassadors from his client city, at his own expense, in exchange for honorary titles and influence, acting as a sort of honorary consul looking after the interests of the other state's citizens. He would promote policies of friendship or alliance, and although not prohibited from going to war on behalf of his own city against the city he represented, he could certainly act as a bridge between warring city-states when it came time for peace negotiations. It was inevitable, however, that a proxenos compromised some of his loyalty to his own city by virtue of his service to another.

There is plenty of evidence that many in this position were active not only in intelligence gathering but also in clandestine activities, from bribery to attempted coups and assassinations. After the Persian War, at some point between 480 and 460 BC, the proxenos of Athens at the city of Zeleia on the Hellespont betrayed both Athens and Zeleia in favor of the Persians, for whom he smuggled gold into the Peloponnese in order to stir up trouble in the Greek alliance. He was subsequently discovered, stripped of his privileges, and very nearly executed by the Athenians.[9] During the Peloponnesian War, a Spartan attack on the city of Byzantium was coordinated with a revolt inside the city by a faction that wanted to withdraw from the Athenian alliance and put out feelers to Sparta; the command of the Spartan force was given to Clearchus, who had been the proxenos of Byzantium at Sparta.[10] In 399 BC, the proxenos of Sparta in the city of Elis, a man named Xenias, attempted to overthrow the government in cahoots with King Agis of Sparta, who was advancing on Elis with his army. The coup failed because Xenias and his followers failed to assassinate the leader of the democratic faction.[11]

All of this goes to show that subversive behavior was a regular feature of the rivalry between city-states and between stronger powers and weaker targets, particularly given the constant threat of war. It could be a real game-changer, and political elites were well aware of the dangers. As we shall see, it also played a powerful role in the struggles between the contemporary equivalent of great power rivals, with significant consequences.

### Sparta, Athens, and the Earthquake of 464 BC

The history of Greece in the fifth century BC is dominated by the Peloponnesian War. Scholars have written reams on the origins of the war and their lessons for contemporary policymakers. Political scientist Graham Allison, observing Thucydides' assertion that it was the rise of Athens and the fear this instilled in Sparta that made war inevitable, went on to posit that there is a tendency toward war when a rising power (Athens) challenges the status quo of a ruling power (Sparta).[12] But the "Thucydides' trap" was heavily influenced by the playing out of subversion between the closest thing the Hellenistic world had to two great power rivals.

The trouble began during the final years of the Greco-Persian Wars, when the anti-Persian alliance of the Greek city-states, known as the Hellenic League, routed the Persians at Plataea in 479 BC. Athens took the lead in pursuing the Persians back across the Aegean. The Spartans, uninterested in expeditions far from their home on the Peloponnese peninsula, ceded leadership of the Hellenic League to Athens.

At first, relations between the two powers remained amicable. Thucydides writes that the Spartans "regarded the Athenians as being perfectly capable of exercising the command and as being also at that time friendly to themselves."[13] But as Athens grew in power and wealth, resentment against her began to brew. At the end of the war, a Spartan faction objected to the rebuilding of the famed Long Walls that protected the road to Athens from the port at Piraeus, 8 km away. When the Athenians ignored the Spartan complaint, the Spartans were said to be "secretly embittered."[14] In 475 BC, an anti-Athenian faction in Sparta proposed going to war to destroy the new Athenian alliance, the Delian League. Nothing came of the proposal, but worries about Athens' growing strength continued to fester. Within a few short years, the Hellenic world began to revolve around the two rivals and their respective alliances, the Peloponnesian League dominated by Sparta and the Delian League led by Athens.

In 465 BC, the growing rivalry came to a head. Athens quarreled with one of her allies, the island city-state of Thasos in the North Aegean, over control of the rich silver mines and trade routes on the opposite mainland. The Athenian fleet sailed to Thasos, defeated the Thasians in a naval battle, and lay siege to the island. In desperation, the Thasians turned to the Spartans for help, and Sparta secretly agreed to invade her former ally.[15]

As Sparta prepared to attack Athens, disaster struck. In the summer of 464 BC, a massive earthquake rocked the Peloponnese. Modern scholars have estimated the force at 7.2 on the surface wave magnitude scale. Ancient sources (Strabo, Pausanias, Plutarch, and Thucydides) put the number of dead at 20,000 and describe a moving scene. Deep fissures marked the land, rockslides cascaded from Mount Taygetos, and the city of Sparta was virtually destroyed. In the aftermath, the subjugated population of Sparta, the helots, took advantage of the chaos to launch a rebellion.[16]

The helots were the backbone of Spartan society, but they were also its greatest weakness. With a status lying somewhere between slave and serf, they were forced to work the land and perform all manner of tasks so that the Spartans could train for war.[17] We are told that helots were oppressed and humiliated by the Spartans, and occasionally more ambitious helots might be assassinated. We are also told that the Spartans declared ceremonial war on the helots annually in order to circumvent any religious offense posed by killing them. Spartans lived in constant fear of a helot revolt; the hostility of the helots toward their masters was so intense that it was said the helots "would gladly eat the Spartans raw."[18] Sparta's enemies considered creating a helot revolt the key to weakening Sparta, while the Spartans themselves were well aware of the danger posed by this potentially traitorous group in their midst. Thucydides noted that when it came to Spartan policy toward them, "security was the overriding consideration."[19] Thus, when the helots rebelled, it was the Spartans' worst nightmare come true.

The helots managed to defeat a Spartan army in the field and retreat to Mt. Ithome, where they dug in and remained through several years of siege. The Spartans eventually requested help from the allies still formally tied to them by the Greek alliance against Persia agreed to in 481 BC. This included Athens. The legendary Athenian general Cimon, who was Sparta's proxenos at Athens, convinced his fellow citizens to send a contingent of 4,000 hoplites and set off for Sparta to assist.

What happened next caused a diplomatic uproar and a political revolution in Athens.[20] Thucydides recounts that the Spartans "grew afraid of the enterprise and unorthodoxy of the Athenians" and "feared that, if they stayed on in the Peloponnese, they might listen to the people in Ithome and become the sponsors of some revolutionary policy." When the Athenian contingent arrived, the Spartans sent them packing with the casual excuse that they no longer needed Athenian help.[21] Cimon, who had staked enormous political capital convincing Athenian leaders that Athens should go to Sparta's aid, was discredited; the event led to his political downfall. In his place, an anti-Spartan faction rose to power in Athens, contributing to the hostile spiral that would culminate in the outbreak of the Peloponnesian War in 431 BC.

Sparta's fear that the Athenians might somehow support the helot rebels was entirely rational. Ithome, where the rebellion took place, was located in the western part of the Peloponnese, which had been conquered centuries before and was historically more restive than the east. Indeed, once the Peloponnesian War had begun, Athens tried to make use of potentially rebellious territories in the region and encourage uprisings of the helots against their Spartan masters by seizing the cities of Pylos and Cythera.[22]

Classical scholars have grappled with the mystery of why the Spartans would invite the Athenians in the first place and then summarily send them away at such huge political cost. There is some speculation that there may have been more than one expedition to Ithome. Plutarch indicates that there were two, and Aristophanes in *Lysistrata* implies that the Athenians actually went to Ithome and helped Sparta put down the rebellion.[23] If the Athenians did spend time in Sparta, we might imagine that something happened during the first expedition, or between the first and the second, to alarm the Spartans about the subversive intentions of their Athenian ally and rival.

These fine details are not necessary to make the point, however. Sparta rejected Athens out of fear that the helots, with Athenian aid, would prove successful in their revolt. In other words, one city-state feared that its rival would support an opposition group on its own territory in order to make gains against it. This falls squarely within our definition of subversion—malevolent behavior on the territory of another against its wishes.

What's more, Sparta's fear of Athenian subversive activities—not just fear of Athens' growing power—caused it to behave in ways that stoked suspicions between the two states, ramping up distrust and hostility and eventually resulting in war. As Richard Ned Lebow has noted, "The Spartans did not vote for war because of their concern for Athenian power. The debate in Sparta was about Athenian motives, not their power."[24] That power was increasingly being used to interfere in the domestic affairs of other states, as Athens engaged in subversion of its allies, instigating regime change, sabotaging defensive fortifications, and meddling in judicial processes and even hostage taking, all in an effort to keep its allies in line.[25] It comes as no surprise that Athens' great power rival, observing this behavior, would be wary of being subjected to the same treatment.

## Subversion During the Peloponnesian War

Athens and Sparta descended into war in 431 BC, and for the next quarter century their battles would shape the fate of the Greek world. Outright hostilities meant that the barriers to subversion, in the form of a need for trust or collaboration, were eroded, and the threat of retaliation was obviated by the existing violence. As a result, subversion was a constant presence, proving a useful tool for taking cities and switching allegiances without sacrificing time, effort, men, and treasure in an assault.

One of the great practitioners of subversion at this time was the renowned Athenian statesman Alcibiades, one of ancient history's most glamorous and naughty figures.[26] Friend of Socrates, ward of Pericles, and a leading general of Athens, Alcibiades would help orchestrate the brief overthrow of Athenian democracy during the war and very nearly effect the same on the important outpost of Samos, all in cahoots with a foreign power.

Embroiled in a notorious religious scandal at Athens in 415 BC, Alcibiades was stripped of his citizenship and properties and banished from the city. He soon fled to Sparta—he had been the Spartan proxenos at Athens—and for the next two years he advised on strategy against the Athenians, fought bravely in battle, and allegedly seduced the wife of the Spartan king. Once more in hot water, he fled to the court of Tissaphernes, the Persian satrap governing the western coast of Asia Minor, just across from the island of Samos.

Plutarch writes that Samos at this time was the most important post in the Athenian empire, for "it was from this headquarters that they sent out expeditions to recover the revolted cities of Ionia, and guarded those which they still retained."[27] Lying a little over a mile off the coast of modern-day Turkey, the island was a rich city-state with the means to defend itself against both Persia and Athens. It maintained its own powerful navy, and it was also the base for the Athenian fleet in the eastern Aegean.

By 411 BC, the war wasn't going well for Athens. After a catastrophic expedition to Sicily in 415 BC, many of Athens' allies and subject city-states had drifted away to Sparta's side in the conflict or been conquered in battle. With each island's revolt or conquest, Athens lost badly needed revenues. The military losses and Athens' increasingly dire financial straits caused grumbling among the wealthy citizens of both Athens and her remaining allies, who chafed at providing all the funding for a failing military policy when the decisions were made by what they considered to be a democratic rabble. Factions among the wealthy began to entertain the idea of overthrowing democracy and replacing it with an oligarchy made up of a few hundred wealthy citizens.

Enter Alcibiades, who dearly wished to have his citizenship (and his property) restored at Athens. Encamped with Tissaphernes on the western coast of Asia Minor, Alcibiades sought to dangle the promise of the Persians' huge financial resources in exchange for overthrowing the democracies at Athens and Samos. They would be replaced by oligarchies of his aristocratic friends and supporters, who could restore him to his former position of power. This scheme appealed to the anti-democratic factions at Athens and Samos as well as the army, which was strapped for cash to pay its men. If Alcibiades could deliver Persian cash to fund the Athenian war effort, they would support the coups.

The first move was to overthrow the democracy on Samos. Thucydides recounts how the Athenians "urged the most powerful men in Samos itself to work with them to try and establish an oligarchy there, despite the fact that the Samians had just been through an internal uprising to avoid being governed by an oligarchy."[28] The Athenian politician Pisander, a close ally of Alcibiades, organized a group of 300 conspirators culled from the Samian upper classes and the hoplites. With the plot in place on Samos, Pisander then sailed for Athens, leading a bloody and successful coup there on June 9, 411 BC.

Once the oligarchs had taken power at Athens, the conspirators on Samos made their move. The terror tactics used by the Athenian plotters—murdering opposition figures and leaving their bodies in public places, for example—were repeated on Samos. But unlike at Athens, the Samian democrats fought back. They rallied the sailors of the Athenian navy, who, coming from the lower classes, were strongly

**Figure 2.2** The Athenian statesman Alcibiades, who left a trail of skulduggery across the ancient Mediterranean world.
*Source*: Painters/Alamy stock photo.

democratic. Together they fought the oligarchs and their supporters and managed to repel the coup attempt.[29]

The oligarchy at Athens was short-lived, lasting only four months before democracy was restored by force. In that time, its leaders tried their hand at fomenting further coups to gain allies. As so often happens with subversion, this backfired. On the island of Thasos, pro-Athenian factions overthrew the democracy and established an oligarchy—which promptly reached out to Sparta and broke away from the Athenian alliance entirely.[30] To make matters worse, Tissaphernes, who had backed Sparta until Alcibiades arrived, shied away from providing the financial support that Alcibiades had promised the Athenians and went back to supporting Sparta.

As for Alcibiades, he escaped without any repercussions. His renown as a military strategist prompted the Athenian navy to recall him once again to Samos, where he was soon back in command and up to his old tricks. In 408 BC, he led the Athenians in the capture of both Selymbria and Byzantium with help from the inside. Xenophon tells us that with Byzantium in particular, Alcibiades, "finding that they were unable to accomplish anything by force, persuaded some of the Byzantines to betray the city."[31]

The Peloponnesian War provided a broad canvas for subversion. We see generous helpings of propaganda and disinformation, from Spartan rumors that Pericles' family had been cursed by the gods to Athenian rumors that Spartans had desecrated religious sites.[32] Support for factions on the inside led to coups in Athens and Samos, and bribery was everywhere. Lacking the usual barriers to subversion, such as fear of retribution or the threat of war, the gloves were off almost all the time.

### Philip of Macedon and the Athenians

Sixty years after Alcibiades had exited the scene, new opportunities for skulduggery opened up in the rivalry between Athens and Philip II of Macedon (382–336 BC). Once again, the persistent threat of war meant that subversion was a constant presence. Philip's territorial ambitions would upend the existing balance in the Aegean. Unafraid to fight, he still opted for subversion whenever possible, particularly against Athens.

Philip II came to power in 359 BC. He quickly revolutionized his army, making it the most advanced in the Greek world, and subsequently conquered his neighbors in quick succession. With his growing power and wealth, he began expanding into the Greek states. His ultimate goal was to force them into an alliance under his command in order to invade the Persian empire's western outposts. Athens, with the most powerful navy in the ancient world, was the ultimate prize. In the course of his expansion, Philip relied on propaganda, bribery, and armed insurgency, cultivating agents on the territories of his rivals just as the Athenians and Spartans had done in previous generations. There is plenty of evidence that he achieved many of his conquests with the aid of pro-Macedonian factions within the target city-states. (This was not unique to Philip. The Persians were engaged in a similar bribery campaign to attempt to sway alliances, just as they had done after the end of the Persian Wars in 479 BC.)

Using a combination of alliance, subversion, and military superiority, Philip quickly extended his influence. By 356 BC, Philip's seizure of the Athenian colonies of Pydna, Potidea, and the wealthy city of Amphipolis brought Macedonia into a formal state of war with Athens. In 352 BC, Philip's forces campaigned as far as the pass at Thermopylae, the crucial bottleneck between steep mountains and the sea that had traditionally been the only viable military route into Attica from the north. It was a harbinger of things to come.

In 349 BC, Philip attacked the city-state of Olynthus on the Chalcidice peninsula. His victory there was preceded by

> the betrayal of 500 Chalcidian cavalry, arms and all, by the two cavalry commanders, one of whom was certainly in a position of some influence in Macedon at a later date, and it was claimed that Olynthus fell by treachery.[33]

The Athenian statesman and renowned Greek orator Demosthenes (383–322 BC), one of Philip's great critics and opponents, tells of Philip separating Olynthus from its allies "by the treachery of sympathetic factions" and then bribing two of its leading citizens to open the gates of the city to the Macedonians.[34] Similar instances occurred with Aristratus of Sicyon and Perilaus at Megara, both of whom turned traitor to their city and aided the Macedonian king. According to Demosthenes, "Philip . . . spent money freely in bribing traitorous persons in all the cities, and tried to promote embroilment and disorder."[35] In 348 BC, on the island of Euboea perilously near to Athens, Philip encouraged factions seeking to unite the cities of the island into a Pan-Euboean League, which would necessitate leaving the Second Athenian Confederacy. Athenian military action to prevent the formation of the League ended in disaster, and the island strengthened its ties with Philip.[36]

Early in 346 BC, news arrived that Philip was marching south. The Third Sacred War had been roiling the Greek states for a decade, pitting the Phocians against Thebes. The Thebans had appealed to Philip for aid, drawing him into the conflict. The Phocians, who were custodians of the pass at Thermopylae, requested military aid from their allies Athens and Sparta. Phocis itself was no stranger to subversion. The

**Figure 2.3** Philip II of Macedon. His use of bribery to subvert potential rivals was renowned.
*Source*: Cromagnon/Shutterstock.com.

Greek historian Diodorus of Sicily wrote that many of the lesser cities "actively supported the Phocians because of the abundance of money that had been distributed."[37] The most recent Phocian leader, the young general Phalaecus, had been removed from the generalship under accusation of pilfering the treasure of Delphi for his own purposes. Now Phalaecus mysteriously regained power, just in time to rescind the call for Athenian and Spartan aid. Rebuffed, the Athenians could only watch and stew in frustration as the Macedonian army approached the pass.

Was there skulduggery involved in Phalaecus' sudden reinstatement at Phocis? There is certainly confusion surrounding this crucial event. *A Dictionary of Greek and Roman Biography and Mythology* notes that Phalaecus was appointed general in 346 BC

> without any explanation of this revolution, but it seems to have been in some manner connected with the proceedings of Philip of Macedon, who was now preparing to interpose in the war. It is not easy to understand the conduct of Phalaecus in the subsequent transactions, but whether he was deceived by the professions of Philip, or had been secretly gained over by the king, his measures were precisely those best adapted to facilitate the projects of the Macedonian monarch. . . . Phalaecus took no measure to oppose the progress of Philip, until the latter had actually passed the straits of Thermopylae, and all hope of resistance was vain.[38]

The classicist George Cawkwell implies that Phalaecus may have made a deal with the Macedonian king, judging from the lenient treatment he received once Phocis was subjugated.[39] What is certain is that in return for allowing Philip to get past Thermopylae without a fight, Phalaecus was allowed to retire unmolested to the Peloponnese with 8,000 mercenaries in tow.

Regardless of whether or not Philip helped Phalaecus regain power, once Phocis had rejected its former allies, the Athenians had no choice but to offer peace terms. The process of negotiating that peace and the repercussions from it—it would end eight years later in war and a staggering defeat for Athens—were the subject of two of the most famous trials of Greek antiquity, one in 343 BC and one in 330 BC. The speeches from those trials provide another glimpse of ancient subversion in action, this time in the accusations of propaganda and bribery that were hurled back and forth between the leaders of the pro-Macedonian and anti-Macedonian factions, the former led by Aeschines and the latter by Demosthenes.[40]

First, the facts. In early April 346 BC, Athens sent a peace embassy to Philip that included among its members Demosthenes, Aeschines, and Philocrates, for whom an eventual peace treaty would be named. The group soon returned to Athens with a counteroffer from Philip that promised peace but excluded Phocis and required an alliance between Athens and Macedonia. During the debates on the counteroffer, a schism appeared between Demosthenes and Aeschines. Demosthenes pushed for Athens to send an army to back up the Phocians, in essence blocking Philip at Thermopylae. (This despite the fact that Phalaecus had rebuffed Athenian aid.) Aeschines, who was known to be close to Philip and his son Alexander, is said to have reported that Philip's goal was to besiege Thebes, not march on Attica, and grant Athens Euboea in exchange for Amphipolis. Aeschines' report of Philip's promises purportedly (according to Demosthenes) led the assembly to accept Philocrates' peace deal. When Demosthenes tried to object, he was shouted down.[41] As a result, Athens did not come to the Phocians' aid, and Phalaecus allowed Philip to occupy the pass at Thermopylae.

Demosthenes would assert in the trials that Aeschines had swayed the *ecclesia* in a direction favorable to Philip's policy because he had been in Philip's pay. His was not a completely outrageous assertion. The historian Donald Kagan notes that "there is a pretty clear indication that Philip did in Athens what he did in other states as well. He bribed important Athenians to be champions of his cause."[42] This was not a matter of mere lobbying on behalf of Philip. Athenian public debate, replete with lashings of propaganda and the occasional lie, was the lifeblood of democracy. Possessing an eloquent representative to sway the democratic assembly could prove a powerful diplomatic tool, even though in this case accusations of bribing an orator may have been more a reflection of the ubiquity of bribery than provable fact.

In the years between 346 and 338 BC, Athens remained convulsed over the potential danger posed by Philip. Demosthenes relentlessly argued that Philip was breaking the peace agreement, using deception and subversion. In Elis, a bloody revolution took place in 344/343 BC that ended with supporters of Philip in power. When the decisive battle of Chaeronea took place in 338 BC, Elis remained neutral. In 343 BC in Megara, only 40 km from Athens, a leading citizen was accused of bringing mercenary soldiers from Philip in an attempt to take over the city.[43] All of these examples need to be taken with a grain of salt, coming as they do from Demosthenes' hostile rhetoric against both Philip and Aeschines, but they are in concert with behavior witnessed earlier.

It is worth noting that Aeschines equally accused Demosthenes of being in the pay of the Persian king, a charge that merely highlights the usefulness and ubiquity of bribery, then as now.[44] It is also entirely possible that Aeschines, flattered by Philip, became his unwitting accomplice because he sought to burnish his own fortunes within Athens. As the scholar Charles Adams put it, "There was no need of bribery with a man whose limited understanding and unlimited vanity made him so easy a tool."[45] This may be a bit mean-spirited toward Aeschines, but it does hint at the reality of promoting a cause using useful fellow travelers. The overall picture is one of Philip using covert subversion and the oratorical power of his supporters at Athens in his ultimately successful campaign to conquer the Hellenic world.

### Et Tu, Roma?

So much for ancient Greece—what about Rome? At first glance, it seems that subversion did not flourish in the Roman world—in the Republic or the Empire. Such behavior was considered suspect by a Roman culture that shunned cunning and deception as unheroic traits. Roman heroes such as Virgil's Aeneas were celebrated for their forthright character; they would never stoop to the same sorts of shenanigans we saw from the Greek Odysseus, for example. In real life, however, evidence of subversive behavior contradicts this. The legendary general Scipio Africanus used subterfuge in his successful campaign against the Nubian forces of King Syphax in 204 BC, so much so that he was criticized afterward by the leading Roman historians Livy and Polybius for his devious behavior.[46] The reality was that there were plenty of examples in the Roman world of both decisive subversion and brutal suppression in an attempt to ward it off, a testament to subversion's perceived power and ubiquity.

During the classical era of the Roman Republic, from roughly 509 BC to 27 BC, Rome was frequently in conflict with her neighbors, giving rise to opportunities for subversive action on both sides. Restive populations under Roman control were easy pickings for adversaries stoking rebellion. The historian Arthur Eckstein writes that

> Pyrrhus of Epirus found support against Rome among Samnite groupings during his invasion of Italy in the 270s; so did Hannibal in 217–210; still later, Samnium was the center of anti-Roman feeling in the rebellion of Rome's allies in 90–88 BC.[47]

Betrayal by agents on the inside was popular. A nine-year-long war between Rome and Tarentum ended in 272 BC with the fall of Tarentum: "The city fell only when an Epirote general left behind by Pyrrhus betrayed it to the besieging Roman army."[48] In 209 BC, the same thing happened again. Tarentum, again at war with Rome, was again betrayed "by a foreigner, one of Hannibal's Bruttian officers."[49]

In another example from 241 BC, a peace treaty between Rome and Carthage designated the Ebro River in northeastern Spain as the military dividing line between the two rivals' interests in the region. Yet Rome maintained protection of the coastal town of Sagentum, 100 miles south of the Ebro. The town could only hold out against Carthaginian pressure by having a close relationship with Rome. This "caused division in the city, which led (with Roman involvement) to the expulsion of a group that advocated accommodation with the Barcids [Carthaginians]."[50] Although the granular detail is lost to time, one sees a Roman finger on the scale.

The danger of potentially treasonous domestic groups—and the fear they inspired—was as much a worry in the ancient Mediterranean as it would prove to be in subsequent centuries. When Mithridates VI, king of Pontus, annexed the Roman province of Asia into his empire in 88 BC, he ordered the massacre of all the Roman and Latin-speaking inhabitants of Asia Minor in a bid to remove Rome's influence. An estimated 80,000 people were killed. The incident, known as the Asiatic

Vespers, became the *casus belli* for the First Mithridatic War between the Roman Republic and the Kingdom of Pontus.[51]

## Conclusion

In considering our examples from the ancient Mediterranean world, two points become clear. The first is that although our ancient cases are spread across a larger expanse of time than events in subsequent chapters, they serve to show that subversion could and did crop up and that much of the evidence in the historical record points to more violent subversion than we will see in later periods. This may be a consequence of the source material; more violent episodes would be more likely to warrant recording and remembering. But there seems to be enough evidence to say that even among the strongest states, subversion or the fear of its consequences played a major role. In 462 BC, the Spartans feared with good reason that the Athenians would use the rebellious helots to weaken or overthrow their regime. In 411 BC, on Samos and at Athens, Alcibiades and his co-conspirators used overt, covert, and violent means to set their oligarchic coups in motion. Sixty years later, Philip of Macedon used bribery, support of opposition factions, and propaganda to facilitate his conquests across the Hellenic world.

Given what we expect to see from our framework in Chapter 1, this is not surprising. After all, the competition over land and resources from colonies meant that war was a constant. As we noted, the threat of retaliation and escalation had less meaning when conflict was always just around the corner. The threat of escalation was no longer a deterrent; in a sense, the escalatory horse had already left the barn. Furthermore, compared to modern-day nation states, the polities of ancient Greece and Rome were fairly permeable targets. Physical and institutional barriers to subversion were low. The result was an impressive array of subversive actions, not merely by strong powers against weaker rivals but also between the largest powers of the region.

The second point is one of continuity. The familiar nature of the tools and behaviors of subversion in classical antiquity, despite the millennia stretching between then and today, is striking. While the arguments and rivalries were very much rooted in their contemporary setting, the attendant propaganda, disinformation, bribery, political manipulation, and assassination are in essence timeless. As we move forward in time with our investigation of measures short of war, we shall explore how these two points fit into subversion's larger story.

# 3

## Early Modern Europe
### Spain Versus England

THE SORT OF subversive behavior on display in antiquity was indeed a harbinger of things to come. Fast-forwarding through the centuries, you can open any book on any period and you'll see rival powers everywhere trying overt, covert, and violent measures short of war to achieve their foreign policy aims.

The scholar Edward Luttwak, in his work on the grand strategy of the Byzantine Empire, shows how Byzantine rulers relied on subversion as the best path to victory. Containing or co-opting their enemies allowed them to avoid war and preserve both their soldiers and their relationships with rivals, who might prove useful allies in future conflicts.[1] As medieval Muscovy rose to dominate neighboring provinces and principalities, fear of subversion was so ingrained that by the sixteenth century, "foreigners in Russia . . . were segregated from the natives in order to prevent subversive influences."[2] That fear came with good reason: The Russian princes themselves had used subversion against other principalities and khanates as they expanded their domains.[3] And the Russians themselves were victims during the Time of Troubles at the end of the sixteenth century, when Poland seized the opportunity created by internal instability to try regime change against its eastern neighbor.

Likewise, in seventeenth-century Japan, the Tokugawa clan rose to power fearful of the danger of subversive elements. Historian Paul Kennedy notes that

> virtually all Christians (foreign and native) were ruthlessly murdered at the behest of the shogunate. Clearly, the chief motive behind these drastic measures was the Tokugawa clan's determination to achieve unchallenged control; foreigners and Christians were thus regarded as potentially subversive.[4]

In their seventeenth-century conquest of China, the Manchus similarly capitalized on the internal dissent and civil unrest that engulfed the Ming Dynasty in its dying decades.[5]

We could pick any number of cases of powerful states undermining one another in this era, but for a particularly rich demonstration of subversion's dynamics, we can pause for a moment in the middle of sixteenth-century Europe and focus on the epic rivalry between France, the Habsburgs, and England.

The European political landscape was in a state of transition. At the beginning of the early modern period, around 1450, Europeans largely shared a sense of identity. Virtually everyone was Catholic, united against the common enemy of Islam. Social and political structures were fairly consistent. Peasants paid feudal dues to their lords and tithes to the church, while cities were run by an elite of guildsmen and magistrates. The aristocracy, higher clergy, and some cities entered into security compacts with the prince, and the whole contractual relationship was mediated through representative assemblies across much of Europe: English, Irish, and Scottish parliaments; the States General of the Low Countries; the Estates General of France; the Cortes of Castile and Aragon; the Diets of Hungary, Poland, and Sweden; the German Reichstag; and so on.

Yet Europe, similar to the ancient Mediterranean world, was also constantly in conflict—king versus king, city states versus territorial princes, emperor versus pope—exacerbated by two great transformational forces. The first was the Protestant Reformation, aided and abetted by Johannes Gutenberg's perfection of the European printing press around 1450. Historian Geoffrey Parker notes that the Protestant revolt created "at the heart of almost every state, a nucleus of zealots prepared to place the advancement of their religion above obedience to their rulers."[6] As the century progressed, Catholic rulers would grapple with Protestant rebels, and Protestant rulers would do the same with Catholics. Both were potential fifth columns for rival states.

The second transformational force was the rise of the House of Habsburg. Previously, France had been the power in Europe to be reckoned with, and other European states had coalesced to block potential French dominance. The pope had sponsored a Holy League in 1511 combining a hodge-podge of European states—Spain, Venice, the Holy Roman Empire, England, the Swiss—to try to kick the French out of the Italian peninsula. But by the early sixteenth century, the Habsburgs were the ones to fear, leap-frogging their rivals through a fortunate succession of marriages and inheritance. After Charles I was elected Holy Roman Emperor in 1519 (becoming Emperor Charles V), he styled himself after his ancestor Charlemagne and had ambitions to unite all of Christendom.[7] His was the first empire in history upon which the sun never set. And although his successor Philip II of Spain swore that he posed no threat to his rivals, the European states of the sixteenth century faced the same problem as those of the twenty-first century: Every move made by the dominant power to preserve the status quo seemed threatening to the neighbors.[8]

These transformations set the stage for great power rivalries centered around the question of Habsburg hegemony and, to a lesser degree, religious affiliation. France in particular fretted about Habsburg encirclement, and her chief goal for the next 200 years would be to make sure that didn't happen.[9] War was frequent, and subversion equally so. France worked steadily to undertake measures short of war in various areas of the Habsburg empire, spreading propaganda and disinformation campaigns, supporting internal factions, arming mercenaries, and stoking rebellion. One of Philip's advisors later laid it out clearly when he warned that the French would

> shelter and stimulate the heresies which lead . . . the Turks to [attack] Christendom. . . . They are the ones who arm North Africa and support Algiers, and supply them with weapons, equipment and other

things; the ones who incite and assist the prince of Orange and the rebels against Your Majesty; the ones who stir up and support the hostile intentions of the princes of the Empire.[10]

By the 1550s, the rivalry would become more complex, and more personal. In 1551, the French King Henry II declared war on the Habsburgs, hoping to recapture areas of Italy and secure French dominance in Europe once and for all. In 1554, Charles countered with a masterstroke, arranging the marriage of his heir Philip to the ultra-Catholic Queen "Bloody Mary" Tudor of England. This brought England into the war on Spain's side. In 1556, ill health forced Charles to abdicate the throne. He split his empire between Philip and his brother Ferdinand of Austria. Philip became simultaneously King of Spain and the titular King of England. Two years later, in 1558, the entire arrangement was upended when Queen Mary Tudor died childless at age forty-two. The English throne passed to Mary's twenty-five-year-old Protestant half-sister, Elizabeth. In the blink of an eye, Philip lost his title as King of England, England for the Habsburgs, and a Catholic land to a Protestant ruler.

For the next forty years, Philip would try to get England back under Habsburg influence; prevent France from doing the same; and, in cahoots with a succession of popes, try to return England to Catholicism and stamp out Protestant heresy. For her part, Queen Elizabeth would maneuver to maintain her throne (and her head) and protect England from the predations of both France and Spain. The cagey dance between the two monarchs would last decades and encompass everything from bold propaganda to armed rebellion and attempted assassination. In the process, the path from diplomacy to war would provide a blueprint for understanding the interplay between subversion's inducements and its constraints.

## Diplomacy

At first, diplomacy was the order of the day. With Mary's death, Philip was under immense pressure to keep England in the Habsburg camp. His councilors warned him of a "domino effect" if he failed, with the rich provinces in the Netherlands and his other possessions in the

Americas and the Mediterranean possibly giving in to rebellion or attack by Protestant or Muslim enemies. The most efficient way of solving the problem would have been to marry Elizabeth. Philip would have regained his title as King of England and that would have been that.

There were of course less elegant solutions. Barring a marriage to Elizabeth, Philip could opt to support a Catholic rebellion in England. This was a more obvious option in 1559, after the new queen implemented a religious settlement that, although moderate toward Catholics, confirmed that she would impose the Protestant faith in her kingdom. Those Catholic subjects who had smugly flourished under Mary now represented a dangerous opposition. Once the ongoing war with France was settled by the Treaty of Cateau-Cambrésis in April 1559, Henry II turned to his former enemy Philip and proposed a joint invasion and the partition of England between France and Spain, aided by Catholic rebels. But Philip's advisors warned that France could not be trusted. Furthermore, the expensive and potentially perilous option of invading England alone and deposing Elizabeth by force risked igniting civil war.[11] Diplomacy was preferable to subversion or invasion, and for the moment, it looked as if the former might prevail.

This was due in large part to Elizabeth, who dangled the possibility of marriage in front of Philip in the months just after Mary's death. Why? Newly arrived on the throne, Elizabeth had to grapple with a host of vulnerabilities. England was an important European country but by no means an equal of the rich and mighty Habsburgs. After the end of the English Civil Wars in 1487, Henry VII had deliberately dissolved much of the army in a successful bid to get the national finances in order, and England's navy had not yet developed into the lethal weapon it would later become. England lagged behind the continental powers in modern arms, and most of the fighting forces she did employ were mercenaries hired from Germany.[12] England was militarily backwards and was already struggling financially under the burden of war with France. She needed a Habsburg ally to protect her from the French, and marriage to Philip was one way to get it.

Both Philip and Elizabeth sought decent diplomatic relations with the other to further their respective goals, and subversive activity of the kind that would later emerge was kept under control, at least for the time being. Even when it would seem that logic dictated otherwise,

**Figure 3.1**  Philip II of Spain tried first diplomacy and then subversion to bring England into the Hapsburg fold.
*Source*: GL Archive/Alamy stock photo.

**Figure 3.2** Elizabeth I of England played a weak diplomatic hand with great skill, fending off subversive threats from Spain, the Pope, and English Catholics.
*Source*: National Portrait Gallery.

diplomacy remained the first choice. The situation in Scotland was illustrative. In June 1559, Scottish Protestants took over the government in Edinburgh, forcing the French regent Mary of Guise to flee. In July, Henry II of France was killed in a tournament, elevating his son Francis and Elizabeth's cousin Mary to the French throne. Mary was Elizabeth's nemesis, raised both French and Catholic, daughter of the ousted Mary of Guise, with a potentially legitimate claim to the English throne through her father, James V of Scotland. With Henry II's death, Francis and Mary designated themselves rulers not only of France but also of Scotland, England, and Ireland. The Protestant takeover in Edinburgh was an affront to the new royal couple. Francis opted immediately for military action, sending a French expeditionary force that drove the Protestants out of Edinburgh.

Elizabeth retaliated by sailing a huge fleet to Scotland and cutting off communications between Scotland and France. Francis turned to Philip, who had by now become his brother-in-law. Francis asked Philip, "since we agree that this is all about religion," to warn Elizabeth to abandon her support for the Scottish Protestants or face the prospect of Philip joining the French against her.[13]

But here realpolitik trumped both denomination and family. Elizabeth had already asked Philip to take her side in the dispute, and he agreed, understanding the "danger that would follow to our dominions if she and her kingdom were lost" to the French.[14] Refusing to back Francis, Philip did nothing to support his fellow Catholics in Scotland because of his need to check the power of the French. His desire for cooperation with England against the French meant that undermining Elizabeth was kept on the back burner, at least for the moment.

Things got trickier still when, after only 18 months on the throne, Francis died unexpectedly in December 1560. Mary was packed back to Scotland to rule over a restive Protestant nation, while her mother-in-law, Catherine de Medici, became for a number of years queen regnant on behalf of her son Charles IX. Unlike Philip, Catherine had no qualms about covert action to gain influence over England. She backed Mary as the legitimate heir to the English throne, sending funds to her Catholic supporters in Scotland. This sparked a subversive tit for tat between Elizabeth and Catherine. Elizabeth secretly sent funds, though not soldiers, to the Huguenots in France, while Catherine tacitly allowed French mercenaries to operate in Ireland in aid of Catholic rebels.[15]

France and England used subversive measures against one another because loss of trust was no barrier; there was already little love lost between the palaces of Paris and London. Yet between Elizabeth and Philip, relations continued to remain focused on diplomacy for nearly a decade after Elizabeth's accession to the throne. Although her early flirtation with a marriage to Philip fizzled out (much to Philip's relief), she began discussions with another Habsburg prince, Charles of Austria, son of Philip's uncle the Emperor Ferdinand. Negotiations took place in 1559 and again from 1564 to 1568, with both attempts aimed from Elizabeth's perspective at securing a Habsburg ally against France. This worked fine for Philip as well because the marriage of Elizabeth to a Habsburg prince (any Habsburg prince) would solve his England problem, especially because England would go to Elizabeth's husband if she were to die childless.

As long as there was the hope of a marriage alliance, there wasn't much of an incentive for Philip to try either subversive action or invasion. And there was a distinct disincentive for supporting Mary. Despite sharing the Catholic faith with the Habsburgs, having Mary on the English throne would have turned England into a French satellite. In 1565, Mary wrote to Philip directly asking for help against Elizabeth, but Philip offered only aid in Scotland.[16] In this instance, the interests of Philip and Spain were not served by promoting a Catholic just for the sake of it. Much better to wait and see what would happen with Elizabeth's marriage and succession, since it was assumed she would marry eventually. Subversion would remain at a simmer as long as there was still a chance of a positive outcome through diplomacy for Philip's designs on England.

## Troubles

But nothing stays the same for long. A tectonic shift in the Anglo-Spanish rivalry began toward the end of the 1560s, resulting in a laundry list of irritations that served to ramp up the level of hostility between the two and usher in an era of increasingly aggressive subversion. In 1566, a rebellion against Habsburg rule in the Netherlands threatened

Philip's control. The reasons for the unrest had mostly to do with local governance and taxation, but a vein of religious discontent ran through it as well. For economic, political, and religious reasons, Philip could not afford to be seen losing his grip on the Netherlands. In 1567, he reacted by creating what would become the longest standing army in the early modern period, the Army of Flanders, under the leadership of the fierce but pragmatic Duke of Alba. As is often the case, a move of strength sowed the seeds of future opposition. It may have been the best option for Philip's PR as a strong ruler, but it massively spooked the French, the Germans, and the English.

The Dutch rebellion was a headline grabber, but there were other issues brewing. In 1567, Elizabeth's marriage discussions with the Habsburg Charles of Austria broke down once and for all, making it abundantly clear that marriage diplomacy was not going to solve Philip's problem with the English. At the same time, Elizabeth's cousin Mary, forced to abdicate the Scottish throne, made a desperate and daring escape from Scotland and arrived in England seeking refuge by the grace of her cousin. No doubt it was probably safer to have Mary in English captivity than potentially scheming against Elizabeth from a position of power in Edinburgh. But Elizabeth now had to contend with the disruptive presence of Mary, a devout Catholic with a possibly legitimate claim to the English crown who could count on many powerful supporters among Catholics in Scotland and England, especially in the north.

Things were also shifting for Philip, especially out on the high seas, where England was beginning to be a thorn in his side. From 1562, Elizabeth had begun to tacitly approve of (and occasionally invest in) English trading expeditions with the Spanish colonies in the West Indies, metaphorically thumbing her nose at Spain's self-proclaimed monopoly on trade in the Caribbean. Then in November 1568, French pirates in the Channel attacked five Spanish treasure ships bound for the Netherlands. The ships sought refuge in English ports, which Elizabeth granted, and the bullion was brought ashore for safe keeping. Just at this moment, news arrived that the Spanish had ambushed and destroyed a slaving expedition led by Sir John Hawkins and Sir Francis Drake. Under pressure from some of her more aggressive pro-Protestant advisors to keep the Spanish treasure, which was destined

**Figure 3.3** The Dutch rebellion in 1567 soon flared into open revolt, creating vulnerabilities for Spain that England would soon ruthlessly exploit.
*Source*: "Sea Beggars Take Den Briel," 1572, anonymous, after Frans Hogenberg.

to pay the army suppressing the Protestant revolt in the Netherlands, Elizabeth agreed. Philip was furious. Egged on by the scheming new ambassador to London, Don Guerau de Spes, Philip and the Duke of Alba retaliated by confiscating English property in Spain and the Netherlands.

Powerful personalities exacerbated the situation. Pope Pius V began pressuring Philip to launch an invasion of England and sort Elizabeth out once and for all; Philip did the equivalent of a royal eye-roll, reminding the pope of the cost of such an undertaking. But relations soured further when Philip refused to let Elizabeth's ambassador to Spain celebrate Protestant mass after he allegedly insulted the pope at a dinner party. And according to historian Geoffrey Parker, Guerau de Spes managed "almost single-handedly" to ruin the relationship.[17]

What do all of these events have to do with subversion? Relations between Elizabeth and Philip were clearly breaking down. Where diplomacy had once been paramount, more underhanded methods would now begin to make their mark.

## The Northern Rebellion

Philip still held out hope as late as 1568 that Elizabeth might come to her senses and recognize the error of her ways. "If I could in any way profitably help her to this end I would do so with all my heart," he wrote to his then-ambassador in London, Guzmán de Silva.[18] But there were too many problems to overcome, and in November 1569, an uprising of Catholic nobles in the north of England, later known as the Rising of the North or the Northern Rebellion, opened up a new phase in the rivalry between Elizabeth and her opponents. The goal of the rebellion was to depose Elizabeth and replace her with Mary. Led by the Earls of Westmoreland and Northumberland, a group of roughly 700 soldiers occupied Durham, then marched south, eventually gathering 6,000 Catholic rebels to the cause. In response, 20,000 English troops under the Earl of Sussex and Baron Clinton managed to disperse the rebels and drive them across the border into Scotland.

The Northern Rebellion was a nasty shock, and Elizabeth responded with draconian legislation and brute force. She declared martial law and demanded a wave of executions. Almost every village in the Yorkshire Dales witnessed a public hanging.[19] The Duke of Northumberland was captured and beheaded. The Duke of Norfolk was imprisoned; his demise would come later after participating in further plots. Altogether, up to 600 of Mary's supporters were executed.

Despite Elizabeth's tough response, the Northern Rebellion seemed to signal to her rivals that she was vulnerable. They seized the opportunity to launch what today would be considered a multipronged campaign of subversion to bring her down. The first salvo was a unique overt propaganda offensive. In February 1570, in an attempt to profit from and capitalize on the momentum of the Northern Rebellion, Pope Pius V sought to whip up public support against Elizabeth by issuing a public decree known as a Papal Bull (from the leaden seal affixed to the end that gave the document its authenticity). Titled *Regnans in Excelsis*, it declared Elizabeth an illegitimate heretic, released her subjects from any obedience to her, and granted all Christian princes permission to invade England. The Bull was a unique propaganda tactic not just because it was overt but also because its impact was amplified by the fact that its author was publicly acknowledged. Catholics, it was thought, would be minded to follow edicts of their pope. The historian J. B. Black writes that Pius well understood the impact of his edict. "Caught between the fire of rebellion at home and the advancing tide of invasion from abroad," he notes, "the Elizabethan government would have been in a parlous position."[20] The Bull gave Catholics permission to overthrow Elizabeth, and its impact would continue to be felt for the next thirty-five years.

But subversive activity by our definition must take place on the territory of the target. The Bull was of no use as a subversive tool unless it could be smuggled onto English territory, translated into the vernacular, and spread among the population. The pope therefore turned to a network of rulers and agents throughout Europe to get the document across to English shores. Copies were sent to all the papal nuncios in the great courts of the Continent for further distribution. By March 1570, the Bull had reached the Netherlands. A month later, it arrived in Poland, with a request to King Sigismund II that it be reprinted and delivered to Danzig and other busy coastal towns where English traders congregated.[21]

Pius was no stranger to subversion. Using a Florentine banker and Catholic adventurer named Roberto Ridolfi as his personal secret agent, he had been clandestinely distributing huge sums of money to Catholic sympathizers for several years prior to 1570. Once the Bull was issued, Ridolfi smuggled at least six copies into England, passing them to Don Gureau de Spes; French Ambassador Bertrand de Salignac Fénelon; and John Leslie, the Scottish bishop of Ross, who was Mary's ambassador to Elizabeth.[22] Gureau de Spes gave a copy to the English Catholic nobleman John Felton, who nailed it to the gates of the Bishop's Palace in London in May 1570, making Elizabeth's excommunication public knowledge. It came too late, however, to make much of a difference with the Northern Rebellion. Given the slow speed of news travel, the uprising in the north was over (in January 1570) before Pius had even issued the Bull.

## Why Subversion Instead of Invasion?

The Northern Rebellion ushered in a new era in Philip's efforts to solve the English problem. He sought a more robust approach, but still he shied away from invasion, shifting his tack from diplomacy to subversion. Why?

There were a number of reasons. One was logistical. As we saw in ancient Greece, Philip of Macedon had sought subversion before invasion because Athens was a hard and dangerous target. The Long Walls between Athens and the port of Piraeus had made the city immune to siege, and the Athenian navy could strike back at Macedonian forces in far-flung locations throughout the Aegean. The same held true to some extent for England, which benefited from good coastal defenses and 20 miles of water between the southern coast and the European continent. England was a tough target for invasion.

Another reason was financial. Philip's empire was stretched on all sides, pouring ever-increasing sums into military engagements against the French, the Turks, and the rebels in the Netherlands. The assembly of Castile, known as the Cortes, wielded considerable power over taxation to support the armies of Spain. Philip did not need the headache or the expense of another war. All things considered, from Philip's perspective, taking England by force would be difficult and costly. Better to play the subversion card and see what gains could be made—after all, subversion is above all cheap.

Finally, internal political conditions in England favored subversion over invasion. Elizabeth was surrounded by an able and astute group of advisors in her Privy Council, particularly William Cecil and Francis Walsingham—known as "Elizabeth's spymaster"—who created a superb intelligence network that would prove capable of thwarting all plots against her. In addition, the Duke of Alba, Philip's governor in the Netherlands, initially advised against invasion because he doubted English Catholics would support a foreign power over an English monarch. With Mary, Queen of Scots now in England and the Catholics in the north already in revolt, subversion looked more promising.

There was a brief moment when things might have turned out differently. Philip had begun funding Catholic rebels in Ireland. When it came to Elizabeth's attention, in early 1571, she sent an envoy to Spain asking for Philip's aid against the Irish rebels and offering to send a new ambassador to Spain to negotiate a settlement of all the outstanding issues. This could have been an example of subversion "working," bringing the targeted party around to a stance more amenable to the subverter. But it was too late. Philip chose instead to escalate, backing what would become the first of a series of plots combining armed insurgency, kidnapping, and assassination to remove Elizabeth and replace her with Mary.[23]

The Ridolfi plot, concocted in the spring of 1571 by the pope's agent Roberto Ridolfi, proposed an invasion of England by 10,000 Spanish troops under the Duke of Alba's command. English Catholics, supposedly inspired by the propaganda of the Papal Bull, would rise up to join them. Meanwhile, Elizabeth would be murdered and replaced by Mary, who would then marry the Duke of Norfolk, the highest ranking noble in England. Catholicism would be restored.

Ridolfi traveled around Europe in a sort of sales tour to promote the idea with Philip, the Duke of Alba, and Pope Pius. Elements of the plot were not new: The uprising in Northern England had sought to depose Elizabeth as well, and after Philip sent the Duke of Alba with his troops into the Netherlands to quash the rebellion there in 1567, the possibility of a Spanish invasion of England had always hung in the air. But despite backing from Philip and the pope, the Ridolfi plot was a spectacular failure. Cecil and Walsingham's spies did their work well, and in April 1571, they arrested at Dover a servant of John Leslie, Bishop of Ross, carrying incriminating letters from Ridolfi in Brussels to his co-conspirators in England. Leslie was arrested as well, along with numerous other nobles, servants, and facilitators. The Duke of Norfolk was tried for treason and beheaded in June 1572. Elizabeth spared Mary's life, but only just, and she further tightened the restrictions of her cousin's imprisonment.

The Ridolfi plot caused the gloves to come off between Elizabeth and Philip, and it proved a turning point in Anglo-Spanish relations. Elizabeth signed a defensive alliance with France in April 1572. More important, she began increasing her material support for restive elements throughout Philip's dominions, including Dutch Protestant rebels in the Netherlands, French Huguenots attempting to settle in Spanish-dominated Florida, and Protestant factions in Portugal after the Spanish annexation of 1580. English privateering against Spanish interests also ramped up. It was a vivid example of the costs of subversion, measured in shattered trust, mutual paranoia, and retaliation.

**Figure 3.4** Elizabeth I receiving the Dutch ambassadors in 1572. Her support for the rebellion in the Netherlands was a thorn in Philip's side.
*Source*: World History Archive/Alamy stock photo.

In 1575, the rebellion against the Spanish in the Netherlands burst into open revolt. Suppressing it caused a further drain on Spain's resources; the 65,000 troops of the Army of Flanders were responsible for more than one-fourth of the total outgoings of the Spanish government for decades afterward.[24] By 1576, Spain was in debt and unable to finance the Dutch campaign; unpaid troops revolted and sacked Antwerp, denting Spain's reputation further. At the same time, English spies intercepted the letters of Don John of Austria, then the current leader of Philip's forces in the Netherlands. The letters revealed that Don John was pushing to use the Netherlands as a base to invade England. Elizabeth's worst fears might now come true.

Elizabeth took this opportunity to strike back hard, using overt and covert methods to weaken the Spanish and distract them from attacking. She increased her funding for the rebels, sending them £100,000 (roughly £40 million in 2024) after the sack of Antwerp and promising to provide soldiers at a later date. In 1577, she even funded a mercenary army of "6,000 Swiss and 5,000 'reiters'" under the Calvinist German prince John Casimir to fight alongside the Dutch. This was a significant shift. When the revolt had first broken out in the mid-1560s, Elizabeth had been reluctant to provide any covert support, fearful of retaliation from Philip and mindful also of damage to her own reputation should she support rebels against their rightful monarch. Now that the stakes were higher and Philip was distracted by financial burdens, Elizabeth was more amenable to risk. Sending substantial funds to the Dutch rebels and supporting Casimir in raising an army allowed her to act while still deflecting accusations of direct involvement in conflict with Spain. (In the end, her efforts bore little fruit. Once in the Netherlands, Casimir's ill-disciplined forces went on a rampage, destroying Catholic churches and alienating the population even more.[25])

Meanwhile, England faced a covert infiltration of newly trained Catholic priests from the English seminary associated with the university in Douai, approximately 120 km from Calais in the Spanish Netherlands. The university had been founded by Philip in 1560 to provide refuge to English Catholics, with many of the top posts held by Catholic professors who had fled the University of Oxford. The seminary gave the English Catholic diaspora an opportunity to continue their training in exile, preparing for the much-anticipated reconversion of England to Catholicism.[26] By the mid-1570s, these eager recruits, with the pope's blessing and encouragement, began to arrive back on English shores; by 1580, Pope Gregory XIII, Pius's successor, was reinforcing them with Jesuit priests.[27] This was a dangerous undertaking; Elizabeth had decreed in 1559 that any Catholic ordained in Europe was a traitor from the moment he returned to England. Arrest, interrogation, and execution lay in store for those who dared the voyage. This forced the priests to be enterprising in their travel plans, often using forged documents and disguising themselves as "merchants, discharged soldiers, returning prisoners-of-war and ransomed galley-slaves."[28] Elizabeth reacted by encouraging loyal Englishman to be on the lookout for the enemy. Soon the southern ports and beaches were crawling with watchers, while agents on the continent sent coded messages to warn of new arrivals. Yet even with woodcut portraits to aid in the hunting, some priests managed to escape to the network of safe houses set up by English Catholics for their protection.[29]

The more the priests came, the more Elizabeth moved to suppress them. In the context of the growing threat of war with Spain, Elizabeth's

reactions to the danger within mirrored what we see in centuries before and after. Fearful of Catholic collaboration with her enemies, she
suppressed those who refused to adhere to Church of England doctrine.
The more Philip and his Catholic allies threatened, the harder Elizabeth
cracked down. Of the priests who returned to England, roughly half
were arrested, and half of these were executed.[30]

As the situation worsened, Elizabeth sought to counter Philip with
both subversive efforts and outright attack. She continued flexing her
muscles far from her own shores in an effort to deflect and weaken
Spain. Sir Francis Drake circumnavigated the globe from 1577 to 1580,
plundering Spanish ports and gathering up treasure as he went. A succession crisis in Portugal in 1580 saw the English supporting Antonio,
Prior of Crato against Philip for the throne (although Philip succeeded
in annexing Portugal). In 1581, the Dutch rebels declared Philip deposed
and named as their sovereign the Duke D'Alençon, later the Duke
D'Anjou, moderate Catholic brother and presumed heir of Henry III
of France. The Duke moved into the Netherlands with a French army
and promptly announced his betrothal—to Elizabeth.

This was a cheeky move. Elizabeth would have gained in Francis an
ally against Spain who, although Catholic, showed signs of moderation
as the self-proclaimed protector of the Protestants in the Netherlands.
The goal was to prevent the Spanish from reconquering their rebellious
provinces, which both England and France believed would be used as a
base from which to attack them.

The potential marriage of the French heir to Elizabeth infuriated
both the ultra-Catholic French Guise family and Philip. He immediately offered financial support to the powerful Duke of Guise and an
alliance with the Huguenot Henry of Navarre, Philip's cousin, if he
would convert and attack Henry III. Soon after, Guise conspired with
an Englishman, Sir Francis Throckmorton, in another plan to invade
England with Spanish troops, depose and assassinate Elizabeth, and
wed Mary himself. Again, Elizabeth's spies proved their worth. They
would do so again in 1586, when Walsingham uncovered a final plot to
assassinate Elizabeth and place Mary on the throne. This time, Mary
was executed.

The Duke D'Anjou had died in 1584, leaving the Dutch rebels
without their self-appointed sovereign. At the same time, William of

Orange was assassinated at the behest of Philip, who had put a huge price on William's head. With both leaders dead, Philip's armies were able to make spectacular gains in the Netherlands. The rebels turned in desperation to Elizabeth, who now was forced to increase her support. Fearful of losing the Protestant territories and concerned about Philip using the Netherlands as the launching ground for an invasion of England, Elizabeth began a massive build-up of English forces in Holland, openly supporting the rebels in exchange for English control over a number of Dutch ports. This overt, violent subversion blurred the line between peace and war.

Philip faced a choice. Subversion of Elizabeth had not achieved his intended goal; indeed, its side effects had worsened relations even if its application had bought both sides some time. By 1585, as Sir Francis Drake began raids against the Spanish mainland near Cadiz, it now seemed that England threatened everywhere—in the Netherlands, in the New World, and now in Spain. The issues at stake had become so contentious, and the rivalry so hostile, that subversion alone was no longer sufficient. In May 1588, Philip's warships sailed for England.

## Conclusion

We have more detail about life in sixteenth-century Europe than we do about classical Greece, but it's fairly clear that the dynamics and tools of subversion were remarkably similar in both periods. In antiquity, we saw overt, covert, and violent acts designed to make foreign policy gains without war. The tools were familiar: propaganda, funds to support opposition factions, incitement to rebellion, and murder. Likewise in the struggle between Philip and Elizabeth, and Catholics and Protestants, the goals of weakening and foreign policy manipulation were pursued with those same familiar tools.

The dynamic of incentives was also the same. When states needed good relations or feared retaliation, subversion stayed in the box. Elizabeth and Philip needed one another against the French in the early years of her reign, and as long as there was a chance of success with the dominant alliance method of the day—marriage—Philip was willing to bide his time and throw the Catholic Mary Queen of Scots under the bus. Likewise, when the Protestant rebellion erupted in the

Netherlands in 1566, Elizabeth shied away from supporting her co-religionists. She needed good relations with Philip against the French, and she also feared what the powerful Spanish army could do if it was provoked into launching an attack against England.

When the dynamic had changed, when hostility had risen to a higher level and Philip and Elizabeth no longer needed one another quite so much against a France riven by religious civil war, Philip opted for subversion over unsuccessful diplomacy. His goal was to overthrow a monarch whom he considered illegitimate. Elizabeth used the same tricks of subversion to defend herself and her kingdom, weakening Philip with increasing support for the Dutch rebels and opposition factions on his other territories in the New World and Portugal. Neither wanted to afford the cost or unforeseen consequences of war. Both sought covert and overt subversion to try to manage escalation; both eventually succumbed to the use of force.

Covert plotting and subversion brought no great gains in the end for Philip and his Catholic allies; indeed, it often achieved the opposite effect from that which it sought. Philip's support of the Ridolfi plot transformed Anglo-Spanish relations and turned Elizabeth into a hostile foe. His embrace of subsequent subversive efforts against her came at the cost of what good will was left between them. By 1588, it had become clear that measures short of war were not going to solve the growing challenge of England. Frustrated by subversion's ineffectiveness, and with more funds from both the annexation of Portugal and the riches coming from the New World, Philip finally launched his invasion attempt.

Elizabeth was somewhat more successful. As the relationship with Spain soured, she became less reticent about supporting the Dutch rebels with cash, implausibly deniable mercenary troops, and finally overt English soldiers. The more she came to the rebels' defense, the more determined Philip became to remove her, but she did manage to stave off Spanish aggression until, having shored up her finances and strengthened her navy, she was in a stronger position to fight back in 1588 relative to the 1560s.

How does subversion in early modern Europe compare with the ancient world? In some ways, our ancient cases show subversion scoring some bigger hits, particularly with regard to bribing factions and buying influence on the inside to aid an adversary. In the sixteenth century, the more violent subversive plots all failed due to stronger institutions and defenses, and less violent activities, both overt and covert, seem to have had less impact as well. Yet overall, a pattern begins to emerge. Unwilling or unable to resort to war, states turned to subversive measures to make gains against their rivals when diplomacy was not delivering. When the target was too strong or the costs too high, subversion stayed at a minimum. When the target was weakened, the costs became more manageable, or the level of hostility ramped up, subversion rose to the fore. The common thread running from antiquity through to the world of the sixteenth century is clearly visible. As we resume our journey across time, we shall see how subversion plays out in a more modern age.

# 4

## The Nineteenth Century
### Skulduggery and Restraint

THE TITLE OF Ludwig Dehio's classic, *The Precarious Balance* (*Equilibrium or Hegemony?* in the original German), captures the leitmotif of nineteenth-century European geopolitics: preventing any state or coalition of states from attaining such a preponderance of power as to allow it to dictate terms to the others. It was a multipolar system of relatively evenly matched powers marked by constantly shifting alliances. And unlike the alliances familiar to us since 1945, these were not chiefly about ties between great and lesser states, but rather pacts among the great powers themselves. The addition or subtraction of such behemoths from a given combination could upend the strategic setting. The potential of these power shifts dwarfed what any state could do internally, at least in the short term. Hence the simple arithmetic and devilishly complex diplomacy of coalitions ruled the day.

If subversion was going to play a major role in this game, it had to promise to affect the politics of alliance formation. Looking inside the era's courts and ministries reveals the frequent presence of factions, each preferring different great power alliances—a fertile field for intervention. This is not to suggest that subversion's other goal, namely weakening a rival, was irrelevant. At least in theory, the prospects there were tempting, too. After all, the European balance was precarious not just because of the uncertainty of alignments but also because the main players in the game were empires, each in its own way a "prison house of nations." Nationalism, ever more potent through the century, was profoundly subversive to empires and whatever balance of power they might form. It opened the door to potentially powerful subversion in aid of national movements inside rivals.

L'Equilibre Européen.

**Figure 4.1** A cartoon depicting the balance of power in Europe.
*Source*: Lithograph by Honoré Daumier from *Le Charivari*, 1866.

This chapter examines subversion's appeal and limits at the dawn, middle, and end of the nineteenth century. The politics of alignment turn out to be central, as expected in a multipolar balance of power system. We observe the temptation to unsheathe the dagger of subversion to weaken great power rivals via supporting national movements, but stronger countervailing incentives ultimately prevailed. Arguably the century's most effective case of great power subversion involved an especially weak target—France in the aftermath of its defeat by Prussia—and an especially subtle subverter, Otto von Bismarck.

## Leaders Matter: Tsar Paul

The fear that one great power might indeed achieve hegemony in Europe, the role nationalism could play in bolstering or undermining state capability, and the decisive importance of alliance politics were all made as real as can be by nearly nonstop wars that engulfed the continent and much of the world between 1792 and 1815. France, its revolution, its nationalism-fueled potential to attain mastery of Europe, and ultimately its emperor Napoleon were at the center of no fewer than seven coalition wars that spanned the decades. And in the midst of all that tumult, the plain fact that leaders can matter in a country's alliance choices also, from time to time, received decisive validation. For a subverter, influencing or, at the extreme, eliminating a leader becomes an attractive proposition.

The century began as the War of the Second Coalition, in which Russia and Britain allied with most of the other great power European monarchies against France, entered its second year. Keeping the Russian ally on board was imperative for Britain, but St. Petersburg's allegiance was not a foregone conclusion. Tsar Paul's court included influential figures opposed to the alliance with the British Empire.[1] Weakened after its defeat in Napoleon's Egypt campaign (among whose objectives was breaking Britain's hold on India), they argued, France seemed less of a threat to the European equilibrium. For his part, Tsar Paul's attitude toward that equilibrium was much like that of his counterparts in other capitals: It was to be preferred to the hegemony of any empire save his own. A temporarily subdued France made the balance seem less precarious and allowed other matters to come to the fore. What

Paul cared about most immediately was Malta, the island base of the storied Knights of St. John that had been taken by Napoleon in his Mediterranean adventure and then by a Britain seemingly intent on keeping it. This irritant fed into a raft of others besetting the alliance. As historian David Schimmelpenninck van der Oye summarizes, "By 1800, Paul was more than ready to reconsider his allegiances."[2]

London officialdom was aware of this wobbliness and had tools in St. Petersburg that might just be able to affect it. Indeed, before the formal alliance, London had not been averse to some subversive meddling to steer Russian policy in a direction beneficial to British interests. This was achieved through the purse of the English ambassador to St. Petersburg, Lord Charles Whitworth. Whitworth was a charming diplomat, independent and resourceful, just the sort of man you would want conducting business in an age of slow communications. Contemporaries and historians alike recognized his attributes: "intelligent, devious, and honest when it was convenient."[3] He moved at the cutting edge of Britain's great power machinations, serving as one of the favorite agents of Lord Grenville, the Foreign Secretary. Whitworth was very much a man who asked forgiveness instead of permission.

He was also not afraid to spend King George's money on His Majesty's "Secret Service," and he often got into trouble for being rather vague about where the money went. An act of Parliament required that funds spent under the heading of "Secret Service" be carefully accounted for, but Whitworth had a long track record of supplying only cursory descriptions in exchange for occasionally eye-watering sums from the bankers.

These monies were liberally applied to promoting policies within Russia that worked in Britain's favor. In 1797, Whitworth managed to get two of Paul's favorites onto the British payroll: the Tsar's mistress, Ekaterina Nelidova, and his valet, Ivan Kutaisov. According to one report, for 30,000 and 20,000 rubles, respectively, the two helped secure favorable terms for England in a commercial treaty then under negotiation. Whitworth's comments in justifying the large sums paid in this arrangement reveal the extent to which bribery was a fact of life. "Both these persons," he wrote, "as they can render extraordinary services, are, from their situation in life, much beyond the reach of an ordinary

**Figure 4.2** Lord Charles Whitworth, London's man in St. Petersburg, "intelligent, devious, and honest when it was convenient."
*Source*: Chronicle/Alamy stock photo.

bribe."[4] Furthermore, in 1798, Grenville authorized Whitworth to draw 40,000 rubles for bribes to ensure that Russia joined the coalition against France. Of this bribe, Whitworth remarked, "It could not have been employed at a more seasonable moment or in a person more capable of making a suitable return."[5]

Clearly, Britain was using gold to steer Russian policy, in the same way that Alcibiades offered bribes to open the gates of rival cities to his ancient armies, or Elizabeth I funded Dutch rebels to weaken her rival Spain. In this instance, British subversive activity was focused on covertly nudging Russian policies in a direction amenable to London.

But there is also circumstantial evidence that Whitworth may have colluded in a more violent and decisive subversive act: the assassination of Tsar Paul in March 1801. This stunning event was sparked by both political and personal factors. Although the Tsar had pragmatic reasons for backing away from the partnership with Britain, Paul's rule struck many contemporaries (as well as later historians) as increasingly erratic. A lifelong manic depressive, moody and capricious, his rethink of Russia's interests in allying with Britain against France occurred even as his rule became more oppressive domestically. Elite differences over alliance politics intersected and fed growing contention over domestic matters. This state of affairs naturally caused intense alarm in Whitehall; with Russia behind him, or even just standing aside, Napoleon constituted a far more serious threat to Britain. And given the evidence about Napoleon's designs on India revealed by the Egyptian campaign, British officials could be forgiven for worrying about another such attempt.

Whitworth was closely associated with a group of conspirators keen to keep the Anglo-Russian alliance alive, including Count Nikita Panin and Count Peter von der Pahlen, the military governor of St. Petersburg. They all shared grave misgivings about Paul's increasingly unpredictable behavior. Paul suspected skulduggery on the part of Britain and Austria (eventually the ciphers were partially cracked and Paul knew full well what was being said about him) and requested that both Whitworth and his Austrian counterpart, Count Cobenzl, be recalled. Both governments obliged, and Whitworth departed St. Petersburg on very short notice in the summer of 1800.

In January 1801, Paul sent Napoleon a startling proposition. He suggested reviving a plan for an invasion of India, rejected some years earlier by Catherine the Great, using a combined Russian and French army. Napoleon gave the offer little heed, finding the idea of 70,000 troops crossing 2,000 miles of inhospitable country a little far-fetched.

Paul, however, was undaunted, and on January 24, 1801, he ordered the leader of the Don Cossacks to raise a fighting force at the town of Orenburg and march on India. Ill-equipped and lacking sufficient provisions, the loyal Cossacks nonetheless struck out in the middle of winter with their artillery and 44,000 horses into the Kirghiz Steppe. Within a month, they had covered 400 miles, nearly reaching the Aral Sea.

Meanwhile, back in St. Petersburg, the intrigue against Paul came to a head. At around midnight on March 23, 1801, a group of inebriated officers and noblemen, led by Count von der Pahlen, stormed into his palace to depose him. In the ensuing confrontation, Paul was murdered, strangled with a scarf.

Contemporary accounts held that the British were somehow responsible. The former vice chancellor, V. P. Kochubai, wrote to his friend Count Vorontsov, "You will see that the English have bought powerful men among us." Olga Zherebtsova, Charles Whitworth's lover and sister of Prince Zubov, one of the leading conspirators, asserted that "English gold" was behind the conspiracy.[6]

Correspondence between Whitworth and his associates, including Lord Grenville, implied that he knew a change of regime was coming; he continued meeting with Panin up until the very eve of his forced departure, and he was also in touch with von der Pahlen. Two months after Paul's assassination, Whitworth received a letter from his successor in St. Petersburg, Alleyn Fitzherbert (later Lord St. Helens), assuring him that "the accounts we had rec'd of a certain transaction were tolerably exact, excepting as to the Hero of the executive part, who was a certain Gen'l Bennigsen." He was referring to Count Levin August von Bennigsen, a German general in the service of the Russian Empire, who joined the group of conspirators at the last moment.

What's more, Whitworth's private papers reveal a prolonged back-and-forth with His Majesty's Commissioners of Audit concerning a secret cache of 40,000 rubles drawn at the very end of his mission. Whitworth eventually turned to the current foreign secretary, George Canning, for help in fending off the enquiry, explaining that

the money was taken up by me as I stated at the time to Lord Grenville, in part to make good some payments on the account of

Secret Service connected with the accomplishment of the object for which the cash subsidy was given.[7]

Once it was established that roughly 12,000 rubles covered closing the mission on short notice, it begs the question of what the remaining 28,000 rubles were for, particularly since Whitworth was leaving the country.

Paul's Indian gambit is perhaps a footnote to the larger history, but Russia's potential for realignment was very real. The archival evidence shows that the India decision was Paul's and Paul's alone.[8] There was little doubt that leader change in this case meant policy change with major implications for power politics. (Indeed, one of the first actions of Paul's successor, Alexander I, was to recall the Don Cossacks, and he reaffirmed the alliance with the British.) We know that there was a confluence of interest between Britain and nobles who supported the alliance on foreign policy grounds and felt increasingly oppressed by Paul's tyrannical rule. We know that Britain used subversion in the past to tweak Russian policy in favorable directions via some of the very same proxies who were intimately involved in the conspiracy to depose Paul.

We have motive, means, and circumstantial evidence. What we do not and cannot know is how important British subversion was. For some historians, it was decisive. Yuri Sorokin notes,

> Knowing the personal qualities of the Russian Emperor Paul I, the British government refrained from diplomatic means of pressure. Almost the only way to prevent the Russian–French rapprochement . . . was the removal of Pavel Petrovich [Tsar Paul] from power.

He concludes that "Whitworth acted as the initiator, the instigator of the conspiracy. He has the dubious honor of transforming anti-Pavlovian sentiment in society into something far more concrete."[9] Others emphasize the indigenous causes and domestic stakes of the coup, stressing the fact that Whitworth was long gone before the action took place. Historian Nadezhda Korshunova summarizes the evidence more circumspectly. "Whitworth did not directly organize and direct the conspiracy, but there is little doubt about the financial participation of the British."[10]

For us, the episode helps explain why the century's statesmen so consistently melded diplomacy and realpolitik with internally focused subversive statecraft. Alliances were decisive yet profoundly uncertain. Different leaders in the same situation could resolve that uncertainty differently. The temptation to directly influence leaders' choices—or the choice of leader—could be difficult to resist.

## Daggers Sheathed: Why Western Powers Chose Not to Subvert Russia

One of the lasting legacies of Paul's move on India was paranoia about Russian designs on the Raj, especially after Russia began expanding into Central Asia toward the second half of the nineteenth century. British insecurity intensified following the Sepoy Rebellion in 1857. Much of that fear featured Russian subversion in the sort of "great game" Rudyard Kipling fictionalized in his bestselling *Kim*. Although it never came to pass, it seemed credible enough in Whitehall. And documents later came to light purporting to reveal that Peter the Great had left his successors a "testament" stipulating that dislodging Britain's hold on India was a central aim of Russian grand strategy. Whenever Russia's designs on Asia came to light, Peter's testament did, too. As late as 1979, after the Soviet invasion of Afghanistan, *TIME* magazine reminded readers of this key documentary proof of Russia's perennial, age-old design to dominate Asia.[11]

The Cossack march to India, aborted though it was, did happen. But Peter the Great's testament? A forgery, concocted by Napoleon's foreign ministry on the eve of his invasion of Russia with the aim of poisoning Anglo-Russian cooperation.[12] It was subversion via disinformation stoking fears of subversion via supporting rebellion to affect alliance politics. It helps hammer home the centrality of subversion—actual and feared—on the century's geopolitics.

In an earlier age, the "great game" between the Russian and British Empires would have joined a befuddling brew of "questions" the unfortunate student of nineteenth-century European history would likely have had to endure—the Belgian Question, the Irish Question, the Eastern Question, the Polish Question, the Ukrainian Question, the German and Italian Questions, and many others.[13] Easy to miss in this morass was that it added up to a subverter's paradise. The great powers of the day were empires dominating ethnic nations that periodically wanted states of their own. In a highly competitive system, why not reach across borders to empower groups within a rival great power with the potential to weaken or distract it?

In all these cases, states had daggers at the hearts of their great power rivals but used them sparingly. The action leaned toward the subtler end of the spectrum: official commentary favorable toward the aspirations of oppressed people, support for or endorsement of a pamphlet or circular expressing sympathy for a cause, and offering exiled revolutionary figures succor from which to influence movements abroad. (London, especially, was host to scores of activist refugees considered subversive on the Continent, Karl Marx being merely the best known). For officials of the day, the spread of subversive words was a serious concern. As the century progressed, ruling elites increasingly believed that public opinion mattered—and that it could be swayed by the written word. Hence, in Austria, the unfortunate target of many of the century's questions, authorities banned publications shorter than a certain length, specifically targeting pamphlets. Historian Holly Case argues that these pamphlets were like the social media of the day.[14] And, precisely because the information space was less crowded than it would become in the twenty-first century, these short, written polemics were thought to be as, if not more, influential.

But in most cases, material support of the violent sort we discussed in Chapter 3 was conspicuous by its absence. Why this restraint? In the voluminous historiography of the era, and in the diplomatic documents on which it is based, two explanations recur and help organize the complexity: trust and escalation. Supporting insurgent national movements inside a rival great power risked alienating its government and its allies, risking cooperation the would-be subverter might need. Worse, it risked war, especially dangerous if the target could count on the support or at least the benevolent neutrality of allies.

Of all the era's questions, the Polish one is most probative. It featured not only a powerful and appealing national movement but also an escape clause from the principle of non-intervention, which might be viewed as a major constraint on subversion, at least of the overt variety. Russia was bound by the terms of the 1815 Treaty of Vienna, which concluded the Napoleonic Wars, to respect certain rights of the truncated Kingdom of Poland around Warsaw—rights that St. Petersburg violated when it sought to put down insurrections in 1831 and again in 1863. Britain and France were rivals of Russia. Critical masses of governmental elites in both countries frequently concluded that a smaller and weaker Russia would be a very good thing indeed. They fought a war against Russia in Crimea with war aims that were explicitly about pushing Russia back to her sixteenth-century borders.[15] The Polish cause was popular with liberal nationalists and much of the public in both countries. When Poles rose up against their Russian overlords in 1831 and 1863, Paris and London could argue that they had every right to intervene in light of the tsar's trampling on the terms of Vienna.

And intervene they did—but only diplomatically, and hesitantly. They sought to bring diplomatic pressure to bear, to "remonstrate" with the tsar, urging restraint toward and concessions to the Poles, arguably to give impetus to the Poles and conclude the crisis with a strengthened Poland and a weakened Russia. London's and Paris' interventionism came a cropper in the first instance on their inability to recruit Austria and Prussia to the cause. These two powers, after all, sat on big chunks of Poland, were implicated in this particular question, and thus were reliable allies (or at least benevolent neutrals) for the Russians. In both the 1831 and 1863 cases, efforts to recruit Vienna and Berlin were unavailing. As the Austrian minister in London put it during the 1863 crisis,

> No one could expect that Austria would embark in an enterprise which in its ultimate result might be to deprive her of a rich and tranquil province. She could not be an accomplice in the work of dismembering her own Dominions.[16]

Clausewitz himself expressed the same concern regarding his native Prussia back in 1831: "The Polish question . . . touches on our highest and most sacred interests and relates to the matter of our very existence."[17] In the 1863 crisis, Prussia's Chancellor Otto von Bismarck had an additional motive: He needed a friendly Russia, else his aim to unify Germany under Berlin's auspices would go nowhere. Anything short of stalwart support for St. Petersburg—which he gave in a formal agreement with the Russians—would likely have eroded the cooperation he knew he would soon need.

Even for London and Paris, the issue of trust wove through the diplomacy in both crises: Unless things could be managed such that victory was assured and St. Petersburg was presented with a fait accompli it would have no choice but to accommodate, the whole endeavor risked alienating a hugely powerful empire for naught. As Lord Aberdeen, head of the Foreign Office, put it as the first insurrection got under way, "Under any other circumstances—in any other times—it would be impossible not to wish well to the Poles, but our great object now is the Peace of Europe."[18] Or as French statesman and orator Alfonse de Lamartine put it when the national revolutions of 1848 again raised the question, "We love Poland, we love Italy, we love all the oppressed nations, but most of all we love France."[19]

But the greatest constraint of all was the fear of escalation. The problem for the Poles was that, time and again, when European statesmen pondered Poland's plight, thoughts turned quickly to war. Case notes, "Plentiful were the assertions across the lifespan of the Polish question . . . that it was not merely about Poland but indeed a 'European question' with the capacity to make or break the peace of Europe."[20] Official Russians signaled time and again that they would fight for the Polish lands they occupied. As one Russian diplomat expressed his empire's stance in 1848,

> Poland as the Poles understand it extends to the mouths of the Vistula and the Danube and to the Dnieper at Smolensk as at Kiev. Such a Poland enters Russia like a wedge, destroys her political and geographical unity, throws her back into Asia, [and] puts her back two hundred years.

And the key was, he added, that "to forbid the establishment of this Poland every Russian will take up arms as in 1812."[21] British and French diplomats in St. Petersburg consistently conveyed this message in 1831 and 1863, urging their superiors not to egg the Poles on. Ultimately, governments in Paris and London believed them, and that is what scuppered hopes for more consequential subversion.

The aborted Anglo-French intervention on behalf of Poland in 1863 provides a telling illustration. Prime Minister Lord Palmerston—as seasoned a statesman as they come—made moves toward intervention only because he reckoned Russia was weak. Defeat in Crimea had weakened Russia more than Britain or France, and it was struggling to cope with the Polish insurgents. As historian George Mosse noted, "What he hoped to do was to force the Russian Government under the threat of possible war with several European Powers to make concessions to the Poles."[22] Palmerston knew all along that war was in the equation, the only question being whether its prospect would scare the Russians more than the British. His whole approach can be seen as a "diplomatic reconnaissance in force" to answer that question. With an actual French military expedition to the Baltic real enough for the Russians to take seriously, and with no support from Berlin or Vienna, he got his answer. "When, towards the end of June, he had convinced himself of the strength of the enemy's position, he was ready to abandon the campaign."[23]

A probative comparison is the experience of the Ottoman Empire. That empire, too, was a congeries of nations in an era of nationalism, and yet when it came to nudging nascent national movements from abroad, the European powers showed less restraint toward Ottoman rulers than they did among themselves. As one historian observes, "Through their wars and support of the separatist goals of rebellious Ottoman subjects, European states abetted the very process of fragmentation that they feared and were seeking to avoid."[24] Russian rulers, who bridled at the very thought that an external hand might dare to stir the Polish pot, were foremost among the meddlers: "Since 1820 Russia had been assiduous in her policy of overtly and covertly encouraging revolt among the Christian Slavs of the Balkan provinces."[25] In hindsight, it may seem self-evident that empires like Russia were at a disadvantage in this game vis-à-vis national states like France; this was less clear then. Pan-slavism, after all, was an ideology many saw as a means to preserve and expand one empire, the Tsar's, at the expense of others, especially the Ottoman.

Why the difference? By the nineteenth century, Ottoman decline had reached such proportions as to exclude Constantinople from the ranks of the great powers.[26] Escalation was comparatively less credible, and so European governments were far more liable to put aside their innate circumspection and conservatism and succumb to the temptation to intervene. What constrained subversion in this case was opposition from European rivals who could threaten to impose costs on any player—usually Russia—that stood to gain too much from destabilizing Ottoman rule.[27] If the Porte were not viewed as such an important element in the vaunted European balance, it would have had to confront much less constrained subversion from the other capitals. This bewilderingly complex diplomatic dance, which generated a major crisis every generation, had a name, of course: the Eastern Question.

So, to those befuddled by the nineteenth century's tangle of "questions," we can offer one important answer in the temptations of and the ultimately more important constraints on great power subversion. Empires were systems of nation states waiting to burst forth, offering tempting targets for rivals. Rulers needed to deter rebellion and foreign meddling. If their power and credibility were great enough, they succeeded. Look beneath the era's diplomatic niceties and convoluted maneuvering, and this is the brutal reality you see.

### Bismarck's Subversive Realpolitik

Hence, we come back to where we started. If it was difficult to affect the scales of power directly through building up your own capabilities or degrading those of rivals, alliances loomed large. And the century's greatest player of that game, a giant of nineteenth-century European politics, was Otto von Bismarck. Students of strategy look to the long career of that Prussian statesman for lessons. One lesson they usually miss is that subversion can be a handmaiden of realpolitik. Historians are now rediscovering what contemporaries knew well—that, as Berlin's ambassador to Paris put it, "the same Bismarck who states that he does not seek to pursue a policy of intervention claims the right to change the governing principles of other countries when it suits his purposes."[28] Subversion figures in many of the German chancellor's machinations over his long career, but two cases loom large: France and Great Britain.

There is little doubt about Bismarck's objective in France in the 1870s: to prevent the formation of a monarchical government in Paris.

His motive was pure realpolitik, touching on both logics of capabilities and motive. He preferred a weaker France and believed that a republican government promised continued internal divisions that would hamstring French power for years. A monarchy, by contrast, would make for a more capable competitor across the Rhine, one more likely to rebuild the army and more prone to a war of *revanche* to reverse the humiliation of defeat by Prussia in 1871 and recover Alsace and Lorraine. Perhaps most important was Bismarck's assumption that a monarchical France would be more attractive as an alliance partner for Austria–Hungary and Russia, fellow monarchies with which Bismarck had established an informal alliance.

The threat of a monarchical restoration in France became real in 1873, when, as Bismarck lamented in a letter to Kaiser Wilhelm I, the French government—previously "weak, civilian and anti-clerical" under Adolphe Theirs—became "strong, militarist, and Jesuit-friendly" under Marshal Patrice MacMahon's presidency.[29] Although ultimately constrained by the institutions of France's Third Republic, MacMahon personally favored a restoration of the monarchy, and like-minded political forces rallied to his presidency. In the face of growing anti-republican sentiment, Bismarck sought to derail royalists and support republicans.[30] Part of his strategy entailed classically complex Bismarckian diplomatic gambits meant to deliver foreign setbacks or otherwise discredit Paris internationally. As useful as such stratagems might be for stacking the deck against Paris in international bargaining, faraway machinations weren't going to affect the French nation's choice of government.

Ambitious aims called for a more audacious effort to produce political effects across the border. And the unique circumstances of the mid-1870s—a weakened France still reeling from a crushing defeat at the hands of the Prussians—allowed Bismarck to seek big effects with subversive words—albeit words threatening war. On three occasions—1873, 1875, and 1877—the German chancellor engineered crises meant to spook French elites and citizens into believing that a monarchy in France meant war with Germany. It was clearly subversion by our definition, as Bismarck was meddling to thwart the domestic political objectives of the French president. But because MacMahon's object was allegedly monarchical restoration, Bismarck's subversion was ostensibly aimed at preserving rather than changing the regime, France's Third Republic.

The details varied, but in each episode, Bismarck faced a challenge: how to get this message to the intended audience without sparking a counterproductive reaction. In this case, concern over escalation had less to do with anything France might do in reply. Rather, the problem was twofold: potential balancing by other great powers and the risk of undermining the republican forces in France. Once Prussia defeated France in 1871 and emerged as a potent German Reich, the other powers were primed to check Berlin if they suspected it of seeking hegemony. Interference in domestic politics was frowned upon, to say the very least, but it was especially alarming if directed against a great power viewed as necessary to uphold the balance of power. And

**Figure 4.3** Otto von Bismarck, dictating the terms of peace to Adolphe Thiers and Jules Favre, Versailles, February 1871, at the end of the Franco-Prussian War. Bismarck would go on to use propaganda and meddling to thwart the return of the French monarchy.
*Source*: Historical Images Archive/Alamy stock photo.

direct endorsement of the republican cause by Berlin would allow the monarchists to brand republican leaders as German lackeys.

Hence, Bismarck needed plausibly deniable but effective means to frighten Frenchmen away from the monarchists. The solution came primarily in the form of a dramatic change in the information environment from what we saw in sixteenth-century Elizabethan England, one that made subversion by word easier than ever: a mass circulation press. After 1815, new technologies allowed mass production of cheap newspapers for an ever-expanding audience. Censorship in France was completely abolished under the Third Republic, which became known as the golden era of French journalism. In the decade from 1860 to 1870, daily press circulation increased from 150,000 to 1 million.[31] The result was a proliferation of news outlets that could be relied on to reprint articles from abroad that would spark controversy and possibly advance the electoral prospects of a given newspaper's favorite party.

Secure in the knowledge that an energetic French press would disseminate alarming news from its German counterpart, Bismarck was able to use various German newspapers at his disposal to pursue a sustained media campaign between 1873 and 1877 that painted the French monarchists as a threat to peace while singing the praises of the republicans. What's more, he had a slush fund left over from the Austro-Prussian War of 1866 (the so-called reptile fund) that he could use to pay for favorable articles in foreign papers as well as the German press and also to compensate clandestine agents operating abroad. The specifics elude us because all of the documents on the activity of German secret agents in France were destroyed in an allied bombing raid in April 1945. Yet we do have evidence that official and unofficial agents worked directly with the French republicans to offer information useful to their case against the monarchists.[32]

In the so-called War in Sight crisis of 1875, Bismarck stumbled into tough external constraints on subversion, culminating in a formal Anglo-Russian warning to Berlin to back off. Yet two years later, when a political crisis in Paris once again raised the possibility of a regime change, the other powers were distracted by Russia's war with Turkey. This time, Bismarck turned up the heat, deploying the press again and buttressing that message with much more direct official warnings of war. Local agents reported great success in creating a climate of fear among French voters. As one French agent put it, "If Bismarck's spies accurately inform him about the terror he inspires in us, he ought to be satisfied."[33] Even though the French press struck back by ironically dubbing Bismarck "the Great Elector of France," German diplomatic reports remained confident that the policy was working.[34] Exactly what role German meddling played in the republicans' victory is impossible to determine, although James Stone, the preeminent scholar of these events, credits Bismarck with "short-term success using these tactics in ensuring the survival of the Third Republic during a critical period at the beginning of 1877."[35]

Bismarck used the same tools a few years later when he took on the strongest power of the day, Britain. Between 1880 and 1885, the Iron Chancellor became increasingly fixated on discrediting his British counterpart, Prime Minister William Gladstone, wreaking havoc on the previously amicable relations between London and Berlin. Bismarck's goal was no less than the removal of Gladstone from office.

The fulcrum of his activity was policy toward Russia. The Russo-Turkish War of 1877–1878, which had so conveniently diverted St. Petersburg and London from Bismarck's subversive campaign against France, had ended with many of the parties dissatisfied with the peace, especially Russia. Furthermore, the episode boosted Gladstone back into the spotlight and paved the way for his run for office in 1880. He campaigned on a platform of liberty for the Slavic Christian peoples in the Balkans from their Turkish oppressors (as mentioned previously, in effect subverting the Ottoman Empire), closer ties with Russia, and hostility toward the Hapsburgs of Austria. This was the opposite of what Bismarck wanted from England.

As a result, Gladstone's victory in 1880 was greeted in Berlin as a catastrophe, and Bismarck set out to secure the Prime Minister's downfall. As in the French case, he first worked to create foreign policy traps for Gladstone. Bismarck's son Herbert expressed the goal with typical bluntness: "that our policy will avail itself of this most favorable moment to squash Gladstone against the wall, so that he can yap no more." In practice, this meant seeking out conflicts where Gladstone would have to choose between his principles and his practicality so that "his prestige will vanish even more among the masses of the stupid English electorate."[36] A campaign of foreign policy annoyances and embarrassments followed; indeed, it has been convincingly argued that Bismarck's sudden grab for colonies in Africa at this time was in part driven by the desire to force Gladstone's hand.[37]

But Bismarck knew that foreign setbacks alone were not enough to unseat his rival. He therefore unleashed a concentrated smear campaign in the capitals of Europe and the German press to amplify Gladstone's every failure. He overtly and covertly supported publications on the failings of the British Liberal government, such as the chaos surrounding

**Figure 4.4** British Prime Minister William Gladstone. Bismarck's policy sought to "avail itself of this most favorable moment to squash Gladstone against the wall, so that he can yap no more."

the Gladstone-supported Irish Land Act in 1881. He distributed critical reports to useful German audiences, including the Crown Prince and the Courts. "Improved" versions were inserted in German newspapers, under the guise of reports from their "special correspondent."[38] This amounted to "the exploitation of Gladstone's Irish troubles by the German government for propaganda purposes," and that was "but one example of Bismarck's strategy."[39]

Bismarck's campaign against Gladstone had a ready and witting ally in Britain: the Tory Party. The British Right had a high opinion of Bismarck, in whom they saw an appealing contrast to Gladstone's tolerant internationalism. On the occasion of Bismarck's sixty-ninth birthday in 1884, the Conservative Party's weekly journal *England* declared that Bismarck was "the greatest man in the world. . . . He has formed a great and invincible confederacy in the heart of Europe," in direct contrast to the "deplorable display of blundering and helplessness which has marked the Imperial policy of Mr. Gladstone for the past four years."[40]

As in the case of France, Bismarck could count on material published in Germany appearing in London. From the 1830s, the British government had started reducing a long-standing tax on newspapers, abolishing it completely in 1855. This resulted in a media boom. Russia was an obvious focus; this is one reason why the Crimean conflict has been called the first media war. Fleet Street became the epicenter of a tsunami of journalism that had a profound impact on the possibilities of inserting information onto an adversary's territory.[41] News clippings from British papers confirm that journalists and the public alike were intently focused on what was being published in other places. The London *Daily News* had regular columns devoted to the news in European capitals and beyond. Correspondents in Berlin provided their British readers with daily updates on the content of, for example, the *North German Gazette*, the *Cologne Gazette*, the *National Zeitung*, and the *Justice* and *Le Figaro* in Paris.

The spat between Bismarck and Gladstone could take the form of propaganda in the papers because there was a virtual guarantee that anything published in the German press would be picked up by English correspondents and relayed back to London. But to take the propaganda effort one step further, Bismarck used his secret "reptile" funds to purchase a news outlet in London, *The North German Correspondence.* And the Chancellor was said to maintain a close friendship with Edward Hermann Steinkopf, the owner of the *Pall Mall Gazette* who also reportedly had influence over the *St James Gazette.*[42] Unlike the situation in 1570, when Pope Pius had to arrange the smuggling of his message onto English soil, the modern press of 1884 made it very easy indeed.

Was Bismarck successful? Did his subversion matter? Gladstone was eventually forced to resign in 1885 after the defeat of his budget, but in fact his reputation was badly dented by the succession of domestic and foreign policy failures, capped by the death of General Gordon in Khartoum in January 1885, and all whipped up by criticism in the press at home and abroad. Bismarck surely had a hand in that.

## Conclusion

The episodes discussed in this chapter feature familiar motives and means. Everywhere we look, the temptations and risks of subversion appear in great powers' strategic calculations. Leaders try to make gains without bearing the costs of war by reaching across borders into the domestic politics of peer great powers. We see systematic efforts to manipulate factions in rival courts, to bribe sympathetic officials and courtiers, and to manipulate the popular press overtly and covertly. We witness something akin to regime change in reverse, preventing the possible formation of an undesired government in a rival great power—though one admittedly in an unusually weak position. But when the target was too strong or too diplomatically important for the era's balance-of-power game, subverters' hands were stayed.

Notwithstanding the continuity in the basic interplay of expected costs and benefits, the subtlety of nineteenth-century subversion stands in marked contrast to the cases discussed in the preceding two chapters. Violent subversion of great power peers—though feared, discussed and pondered as an option—is conspicuous by its absence. Elaborate efforts went into ensuring the deniability of the covert campaigns we discussed. One difference that leaps out when comparing the cases in this chapter to those in the previous ones is the prevalence of great power war. Nearly constant in the preceding chapters, after 1815 wars among the international system's top dogs became much less frequent.

And those that did occur were shorter. The result was to make the distinction between peace and war that we emphasized in Chapter 1 far more salient. Nearly constant great power war in the ancient and early modern worlds weakened constraints on subversion. Long periods of great power peace in the nineteenth century heightened the significance of those constraints.

This chapter reflects the pattern that we've already highlighted, one in which the tools and behaviors of subversion remain consistent over time while the frequency of decisive great power subversion seems to recede. Keeping this in mind, we now turn our attention to the familiar territory of subversion during the twentieth century and the Cold War.

# 5

## The Twentieth Century

### Searching for the Silver Bullet

MOST OF WHAT is written about subversive statecraft is about the twentieth century. But in this vast literature, you won't find an answer to this chapter's driving question: How did subversion's role in great power rivalry change from what we've observed across preceding centuries? Bearing in mind that we're focused on direct meddling by rival great power peers in each other's domestic affairs, the answer is surprising: very little. The same mix of incentives and constraints that governed subversion in previous centuries continued to limit its potency in the tumultuous twentieth century. But the pace did quicken. Two world wars and rapid technological, political, and geopolitical change fed an accelerated cycle: Great hopes for (and fears of) subversion's potential to decisively affect major power rivalries repeatedly emerged, new tools for meddling were put into play, defensive reactions followed, leading to a new equilibrium with subversion back in its box.

We arrive at that conclusion by examining three fraught periods in great power politics—the 1930s, the early Cold War, and the "new" Cold War in the 1980s. In each, we highlight the most probative cases that make for instructive comparisons: those with relatively abundant evidence in which there were good reasons to think conditions were especially favorable for the subverter. Remember: Our focus is on peacetime subversion among great powers because we already know from the massive scholarly edifice of studies on covert statecraft that great power subversion of smaller and weaker powers was rampant and often consequential, and that great powers took the gloves off when subverting each other in war.

## Subversion in the Peak Twenty Years' Crisis

It is difficult to identify a more intensely competitive great power setting than what E. H. Carr dubbed the "Twenty Years' Crisis"—the interval between the world wars when declining status quo powers struggled to fend off rising dissatisfied challengers while trying to avoid being dragged into a war by entangling alliances, as had happened in 1914. In light of the preceding chapters, it comes as no surprise that if you look beneath the surface of the high politics Carr and other scholars of international politics focus on, a stunningly complex netherworld of measures short of war comes into focus. The great powers had taken the gloves off subversion during the Great War. Institutional memories and, in some cases, operational networks from wartime lingered into the post-war period. As the post-war period began to look ever more like a pre-war period, the subversive competition intensified.

### The Undercurrent of Subversion

Two major forces cut across borders in ways that opened doors to subversion: ideology and national identity. In Europe, the challengers— Germany, Italy, and the USSR—were each ultimately governed by a leader espousing a threatening ideology with adherents within the defenders who might be mobilized for subversive ends. If nineteenth-century empires were preoccupied by the potential dagger of subversive national feeling abetted from abroad, the twentieth century's major democratic powers—the United States, Britain, and France—fretted about "fifth columns" inspired by the ideologies—and aided by the pocketbooks—of great power rivals. Furthermore, the war had shown in spades how subversive national self-determination could be, helping propel the breakup of three great empires. One needed to look no further than Berlin's "hybrid war" efforts to mobilize German speakers in Czechoslovakia and Austria to see that national identity was a potent part of the mix in the new geopolitical setting.

The USSR's interwar experience reflected the most exaggerated fears and hopes about the subversive power of both factors. The ideology story is well known, featuring the creation of the Comintern and its use as a tool of revolutionary realpolitik. But hopes for dramatic subversion of capitalist rivals soon morphed into trumped-up fears that external forces might exploit intra-party dissension to undermine Stalin's rule. Each wave of internal repression in the Great Terror was accompanied by ever more outlandish claims of foreign subversion as formerly loyal Bolshevik leaders were coerced into confessions of working for foreign intelligence services in elaborate show trials. Tens of thousands of less famous comrades met similar fates in dingy rooms in the basement of the Lubyanka and other NKVD redoubts. Exaggerated fears of political subversion by ideological adversaries were baked into Soviet rule.

Less well known is the story of how hopes and fears about subversion via national identity influenced the very structure of the USSR and the country's nationalities policies. The creation of the USSR's federal structure, with national republics in the borderlands enjoying (at first) limited cultural autonomy, was partly an attempt to undermine rivals via subversion. Ukraine was the showcase. Vladimir Putin's claim that Lenin "created" modern Ukraine is a tendentious reference to the early, optimistic phase of this subversive policy: to foster appealing ethnic republics to attract co-nationals across borders and undermine rivals. Historian Terry Martin dubbed this the "Piedmont principle," referring to that Italian state's role as the nucleus driving Italy's unification. Soviet Ukraine would be to Ukrainians under Polish, Romanian, and Czechoslovak rule as Piedmont was to fellow Italians during that country's unification.[1] An attractive Soviet Ukraine made for a far better base of subversive operations among co-ethnics across the border than a Russian-dominated USSR.

The same went for other borderland republics (Moldavia, Karelia, Belarus, etc.)—but not for long. As Soviet rule became more repressive and violent, as the peasantry suffered under brutal collectivization, the Piedmont principle reversed: Co-nationals across borders were doing better. Ukrainians under Polish rule weren't being murdered and starved en masse. Worried that Poland would do unto the USSR just what the Bolsheviks had tried to do to Poland, Stalin wrought massive repression on Ukrainians. So Stalin's wave of repression engulfed not only so-called class enemies but also entire ethnic populations accused of being susceptible to foreign subversion. In extremis, whole populations—Chechens, Crimean Tatars, and Volga Germans—were brutally packed on trains and exiled to Siberia. To be sure, there were foreign operations in play that sought to nurture subversive action among Soviet national minorities—but these were pinpricks compared to the violent repression Stalin unleashed.[2]

The Soviet story shows how great power subversion can be important historically and politically even when it does not yield big geopolitical payoffs. The USSR made itself into a tough target for external subversion in part by fetishizing counter-subversion to the point of a morbid paranoia that ultimately did more damage to Soviet power than anything the foreign intelligence services could have dreamt up.

### Democracies in the Crosshairs

But what about the seemingly vulnerable democratic targets? Not surprisingly, authoritarian adversaries took shots at subversion. Berlin funneled support to the German–American Bund, the Friends of New Germany, and other sympathetic groups in the United States; Germany and Italy were important financiers of the British Union of Fascists and its leader Sir Oswald Mosley; and the Kremlin diverted scarce resources to subvent communist parties operating in its democratic great power peers (Germany and Italy having outlawed opposition parties early in the decade).

How did it all play out as the crisis came to a head in the mid- to late 1930s? Much as it had in the previous century, it turns out. Despite new technology like the radio, compelling transnational ideologies like fascism and communism, clever new organizations to mold those ideologies to strategic ends like the Comintern, and seemingly vulnerable targets mired in the Great Depression and riven by class struggle, subversion remained a sideshow in this dangerous multipolar game. Why?

Part of the answer lies in the perennial challenge of how to support a sympathetic political movement within the target without compromising its effectiveness—an especially acute problem concerning right-wing nationalist ideologies like fascism. If your slogan is "America first" or "Britain first," being seen to take money from a foreign power was not a good look.[3] And then there was defense. The U.S. House of Representatives Special Committee on Un-American Activities, of later McCarthyite infamy, dates from this era, having been formed in 1934 to consider responses to Nazi meddling. The Committee exposed examples of brazen subversion by Americans on the German payroll, including the case of an American agent for Berlin who inserted pro-German propaganda into the Congressional Record and distributed it to millions of Americans by using the congressional franking privilege, courtesy of sympathetic legislators.[4] The result was the U.S. Foreign Agents Registration Act, which Franklin Delano Roosevelt (FDR) signed into law in 1938 and remains in force today. Much more extreme measures—such as secret prosecution and internment of fascists by MI5 and the British Security Service, witch hunts for communist subversives, and, shamefully, the wartime internment of Japanese Americans—were so repressive as to forever tar the very idea of counter-subversion.[5]

But the main story was that the strategic setting made subversive fifth columns into potential diplomatic liabilities. Germany wanted the United States to follow a policy of benevolent neglect of European affairs. For most of the latter 1930s, this seemed a real possibility that was only being undermined by scandals swirling around Nazi support for U.S. isolationists.[6] Berlin understood this and curtailed support even though having American co-believers was gratifying ideologically. Once the battle for U.S. alignment became acute after the fall of France, the Germans did attempt to support isolationists but had to contend with a new actor on the American internal scene. Under instructions from Winston Churchill, MI6 set up a covert action shop in New York—British Security Coordination (BSC)—that unleashed a series of operations to influence U.S. public opinion, counter Germany's subversive efforts, and tar America firsters with the brush of treasonous collaboration with the Nazis.[7]

In hindsight, the British operation appears to have been far more effective than the German operation, but the main reason was that London was working with, not against, the U.S. government: MI6 acted with FDR's blessing and the active support of J. Edgar Hoover's Federal Bureau of Investigation (FBI). The FBI was still cutting its teeth as a counter-intelligence agency, and Hoover welcomed British assistance as his agency expanded in response to "fifth column" fears made all too real in Hitler's European conquests.[8] (Once the United Kingdom became a belligerent in the war, the U.S. Neutrality Act forbade FBI–MI6 collaboration against German subversion, so a covert operation was the only way to continue it.) As controversial as the BSC operation would have been had it been exposed, it reflected rather than changed the policy of the sitting U.S. government.

Britain's fascist movement was stronger than its U.S. counterpart, but the same pattern played out there. Evidence from Italian archives suggests that Rome imagined for a time that Mosley and the British Union of Fascists might actually gain political power, but ultimately the aim was to blunt British opposition to Italian designs in Africa.[9] Once officials in Rome lost confidence in Mosley's ability to influence British policy, they dropped their subsidy and focused on sympathetic conservatives in parliament and Whitehall. The same went for Berlin: Why risk alienating a British government following an appeasement strategy by supporting fascist troublemakers? To be sure, Joseph Goebbels was unable entirely to resist entreaties for funds coming from Mosley's glamorous Nazi-connected wife, Diana (née Mitford), but they came with the injunction that "Mosley must work harder and be less mercenary."[10]

The constraining power of the strategic situation itself is clearest in the case of the French Communist Party (PCF), for there the other constraints were weaker. Perhaps no tool has ever existed with as much potential for great power subversion as the Communist International, which comprised parties throughout the world—including within rival great powers—operating at times in an atmosphere in which very large fractions of the population expressed sympathy not only for the local communist party but also for the Soviet Union and everything they thought it stood for. The constraint that "my country first" nationalism imposed on fascist internationalism hardly applied to parties based on transnational class solidarity. Stalin could issue orders for actions in support of Soviet foreign policy and expect them to be implemented by party leaders in target countries, in some cases with hundreds of thousands of faithful followers.[11] And therein lay the dilemma for the democracies, for if a big chunk of the electorate feels sympathy for a foreign power and organizes a mass party around that idea, the government of a liberal polity has limited options for defense.

More than any major power, France exemplified this subversive potential. Generations of French working people were raised in a pro-Soviet communist party culture, loyally following the party line as defined by leaders who took their cues from the Kremlin.[12] Make no mistake, this was a case in which common knowledge of the party's loyalty to a foreign power was an asset, not a liability. Moscow's implausible denials of the connection were to smooth diplomatic conversations only. And the line from the Soviet leader shifted with every realpolitik maneuver Moscow saw fit to execute—eventually including support for the Hitler–Stalin pact and opposition to French rearmament as the Nazi war machine threatened France.

No government today possesses anything remotely like this, a popular, legitimate political party in another great power at its beck and call. Yet the PCF never figured especially importantly in Stalin's grand

**Figure 5.1** Comintern poster, 1920. Perhaps no tool has ever existed with as much potential for great power subversion as the Communist International.
*Source*: incamerastock/Alamy stock photo.

strategy throughout the 1930s' geopolitically fraught denouement.[13] Why? The PCF's impressive potential as a subversive instrument was only possible because its connection to Soviet statecraft was common knowledge. Sure, Stalin maintained a charade of Comintern independence that allowed him to implausibly deny its official role, but serious people were not fooled. Even without the documents we now have that tell the story in detail, the PCF's very subservience gave away the game.

As a result, if Stalin seemed to authorize actions by the party that challenged Paris too frontally, he risked alienating the government of a great power. And Moscow needed cooperation that it could not obtain if local communist activities sparked retaliation by more establishment parties. Whether it sought diplomatic recognition, trade deals, technology transfer, military cooperation, or alliances to balance Germany, Moscow could be thwarted rather than assisted by overzealous action by local communists. The game was about nudging French policy, not undermining the French state, and so the PCF had to be wielded as a scalpel, not an ax.

These tensions came to the fore during the so-called popular front period from 1934 to 1939. With Moscow's encouragement, the PCF moved toward an inclusive front with parties of the left against fascism domestically and Nazi Germany internationally. Stalin's policy in this period was to avoid being tricked into taking on Germany alone. He wanted to do to Britain and France what he (rightly) assumed they were trying to do to him: pass the buck, doing everything possible to deflect German power toward the West, and doing everything possible to induce the Western powers themselves to step up to the plate and take on Germany first.[14]

From that perspective, the worst thing for Moscow was to feed the already deep wellsprings of the Western powers' mistrust of the Soviet Union and create a sense of unity between Germany and the democracies in their opposition to communism. That mistrust was "justifiable," historian Jonathan Haslam argues, in part because of the Comintern's past subversive actions against France and Britain (and their empires).[15] That delayed cost of prior subversion limited the degree to which Stalin could now support a forward-leaning stance for the PCF. The evidence shows him trying to make use of the party to forward his objective—especially forging and sustaining the 1935

Franco-Soviet pact to contain Germany—but unable to go too far.[16] On Moscow's instructions, the party flipped its long-standing position against "bourgeois militarism" to support rearmament, much to the consternation of its core membership. But the more popular the party became, and the more energized its membership became, the more the specter of the "red menace" appeared, which would weaken the already wavering French commitment to collective security. Should the communist party become too big a threat to the French establishment, it could drive the French and possibly even the British center-right into an appeasement stance.

### Early Cold War: High Hopes

Slowly but steadily, it became apparent in Moscow and Washington after 1945 that looming before each was the potential for a gigantically expensive exercise in traditional statecraft: creating a balance of power to contain the other superpower. The costs that entailed seemed daunting, but in the immediate wake of history's deadliest war (and with atomic weapons entering the picture), the costs of reverting to war to settle East–West disputes were too huge to contemplate. Hence the appeal of measures short of war as substitutes for or complements to balancing via arms buildups and alliance commitments. Each side had just ramped up tools for subversion from propaganda to sabotage and insurgent operations as part of its war effort. Each had tools at its disposal that might be used to subvert the other to weaken either its capability or intent to balance. In the West, there were communist parties and various and sundry sympathizers, and at least some political forces with doubts about making major commitments internationally; in the East, anti-communists, nationalists, and various other potentially subversive forces existed, along with contacts and networks for influencing them, ready to be picked up from their former Nazi masters.

How did subversive statecraft interact with traditional balancing as the Cold War dawned? Of course, we now know that balancing ("containment") would dominate subversion ("rollback"). And we know that Stalin preferred suborned communist-led buffer states in Central Europe to the risks of spreading revolution westward. But scholars' probing of ever more formerly secret documents has uncovered just how slow the process was on both sides. It took time for Moscow and Washington fully to come to terms with the fact that they could not subvert the other side's consolidation of a balancing alliance.[17]

### Stalin Banks on Balancing

If Stalin was going to take subversive action to impede the consolidation of an anti-Soviet bloc, the most obvious place to start was Western Europe, home to potent communist parties. France was a promising target. The PCF was at its peak, basking in the glory of its role in the resistance and, for a time, was France's largest party. Its leader, Maurice Thorez—having spent the war penning inspirational missives from "somewhere in France" while in fact safely ensconced in Moscow—served briefly as prime minister. French politics were poisonously polarized and seemed ripe for subversion. What could go wrong?

From 1944 to 1947, the instructions from Moscow were to support "national unity" in cooperation with other political forces as the best means of reducing British and American influence. A turning point came in 1947 with the expulsion of the PCF from government, the announcement of the Marshall Plan, and a Moscow-approved mass mobilization of the communists in opposition. At first glance, this nationwide campaign, which included mass strikes that at times turned violent, constitutes bold subversion. But Stalin probably knew that unleashing the PCF in this way stood scant chance of changing France's anti-Soviet course. And he rejected an option that local party leaders in both France and Italy considered: armed insurrection.[18] His reasoning can be pieced together from his conversations with communist leaders: It was simply too dangerous.[19] The path to escalation was on display in Greece, where the communists had taken up arms in a bloody civil war. Were such a conflict to occur in a major Western power with Anglo-American forces on the scene, its spread—possibly to involve the Soviet Union itself—was a frighteningly real prospect, especially given the other mounting sources of East–West tension.

The United States had a vast arsenal of tools—notably the massive economic resources underwriting the Marshall Plan—to draw France, Italy, and the smaller powers close. And Washington did not shrink from its own major covert action to support non-communist parties.

**Figure 5.2** Communist rally at the Chateaudun crossroads, Paris, June 20, 1946. As newspapers warned of civil war, French authorities "approached the situation as that of an essentially subversive and insurrectional character." *Source*: Roger-Viollet Gallery.

It worked with a powerfully motivated French political and military establishment, which "approached the situation as that of an essentially subversive and insurrectional character."[20] Given those advantages, Soviet subversion that posed a real threat to the formation of a Western alliance was a measure too close to war for Stalin. Creating his own sphere was taxing enough to preclude taking much larger risks to subvert the formation of the Western bloc.[21] The prize was the creation of a secure sphere of influence in those areas where his military power stretched. Subversion continued to be a useful tool at the margins for complicating matters for the rival, but it would remain at levels that would not, in Stalin's estimation, risk an aggressive response from the West.

In short, Marshall Plan money, the Central Intelligence Agency's (CIA) own covert support for non-communist parties, and Stalin's circumspection ultimately consigned Soviet subversion via Western Europe's powerful communist movement to a supporting role in early Cold War geopolitics. Moscow settled into a pattern of using communist parties in Western Europe in opposition to try to frustrate the consolidation or strengthening of the West. The PCF scored a victory (in cahoots with Gaullist forces) in defeating the European Defense Community in 1954 in the National Assembly—a significant win against U.S.-sponsored balancing, but a temporary one. Ultimately, although the PCF would long remain a mass party giving steadfast backing to Soviet policy aims, for the bulk of the Cold War, Moscow was happy to deal with Gaullist presidents who steered a quasi-independent course within the West.

Given much weaker communist parties in the United States and United Kingdom, the prospects for high-impact subversion there were even dimmer.[22] Ever opportunistic, Moscow worked with the tools it had to complicate matters for its rival. The Kremlin maintained its elaborate spy network and sought out sympathetic figures who might prove useful in advancing Soviet foreign policy. An example from these years made headlines on May 18, 1948. Radio Moscow broadcast a lengthy message from Stalin responding to an open letter from U.S. Progressive Party candidate Henry Wallace. The Kremlin tyrant praised Wallace's proposals for settling the issues that were driving the USSR and United States toward a cold war. Even sympathetic observers noted how favorable those ideas were to Moscow's official positions. Thanks to historian Benn Steil's extensive research in Russian and U.S. archives, we now know that this was no coincidence: Stalin himself had suggested most of them in a complex back-and-forth with Wallace via Moscow's ambassador to Washington, Andrey Gromyko, and his boss, Foreign Minister Vyacheslav Molotov.[23] There's a word for these surreptitious dealings: collusion.

Wallace's motive was to bolster his campaign by presenting himself as the man who could avoid a cold war and tarring Truman as a belligerent hawk. According to Steil, he was so desperate for the imprimatur of a statesmanlike dialogue with Stalin that he was happy to present many of the Soviet leader's stances on the Cold War as his own. For his part, Stalin took the opportunity offered by Wallace's ambition, almost certainly not with any delusions about the former vice president's quest for the White House. His game was likely subtler. Moscow had just leaked details of a secret approach to Molotov by U.S. ambassador Walter Bedell Smith in a way that made the U.S. administration look eager to deal in private but bellicose in public. Bolstering the forthright

Wallace's approach put Truman's policy in a bad light. The result, in the State Department assessment, was "a temporary propaganda victory."[24]

Hence, Soviet subversion against the main great power adversary in the early Cold War amounted to a handy handmaiden of Machiavellian public diplomacy.

### George Kennan and "Rollback"

As the Cold War dawned in Washington, meanwhile, no one knew that "containment" would work, so key decision-makers reached for another tool: subversion, including violent subversion, of the Soviet superpower. It failed, and we ended up with the Cold War of memory, but the flirtation with a proxy war on the territory of a great power peer in peacetime speaks volumes about the subject of this book.

The attempt at direct, violent subversion of a superpower peer was but the tip of a long spear that included similar operations against the emerging Soviet-supported communist satellite regimes in central Europe as well as the vast panoply of nonviolent measures. But it looks on the surface like an extraordinarily bold subversive operation, much like what big powers often do to small ones in peacetime, and like what some great powers attempt against each other in war. Indeed, many of the people who conceived and ran the program were coming fresh from the experience of running such operations in wartime German-occupied Europe.[25] What explains this dramatic effort, and why did it end in ignominious failure?

Let's look at it through the fertile mind of the man who would later be heralded as the "father of containment," George Kennan. It's July 1947. Kennan had already penned his "long telegram" from Moscow on the Soviet threat. A public version was just out in *Foreign Affairs* under the pseudonym "Mr. X." There he explained why Moscow was so unalterably hostile to the West that a diplomatic settlement of the world war—a swirling mass of issues in which the fate of Germany was primary—was unrealistic. The massive Red Army, which had, more than any other force, defeated the most fearsome military machine the world has ever known, sat in the center of Europe. And the Kremlin also controlled a worldwide subversive network of communist parties that it was using to weaken and frustrate efforts of the Atlantic powers.

For Kennan, the overarching challenge now was to create such a powerful counterbalance to the Soviet Union that its expansionary impulse could find no outlet.

As that message resonated in Washington and allied capitals, Kennan was wracked by doubts. He did not know if such a counter to Soviet power was feasible, how much it would cost, whether public opinion in democracies would support it, and whether another war could be averted. There was no precedent in history, most certainly not in the American experience, for what we now know ended up happening: the creation of a durable, powerful, institutionalized North Atlantic Treaty Organization (NATO) complete with a large, permanent U.S. military presence in Europe, the whole rivalry stalemated by mutual fear of nuclear annihilation. If you'd spelled out that vision to him in 1947, he'd have been appalled, seeing such an outcome as a dangerous threat, especially to American democracy at home. For Kennan, division of Europe was a defeat; victory was some kind of arrangement that got Soviet power out of central Europe. What he wanted was a more traditional balancing coalition comprising rebuilt great powers in Europe backed by a distant but supportive America.

Even before Moscow's acquisition of atomic weapons, war was too frightening to contemplate seriously. Diplomacy, too, was completely stalled with the breakdown of the foreign ministers conference trying to settle the German Question. Stalemated diplomacy meant there was little to bargain with, few realistic carrots to offer. This was the hothouse that nurtured the strategy of "measures short of war" against the USSR. The solution developed by Kennan and his policy planning staff, and supported in various highly secretive committees in Washington, was to combine a strategy of rebuilding and drawing together the Western allies with subversion operations that would "reduce the power and influence of the USSR to limits which no longer constitute a threat to the peace, national independence and stability of the world family of nations" and "bring about a basic change in the conduct of international relations by the government in power in Russia, to conform with the purposes and principles set forth in the UN charter."[26]

It was time to reach across the USSR's borders and make things happen on its territory that would affect the balance of power.

**Figure 5.3** George F. Kennan, member of the State Department Policy Planning Staff, sits at his desk, June 25, 1947, Washington, DC (AP photo/John Rooney). Kennan stated, "The political warfare initiative was the greatest mistake I ever made."
*Source*: Associated Press/Alamy stock photo.

Collaborating with former Nazi officers who had developed networks in the region during the war, and building on already established operational contacts, U.S. officials sought to channel material and human aid to anti-Soviet insurgents in Ukraine, Moldova, and the Baltic states, whose numbers exceeded 100,000.[27] According to operational commander Harry Rositzke, in Ukraine's Galicia region alone, the United

States supported approximately 30,000 rebels with airdrops of medical support, cash, and wireless radio transmitters:

> These cross-border operations involved enormous resources of technical and documentation support, hundreds of training officers, thousands of safe-houses, and, above all, hundreds of courageous men who preferred to fight the Russians or the communists rather than linger in DP camps or emigrate to Brazil. Scores of agents paid with their lives for our concern.[28]

And Kennan was not alone. Across the pond, his British counterparts were reaching the same conclusions. As historian Calder Walton reconstructs the mood in official London,

**Figure 5.4** Fighters of the Lithuanian anti-Soviet resistance: "These cross-border operations involved . . . hundreds of courageous men who preferred to fight the Russians or the communists rather than linger in DP camps or emigrate."
*Source*: Harry Rositzke, "America's Secret Operations: A Perspective," *Foreign Affairs,* January 1975, p. 335.

Britain's senior policymakers and civil servants were sharpening their own covert action knives. Labour foreign secretary Ernest Bevin was initially skeptical about letting MI6 and the CIA's dogs of war loose because of the reaction it might engender from Stalin. But Bevin's resistance towards covert action softened as he struggled with successive diplomatic failures with the Soviet Union and meetings of foreign ministers. He agreed to a policy of covert action in Eastern Europe. . . . In a report kept classified for seven decades, MI6 chief Menzies offered a menu of dirty tricks, ranging from propaganda, bribery, and blackmail . . . to more sinister acts like arson, sabotage, kidnapping, and "liquidations"—apparently a euphemism for assassinations.[29]

The fate of these operations was ugly. Much later, in retirement, CIA officers, including Rositzke, would look back with profound regret at their role in sending Ukrainians and Balts to their deaths at the hands of Stalin's police state, for no discernible end. John Paton Davies, who worked with Kennan on the policy planning staff, concluded in a 1994 interview that the rollback operations "were unnecessarily dangerous and provocative."[30] A CIA study declassified in 1998, while justifying the operation in light of the tough circumstances, ruefully concludes that "the CIA's efforts to penetrate the Iron Curtain using Ukrainian agents was [sic] ill-fated and tragic."[31] Bureaucratically, the operations were a mess.[32] Neither President Truman nor President Eisenhower intervened to impose a clear organization, until 1956, when Eisenhower convened a top secret commission to examine these operations that concluded with a pungent, no-holds-barred critique.

That bureaucratic incoherence was mainly the result of strategic incoherence that even Kennan's storied mastery of the English language could not overcome. What was the purpose? The answers were varied and contradictory. The headline aim sometimes was regime change. But against the USSR? Cooler heads realized that supporting insurgents in Ukraine and the Baltics wasn't going to end with the toppling of the Soviet communist party. Stalin's USSR was one of the toughest counterinsurgents in history. The dictator had spent the 1930s terrorizing his population, accusing masses of innocent people of fictitious subversive plots. The entire regime ran on morbid, pervasive suspicion of fifth columns. The notion that the pinprick operations the CIA ran at the Cold War's dawn would move the needle on Soviet political stability was farcical.

So perhaps the rationale was to weaken the Soviet Union by causing it to divert resources to combating the insurgents? One U.S. official saw the goal as "throwing grit into the machine of communist regimes;" another ventured that it was "to get in there and do something that would put a frown on Uncle Joe's face."[33] But would it be a frown or an amused smile? The problem by 1949 was the lack of an operating base anywhere near Soviet territory, creating formidable logistical problems. Without a nearby safe space, any hope of a sustained insurgency was forlorn; ultimately, the Ukrainian fight ran its course largely independent of the U.S. efforts to aid it.[34] So maybe the goal was to prepare for a possible war, in which case networks of operatives on Soviet territory would be helpful? Or perhaps it was to use insurgent agents to gather intelligence to assess Soviet intentions now? All these rationales can be found in the documents, yet they are contradictory. Using agents to conduct sabotage operations and impose costs on Moscow now undermines their use as sleeper cells for a possible World War III or as ongoing espionage assets. If peacetime espionage or wartime sabotage are your aims, you can't undertake subversion.

This kaleidoscope of rationales was itself the effect of a larger strategic reality. The Soviet Union was an extremely tough target with a home field advantage and the capacity to retaliate. Its counter-intelligence operation was massive and wily—and had little difficulty penetrating the insurgent movements. It ruthlessly rolled up the "rollback" networks. Because of its overwhelming home field advantage, Moscow never needed to escalate in response. Had it felt the need, its capacity to do so was fearsome. As Eisenhower's secret commission concluded, "Careless implementation [of this policy] might well create situations which the USSR would consider grounds for war."[35] Doing anything serious required a big operation, and a big operation could not be conducted in a non-escalatory way. Eisenhower administration national security documents reflected the changed tone, emphasizing that subversive measures short of war were unlikely to "stimulate major change"; that the aim in undermining the Soviet Union was "evolutionary rather than revolutionary"; and that "no political warfare strategy can in any sense substitute for adequate military, political, and economic programs designed to strengthen the Free World."[36] Slowly and fitfully, the U.S. government came to terms with the fact that subversion could not substitute for conventional balancing.

Just as Stalin ended up placing his bets on horrifically expensive balancing rather than subversion, the United States ultimately implemented the containment grand strategy we came to know—precisely the outcome Kennan so ardently wished to avoid, to the extent that he was pushed to experiment with a subversive strategy he later came to regret. He told the Church Senate investigative committee in 1975 that "the political warfare initiative was the greatest mistake I ever made. It did not work out at all the way I had conceived it."[37]

## Mature Cold War Subversion: Covert Harassment

After the failed kinetic political warfare operations of the early Cold War, the United States backed away from violent cross-border subversion of the Soviet Union, and indeed the Soviet bloc. Against weaker adversaries with less diplomatic clout, such restraint was conspicuous by its absence. Even China, with its vast potential, remained weak, isolated, and hostile for the first years after the communists' victory in 1949. Washington did not truly give up on even violent subversion until the U.S.–China rapprochement in the 1970s. By then, China had not only acquired nuclear weapons but also, in the Nixon–Kissinger strategy, assumed diplomatic value far too great to risk by alienating Mao with pinprick operations in places like Tibet.[38]

It was the East Berlin uprising in 1953 that crystallized a red line concerning subversion of the Soviet bloc: Fear of escalation kept the Eisenhower administration's support to nonviolent means.[39] Washington gravitated to subtler, more arm's-length strategies, including continued indirect efforts to support nationalist and dissident movements within the Soviet Union, an array of direct information operations, and a sustained effort to undermine the Kremlin via the use of émigré-staffed radio stations.[40] An indicator of U.S. circumspection about bolder subversive operations was the negative reaction in the government decades later when CIA director Bill Casey advocated ramping up the operation in support of anti-regime insurgents in Afghanistan to funnel support to Islamist anti-Soviet operatives in the Tajik Soviet Socialist Republic.[41] For their part, the Soviets sustained and developed an elaborate toolkit for subversion, including communist parties, front organizations, propaganda, and elaborately organized disinformation campaigns.

Neither side wholly reconciled itself to the constraints on subverting the rival. Always, clever minds in each capital sought some silver bullet workaround that would have real effects on the competition without risking escalation or a dangerous poisoning of relations.

## Cold War Radio

Washington's coterie of political warriors came to view radio as a major Western advantage. The Soviet Union was a very tough target for violent subversion, and its fearsome counter-intelligence capabilities severely restricted other forms of active measures. But its stifling, obsessive, ham-handed control over the internal information environment was vulnerable to simple truth-telling. U.S. radio ~~propaganda~~ exploded after 1945. Radio in the American Sector (RIAS) broadcast from West Berlin into East Berlin and East Germany, becoming phenomenally successful with listeners on the other side of the Iron Curtain.[42] The Voice of America (VOA), inaugurated in February 1942 to combat Nazi propaganda, eventually broadcast in 48 languages worldwide. As "white" propaganda, its links to the U.S. government were freely acknowledged and its content designed to present the best aspects of American society. Musical programming, particularly jazz, was a powerful soft weapon in the war for hearts and minds. But enterprising Cold Warriors, among them George Kennan at the State Department and Frank Wisner at the Office of Policy Coordination, wanted a covert operation to work alongside the overt one. The result—Radio Free Europe (RFE) and Radio Liberty (RL)—came to be classed among the most effective elements of U.S. psychological warfare in the history of the Cold War.[43]

Radio Free Europe, which began broadcasting into Soviet satellite states on July 4, 1950, was the collective brainchild of Kennan and Wisner, along with former Office of Strategic Services veteran and future CIA head Allen Dulles. Dulles and a group of illustrious private citizens formed the National Committee for a Free Europe to provide cover for RFE as a private, nongovernmental entity. RL, which began broadcasting into the Soviet Union on March 1, 1953, operated along the same lines as RFE, working out of their joint headquarters in Munich's Englischer Garten. Just as RFE used refugees and defectors from Eastern bloc countries to broadcast back into their homelands, so RL harnessed defectors and members of the Russian diaspora to broadcast back into Russia. Within 18 months of its first broadcast, RL had added Ukrainian, Belarusian, and 15 other local languages of the Soviet Union to its programming. Funding came from the CIA, carefully concealed behind the ongoing front of RFE/RL as a private enterprise.[44] And it did more than broadcast messages. A CIA report from 1970 documented more than 2.5 million "ideologically objectionable" books and periodicals distributed into the Soviet Union and Eastern Europe within the previous two decades.[45]

After 1989, RFE/RL and their associated programs came to be viewed as a far-seeing investment in consciousness raising in Central Europe and the USSR that paid off in communism's swift collapse. Evidence poured forth from the region of the key role the radio "voices" played in informing citizens and inculcating skepticism about their communist rulers' legitimacy. But that is hindsight. The bulk of evidence from the mature Cold War reveals more prosaic aims: to help foment dissent, impose costs on the Soviets, embarrass them, and put them on the back foot. And by those more modest lights, the program seemed at the time to be a smashing success. After all, the targeted regime in Moscow constantly complained about the radio broadcasts and devoted enormous resources to jam them.[46] Within minutes of the first broadcast in March 1953, the Soviets began jamming the frequency.[47] According to the CIA, offense had the advantage here: "The $150 million spent annually by the Russians for jamming operations which are only marginally successful is indicative of the value of Radio Free Europe and Radio Liberty which cost less than $35 million to operate." Based on evidence from defectors and legal travelers, the CIA asserted, "It is generally agreed that RL merits a significant share of the credit for the increasing manifestations of dissent and opposition among the Soviet intelligentsia."[48]

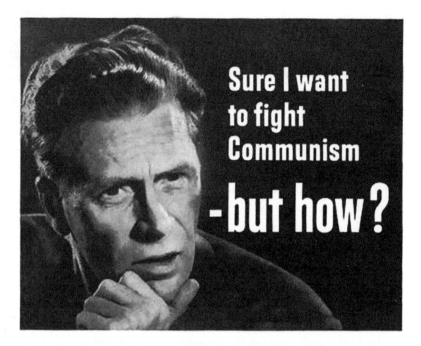

## With "TRUTH DOLLARS"–*that's how!*

Your "Truth Dollars" fight Communism in it's own back yard—*behind* the Iron Curtain. Give "Truth Dollars" and get in the fight!

"Truth Dollars" send words of truth and hope to the 70 million freedom loving people behind the Iron Curtain.

These words broadcast over Radio Free Europe's 29 transmitters reach Poles, Czechoslovakians, Hungarians, Romanians and Bulgarians. RFE is supported by the voluntary, cooperative action of millions of Americans engaged in this fight of good against evil.

*How do "Truth Dollars" fight Communism?* By exposing Red lies . . . revealing news suppressed by Moscow and by unmasking Communist collaborators. The broadcasts are by exiles in the native

tongues of the people to whom they are beamed.

Radio Free Europe is hurting Communism in its own back yard. We know by Red efforts to "jam" our programs (so far without success). To successfully continue these broadcasts, even more transmitters are needed.

*Every dollar buys 100 words of truth.* That's how hard "Truth Dollars" work. Your dollars will help 70 million people resist the Kremlin. Keep the truth turned on. Send as many "Truth Dollars" as you can (if possible, a dollar for each member of your family). The need is now.

FIGHT COMMUNISM

with "TRUTH DOLLARS"

## *Support* Radio Free Europe

*Send your "Truth Dollars" to* CRUSADE FOR FREEDOM *c/o your Postmaster*

**Figure 5.5** 1950s USA Radio Free Europe magazine advertisement. CIA funding for Radio Free Europe and Radio Liberty was covert until 1972.
*Source*: Retro AdArchives/Alamy stock photo.

*Front Organizations*

Radio-borne propaganda's success was an exception to the rule: Through much of the latter Cold War, Americans fretted that the Soviets had a subversive advantage. Moscow's Cold War use of "front organizations" that could channel Communist Party organizational savvy and funds from the Central Committee's International Department to various peace and disarmament movements is a case in point. Precise numbers are murky, but there's little doubt that these were major operations. GRU defector Stanislav Lunev claimed that the USSR gave $1 billion to American anti-war movements, more than it gave to the Viet Cong. A State Department official told *TIME* magazine that the KGB may have spent $600 million on the peace offensive of the early 1980s. In various reports, the FBI and Britain's MI6 suggested comparable numbers for other periods.[49]

There is no need to accept those numbers at face value, or to buy the old Cold Warhawks' view that these indigenous, popular, and sincere mass movements were created or controlled by the Kremlin, to appreciate the significance of Moscow's efforts. For starters, they were far more organized, directed, expensive, and substantial than any subversive effort emanating from Moscow in recent times, 2016 included. The key aim was modest: bolster opposition to U.S. policies that could make Cold War competition more expensive for Moscow and strengthen the Soviets' diplomatic position by nudging popular movements to direct popular political pressure at Washington. And it is just possible that they were the most successful such operations the Soviet Union ever mounted.

The first phase from 1946 to 1956 was organized by communists under the auspices of the Moscow-funded World Peace Council (WPC).[50] The communists' leading role was clear, but the movement was hugely diverse, headlined by a star-studded cast of intellectual and scientific leaders from the Soviet Union and throughout the West. It began with mass petition campaigns, the best known being the Stockholm Appeal calling for the prohibition of nuclear weapons. The trademark communist organizational prowess yielded thousands of local peace committees to collect signatures—nearly 500 million by the end of 1950, a quarter of the world's population. Moscow then directed the movement to

support its diplomatic push for a great power pact of collective security in Europe. This time, 600 million signatures were gathered, but a
much greater proportion came from the USSR and China, reflecting a
challenge Moscow's men on the WPC reported to their masters. Soviet
writer Ilya Ehrenburg's memos back to the foreign ministry stressed the
contradiction posed by demands for a broad peace movement that was
also a direct tool of Soviet foreign policy.

The Soviet invasion of Hungary in 1956 fractured global communism
and the peace movement it nurtured. The ostensible goals—nuclear
abolition and a collective security pact in Europe that would exclude
the United States—were not achieved. But, thanks to the movement,
Soviet proposals dominated the 1955 Geneva Summit. In Washington,
President Eisenhower received a report on opinion polling that seemed
to show a Western public alarmingly persuaded by Soviet proposals
which raised "disquieting doubts about the future of NATO." As historian Geoffrey Roberts notes, "By the time a second conference of
foreign ministers convened in November 1955, the Western powers had
been forced by public and political opinion to put forward their own
proposals on European collective security."[51] Putting your rival on the
back foot, and inducing it to negotiations it originally opposed, on
terms you define, is not regime change, it's not the assassination of a
hated leader, and it's not even a massive drain on rival resources. But
in the real world of diplomacy, it's not half bad. And as important as
the indigenous sources of the peace movement were, there is no way it
would have assumed its size, coherence, and specific policy direction
but for the Soviet operation.

The next phase was marked by greater subtlety and a proliferation
of front organizations meant to resolve the contradiction Ehrenburg
stressed: how to attract the independent supporters necessary for a
broad and credible movement while still bending it to Soviet policy. As
a CIA report noted, the front organizations, covering interests ranging
from peace to student issues, women's issues, religion, and science,
posed a challenge to the democratic West: "They are difficult to trace
and to deal with because they fall into the gray areas between a legitimate exchange of ideas and an active measures operation."[52]

Numerous campaigns took a similar form, combining traditional
diplomatic proposals meant to resonate with peace movements

and pressure Washington with propaganda aided and abetted by Moscow-funded front organizations. The movements Moscow sought to influence did contribute to real policy effects. Examples include President Jimmy Carter's decision to cancel a planned deployment of the enhanced radiation weapon (ERW), the so-called neutron bomb; President Ronald Reagan's move toward a "dual track" decision to counter intense pressure against a new U.S. deployment of intermediate-range missiles in Europe by offering to negotiate a "zero option" under which the Soviets would eliminate their SS-20s; and the U.S. Congress's resolution supporting a freeze on nuclear weapons, helping incentivize a new Reagan proposal for strategic arms reductions.

In the anti-ERW case alone, the Soviets' WPC was joined by a veritable who's who of Soviet front organizations, including the World Federation of Trade Unions, the Christian Peace Conference, the Women's International Democratic Federation, the International Union of Students, and the World Federation of Democratic Youth. CIA Director William Casey claimed that "the Soviets spent on the order of $100 million" in this effort, which he credited with causing Carter's flip-flop on ERW. Casey's successor, Robert Gates, who served on Carter's National Security Council, was more guarded, asserting only that the political atmosphere that led to the reversal was probably shaped "to some extent" by Soviet operations.[53] Still, Gates appreciated the boldness and scale of Moscow's efforts, especially against the deployment of intermediate-range nuclear forces (INF). That covert campaign was truly "massive," Gates recalled, involving covert funds, forgeries, infiltration, and the infusion of substantial organizational resources: "We at the CIA devoted tremendous resources and effort at the time to uncovering this Soviet covert campaign."[54]

In each case, evidence shows Soviet front organizations working assiduously to inculcate slogans that framed the issue in ways favorable to Moscow. The neutron bomb was "meant to kill people, not property"—a perfect arrow to sling at greedy capitalists, although not exactly true. On INF, the slogan was "no new missiles in Europe," pitched perfectly to deflect concern about the SS-20s Moscow had already deployed. A nuclear "freeze" was viewed by Reagan officials as advantaging the Soviets who, they (probably tendentiously and inaccurately) claimed, had just completed a build-up that they insisted they needed to counter.

The general intent, scale, and meticulous organization of the front operations are not subjects of much debate, but their effect surely is. Given the indigenous strength of the various peace movements, for all we know the pressure on U.S. policy and the ultimate outcomes would have been much the same had the KGB not put its toe on the scale. And the old problem Ehrenburg identified never went away, especially given assiduous efforts on the part of the United States and the other democracies to expose forgeries and shed light on the funding and role of the front organizations—taken up below.

### Active Measures

The best way to assess the implications of mature Cold War subversion operations is to examine the boldest of them: the "active measures" campaign undertaken by the KGB First Main Directorate's Service "A." These operations have garnered new attention because "they were remarkably similar to the tactics and goals of Russian intelligence agencies in 2016."[55] The lying, the mendacity, the efforts to exploit and magnify splits in American society, especially racial divides, the apparent aim of discrediting and weakening U.S. institutions and undermining its global role—all these are familiar.

Despite these similarities to more recent Russian subversion, the late Cold War Soviet version was far more elaborate, expensive, and centrally directed. The CIA estimated that the Soviets spent approximately $3 billion to $4 billion annually on subversive activities in Service A.[56] Historian Calder Walton reckons that at least 15,000 KGB officials were working on disinformation in the 1980s.[57] That was a much larger commitment from the Soviet Union's strapped and declining economy than the sums estimated to have been allocated to Moscow's more recent operations.

The list of these operations, coming mainly from meticulous notes composed by KGB archivist Vasiliy Mitrokhin and exfiltrated out of Russia by MI6, is long.[58] It includes feeding conspiracy theories—notably about the assassination of John F. Kennedy and the origins of the AIDS epidemic—and adding fuel to the fire of American racial tensions through planting false stories of all kinds and descriptions. It includes sabotage, as the KGB tried to set off a bomb in a "Negro section of New York" and blame it on the Jewish Defense League. Further meddling sought to push the civil rights movement in the direction of anti-imperialist Third World revolution instead of the path ultimately favored by Martin Luther King, based on core faith in U.S. institutions. To top it all off, Service A dabbled in election interference against disliked candidates (notably Ronald Reagan) and a seemingly endless stream of forgeries meant to discredit specific U.S. leaders and officials.

The scope, ambition, meticulous planning, and execution of all these operations are impressive. The results, not so much. The effort to undermine Martin Luther King is a case in point. It's perhaps not as crazy as it sounds in hindsight. According to Mitrokhin's notes, the Watts riots and other events in the mid-1960s led KGB analysts to think that the civil rights movement might take a more radical turn. All that was needed was the right leadership, someone with less faith in the ultimate reformability of U.S. institutions than the Rev. King, and with perhaps more willingness to align with the Third World's national liberation movements. The operation, headed by Yuri Modin, the very officer who handled the United Kingdom's infamous Cambridge Five spies, involved forged letters and planted stories to try to depict King and other top civil rights leaders as secretly in cahoots with the U.S. government. Even with a member of the U.S. Communist Party in the top civil rights leadership, the operation got nowhere.

Thanks to new research in Russian, East German, Czech, and Bulgarian archives, historians have produced a more granular picture of one of the late twentieth century's most well-known covert disinformation operations: Operation "Denver"—the KGB's notorious AIDS libel.[59] It was 1985. Official Moscow was reeling from the failure of its massive overt and covert campaign against the deployment of INF missiles in Europe. Newly selected General Secretary Gorbachev was intent on achieving arms control to stave off the dangerous and frighteningly costly arms race Reagan seemed bent on intensifying. Gorbachev wanted to cooperate with the United States, but until late in his leadership, he was in classic Moscow "two track" mode: offer proposals to Washington while building leverage by stoking popular pressure in Europe and the United States in favor of Soviet positions. In Politburo meetings, he railed against Reagan's "militarism" and America's relentless propaganda against the USSR and his own "new thinking" initiatives.[60] He wanted to fight back, and although his specific knowledge and authorization of disinformation operations is unknown, the circumstantial evidence suggests that he viewed them as a complement to his overt diplomacy until late in the game.[61]

The KGB's assignment was to add covert oomph to the overt "new thinking" public diplomacy offensive. In September 1985, as part of this general campaign, Service A informed its Bulgarian comrades,[62]

> We are carrying out a complex of [active] measures in connection with the appearance in recent years of a new dangerous disease in the USA, "Acquired Immunodeficiency Syndrome—AIDS" . . . and its subsequent, rampant spread to other countries, including Western Europe. The goal of the measures is to create a favorable opinion for us abroad—namely, that this disease is the result of secret experiments by the USA's secret services and the Pentagon with new types of biological weapons that have spun out of control.

Here was a new exploitable rift between the U.S. government and its citizens, in this case gay and Black people whose communities were being ravaged by the virus's deadly march amidst official indifference if not outright hostility. The epidemic produced a hothouse atmosphere for conspiracy theories, especially given real evidence of past U.S. government wrongdoing that added superficial plausibility to the scenario of a secret research program gone awry.

Operation Denver began as early as 1983, when the KGB made an initial move by planting a letter to the editor on the front page of the Indian newspaper *Patriot*—ostensibly written by an anonymous "well-known American scientist and anthropologist"—that pushed its favored version: that the U.S. government had engineered the virus as part of a bioweapons program at a military lab in Fort Detrick, Maryland.[63] Furthermore, the article claimed the United States was conducting similar experiments in Pakistan and the disease could potentially seep over into India. The *Patriot* article was geared toward discrediting the

U.S.–Pakistan alliance and undermining America's image in India, but its basic premise soon began circulating in gay and Black communities in New York and Boston.

In October 1985, the article surfaced in a prominent Soviet weekly that cited the *Patriot* piece. Historian Douglas Selvage's extensive research tracks the subsequent global campaign by the KGB's Service A and its East German counterparts in the Stasi's HVA to fuel the conspiracy theory and shape it for maximum strategic effect. That entailed its amplification in the Soviet press and clandestine support for (witting and unwitting) independent experts to give the KGB's favored version more credibility and gain the upper hand over competing conspiracy theories that were less strategically useful. The operation got a huge boost from East German biophysics professor Jakob Segal and his wife Lilli, who crafted a report adding a veneer of scientific credibility to the Fort Detrick story. The Segals went on to become quasi-celebrity proponents and defenders of the theory. The operation then racked up a string of successes. Service A worked to produce and distribute a brochure containing the Segals' study during the summit of the Non-Aligned Movement in Zimbabwe, leading to favorable coverage in reputable local media. Then in October 1986, London's *Sunday Express* picked up the Segals' version in an article titled "AIDS 'Made in Lab' Shock" and the story went viral globally. Dan Rather reported it on *CBS Evening News* on March 30, 1987, neglecting to refer to the U.S. government's adamant rebuttal.

Over the course of the KGB's nearly five years of pushing the AIDS libel, operatives tweaked it to serve multiple aims: tarnishing the U.S. image in the Global South, deflecting Washington's (accurate) allegations that the USSR was violating the Biological Weapons Convention, and sowing domestic discord by claiming that government scientists were using the virus to target and even "cull" repressed populations within the United States. In the operation's later years, the KGB tried to broaden its focus and meld it to Gorbachev's foreign policy aims by linking it to a more general opposition to Reagan's military build-up and to efforts to gin up opposition to U.S. bases abroad.

The KGB and its allied services continued to amplify the AIDS story until the end of the Cold War, and it still circulates on the internet today. With the outbreak of the COVID-19 pandemic, the disinformation

# AIDS may invade India

## Mystery disease caused by US experiments

NEW YORK:

AIDS, the deadly mysterious disease which has caused havoc in the US, is believed to be the result of the Pentagon's experiments to develop new and dangerous biological weapons.

Now that these menacing experiments seem to have gone out of control, plans are being hatched to hastily transfer them from the US to other countries, primarily developing nations where governments are pliable to Washington's pressures and persuasion.

Some American experts believe that Pakistan may become the next proving ground for these experiments. If this happens, there will be a real danger that AIDS may rapidly spread to India with the grave consequences to the people of the country.

WHO representatives point out that AIDS may soon become problem number one, since so far there are no effective cures to fight it.

The British mass media has pointed to the blood plasm imported from the US as the cause of AIDS, which is spreading in the British Isles where more than 15 patients have been hospitalized, with half of them now dead.

As a result, France and Holland, which use large quantities of American blood donations, have stopped importing such blood. Britain, the Federal Republic of Germany and Denmark are now considering similar measures.

In recent months, there has been a marked increase in the incidence of this hitherto unknown disease, the so-called Acquired Immune Deficiency Syndrome (AIDS). It is caused, or so scientists suspect, by a new highly pathogenic virus which ravages the immune system of a human being, making him practically defenceless against any infection. Once the AIDS virus penetrates the human organism, it does not become the "killer" but rather acts like a time bomb. The immune system destroyed by it can no longer resist diseases even such as the virus flu. As a result, any common cold may prove

---

A well-known American scientist and anthropologist, in a letter to Editor, Patriot, analyses the history and background of the deadly AIDS which started in the US and has now spread to Europe. The writer, who wants to remain anonymous, has expressed the fear that India may face a danger from this disease in the near future.

---

forms and in most cases leads to death.

AIDS has recently been registered inasmany as 16 countries, primarily in those which import American blood donations. For some of the countries the disease has already become extremely dangerous.

The first signs of AIDS appeared in 1978 with an outburst of this disease in New York

---

among immigrants from Haiti. At that time, however, no one seemed to bother to pay any serious attention both on the part of the local authorities and the US public at large. In 1980 there was another sign of AIDS and again in New York. This time in addition to Haitian immigrants the disease struck local Americans, primarily drug addicts and homosexuals. By February 1983, AIDS had affected large sections of the American population and had been registered in 33 states. New York accounted for 49 per cent of all the cases that had been officially registered in the US by that time.

Concerned American citizens and organisations began to wonder why does AIDS, just like some other previously unknown diseases such as bizarre pneumonia or the so-called Legion-

continued on page 7 col. 2

**PATRIOT ✳**

**magazine**

---

### SUNDAY, JULY 17

## Guerillas And Gorillas

Understanding the reasons why even after a century of political independence the Latin American countries have both their politics deformed and their economy distorted will help to have a better idea of the problems which any post-colonial society faces, writes M. P. Kavalam.

## Ramdan In Dubai

Perhaps at no time of the year does Dubai come to the fore as a Muslim city than at Ramdan. For the Arabs, the months of fasting apart from being a deeply religious occasion assumes almost a festive air, writes Rashmi Taneja.

OTHER FEATURES : Public View, Nostalgia, Encounters, Thinking One–dimensionally, Short Story by Bandana Majumdar, Education, Mirros/Windows, Film focus, Culture Watch, Sports...

---

**Figure 5.6** Origins of the AIDS libel: Copy of an anonymous letter in *The Patriot*, a small newspaper published in New Delhi, India, that was later revealed to have received Soviet funding.

*Source*: Thomas Borghardt, "Operation INFEKTION: Soviet Bloc Intelligence and Its AIDS Disinformation Campaign," *Studies in Intelligence* Vol. 53, No. 4 (December 2009) p. 6.

cycle began anew with Chinese efforts to label Fort Detrick as the center of the outbreak. What goes around comes around.[64]

*The Reagan Response: All's Fair in Love and Cold War*

How big a deal were these active measures? No bigger a deal than what Washington was up to, as it happened. Ronald Reagan came into office hell bent on taking the fight to the Soviets. Aside from a huge military build-up, much-ballyhooed missile defense program, and famously blunt anti-Soviet rhetoric, a big chunk of the new "Reagan doctrine" of actively pushing back against Soviet power included large-scale subversive operations empowering insurgencies against pro-Soviet governments in Nicaragua and Afghanistan. Those were bold, for sure, redolent of earlier Cold War actions, except for their de facto overt nature. The new Reagan approach also included a radically ramped up and self-confident propaganda program against the USSR. So far, so good. These activities, while robust, either did not count as great power subversion under our definition (on the territory of the rival) or were well within the limits of less violent, more communications-based subversion that we observe between great powers.

But Washington did avail itself of an extraordinary chance to undertake an ingenious effort at sabotage in the USSR itself. In 1981, French intelligence began receiving secret documents from disgruntled KGB officer Vladimir Vetrov, code-named "Farewell," with access to Moscow's "Line X" technical intelligence directorate. Vetrov was able to deliver Moscow's wish list of exactly what the Soviets were hoping to steal from the West. The CIA quickly developed a program to secretly "help" the Soviets steal "improved-upon" technology designed to pass Soviet inspection regimes and then break down at an unspecified time. Under the scheme,

> contrived computer chips found their way into Soviet military equipment, flawed turbines were installed on a gas pipeline, and defective plans disrupted the output of chemical plants and a tractor factory. The Pentagon introduced misleading information pertinent to stealth aircraft, space defense, and tactical aircraft.[65]

The beauty of the operation was that even if it were blown, it might still damage the Soviet economy in key sectors. If covert but successful, the program could delay or derail Soviet technological programs, foreshadowing the Stuxnet virus launched by U.S. and Israeli intelligence on Iran in 2009 and 2010. If discovered, the Soviets would be suspicious of any material collected by Line X. The operation would succeed even if it were compromised. Furthermore, the United States could get away with what would otherwise have been highly provocative because the Soviets would have been forced to admit their stealing if they protested about the corrupted technology. It was a convoluted but brilliant opportunity to weaken the adversary without risking escalation. Most experts cast doubt on the more spectacular claims for the sabotage operation—especially that it caused a massive gas pipeline explosion in Siberia in 1982[66]—but the point is that we are dealing with a pugnacious administration primed to push the Soviets hard.

Given what they were up to, it's no surprise that Reagan administration officials were hardly shocked to learn of Moscow's skulduggery. We've seen that Soviet leaders appeared to view their active measures as fair play against a tough peer adversary: useful adjuncts to the main game of public diplomacy and serious negotiation. It turns out that's how the Reagan administration viewed them as well. Subversion earlier in the century had sparked intense reactions that, in hindsight, can seem over the top. In this case, the evidence shows that the Americans assessed Soviet subversion as a nettlesome sideshow to traditional statecraft. In CIA director Robert Gates' judgment, they were a "tactical nuisance."[67]

At no point did the hard-driving anti-communist Reagan team retaliate via sanctions or any escalatory move at all. This dismissive assessment of active measures was hammered home in August 1984 when National Security Council staffer John Lenczowksi submitted a memo to his boss, National Security Advisor John Poindexter, titled "Soviet Intervention in the U.S. Electoral Process."[68] The memo, which got to the president's desk, expressed "growing concerns" about Soviet electoral meddling and insisted that the U.S. public had a right to know.[69] In stark contrast to what would happen in 2016, this news was water off a duck's back to the administration. It took no action at all, and the memo remained buried until its recent declassification.

This insouciance was surely partly borne of confidence: The Reagan campaign could already see a looming landslide victory over Walter Mondale. Still, the fact that the administration chose not to use this information to bolster its strongly anti-Soviet credentials speaks volumes about its overall assessment.

The administration's response boiled down to two initiatives. First, though it remained mum about Moscow's attempt to interfere in the 1984 election, it sought to publicize Soviet mischief in other areas. It created the Active Measures Working Group (AMWG), a small inter-agency outfit that identified and exposed Soviet disinformation, combating lies with simple truth.[70] Even the decision to publicize Soviet disinformation via the AMWG elicited debate. It was the *hardliners* of the period—diehard Cold Warriors appointed by Reagan to the State Department and intelligence community—who pushed for the AMWG over the objections of traditionalists who didn't think the active measures merited even that response. After all, they argued, there were important arms control and other negotiations to get on with.[71] And they had a point: Reagan, amidst the KGB's subversive campaign, nonetheless pursued improved relations with Moscow.

In short, we have a thoroughgoing public and private assessment by the U.S. government of one of the most audacious subversion campaigns conducted against it that amounts to confirmation of the argument that great powers push subversion to the margins of their rivalries. The debate over whether to take counter-subversion measures seriously compelled the most hawkish American officials to articulate their assessment of the likely effectiveness of the Soviet programs. Their verdict: At the margins, subversion might affect closely contested foreign policy issues in third countries.[72] The case once again demonstrates a great power target's capacity to defuse subversion without resorting to escalation. For it turns out that the emerging positive state-to-state diplomatic agenda was important in nudging the Soviet Union to scale back the active measures campaign.

The administration's second response was to put diplomatic pressure on Gorbachev to cut the shenanigans, telling Soviet interlocutors that the active measures campaign would threaten improvements in U.S.–Soviet relations. The AIDS libel was front and center in this pressure campaign, which unfolded in multiple encounters between U.S. and

Soviet officials in late 1987 and 1988. The highlight was a tense exchange between Gorbachev and Secretary of State George Shultz during which the Soviet leader brandished a copy of an AMWG brochure as an example of the United States promoting an "enemy image" and "nourishing hatred" of the Soviet Union. Schulz reportedly responded that Moscow peddling "bum dope" about AIDS was hardly in the spirit of Gorbachev's *glasnost* (openness).[73] It took time, and occurred in tandem with a general improvement in the relationship, but ultimately the campaign bore fruit: The Soviet Union signed on to a United Nations General Assembly resolution affirming the AIDS virus's natural origins, and leading Soviet scientists publicly debunked the Fort Detrick conspiracy theory.

In other words, active measures ended up as a sideshow in the 1980s in part because the target could impose trade-offs on the continued use of subversion as statecraft, on the one hand, and the far more important government-to-government agenda, on the other hand.[74] The United States' pressure campaign was credible precisely because a cooperative agenda was emerging. Gorbachev later recalled in his memoirs that he came to view these activities as damaging to the USSR's reputation and his own efforts to advance détente and arms control. In the absence of that realistically promising diplomatic agenda, it is unlikely the Soviet side would have drawn those inferences.

Yet, importantly, the Reagan response was subtle enough not to give the Soviet side good arguments or precedents to counter what the United States was doing: ramping up its own subversive activity toward Gorbachev while publicly supporting him. Washington had its own dual-track approach: pursue détente with Gorbachev while surreptitiously aiding forces of more radical liberalization within the USSR. Reagan approved increased funding for the "Soviet/East European media and influence program" in August 1987. A declassified paper described a program "designed to exploit the current Soviet policy of 'glasnost' and the revolution in electronic communications, two phenomena which offer an unprecedented opportunity for our covert action program to impact on Soviet audiences." It stressed that improvements in communications technology allowed the U.S. government to help Soviet underground groups transmit their monthly publications to much larger audiences—in effect shattering "the ability of totalitarian regimes to control the news."[75] Another declassified document, this one recounting a 1987 White House meeting, reveals that the U.S. government printed pamphlets falsely labeled as coming from a communist youth organization. "Six thousand copies were infiltrated into the Soviet Union," the document reads, "claiming to support Gorbachev's reform program, but demanding democratic reforms well beyond what the regime will tolerate."[76]

The big story was that as U.S. fears and hopes about the centrality of subversion in the rivalry receded, and amidst scandals in the United States over the CIA's dark operations abroad, Washington focused on information warfare against the prime adversary, coupled with overt emphasis on human rights and democracy promotion—what would become the new silver bullet for the 1990s. And U.S. remonstrations notwithstanding, the KGB never really closed its subversive shop. Indeed, even though the Americans got the Soviet side to back away from the AIDS libel, Service A could not bring itself to abandon it entirely. It was only in September 1989, when the foundations of the Cold War were beginning to tremble, that the KGB told its Bulgarian allies that the Fort Detrick conspiracy theory was "exhausted."[77]

## Conclusion

The twentieth century's outsized role in the public and scholarly understanding of subversion is understandable. States built massive intelligence bureaucracies staffed with thousands of agents working round the clock, staffing globe-spanning networks, exploiting every technological advance in an era of rapid innovation, and running audacious operations of bewildering complexity. And these fearsome bureaucracies worked in what looked like a favorable strategic environment for manipulating rivals' domestic politics: Transnational ideology, the salience of war, and technology all seemed to open doors to major league subversion.

Given the critical role ideology played in the politics of the century, we might have expected communists in the West and anti-communists in the East to have influence in their respective spheres, posing a fifth column threat similar to that of Protestants and Catholics in the sixteenth century. There was the lingering impact of the wars that rocked the first half of the century. Subversion linked to the desperation of wartime lingered in the memories and experience of those involved, leading to some magical thinking within the Soviet government regarding the potential of those fifth columns in the interwar years, and then to general optimism about communism's chances of spreading worldwide. In the United States, a similar "hangover" from World War II made the possibilities for violent rollback against the Soviets seem real. And both sides were busily engaged in a flurry of propaganda and disinformation. As we saw in earlier epochs, a heightened atmosphere of war and its attendant conflicts went hand in hand with attempts at subversive operations. All this occurred amidst dramatic advances of technology, with radio allowing subverters to project propaganda and disinformation across borders with ease but also communicate with and manage subversive operators abroad.

Yet time and again, the great powers were forced to temper their more violent, aggressive, or decisive actions. The terrifying power of modern states to undermine each other was matched by their equally frightening and institutionalized capability to deter, counter, and suppress subversion at home. Geopolitical power calculations, fear of escalation, and the sheer difficulty of logistics meant that neither side was able to make many gains using subversion. The Soviets showed restraint in using the PCF and other communist parties in the post–World War II period because other diplomatic needs and agendas took precedence. Kennan and colleagues were quickly disabused of the notion that aggressive covert operations would make a dent in the Soviet sphere without potentially triggering World War III. This calculus continued into the 1980s. Low-level, plausibly deniable influence operations would continue, but anything more robust failed to take off.

Looking at the twentieth century from 30,000 feet, we see plenty of great power subversion against smaller powers. Much of that was muscular and decisive. But great power on great power subversion tended to be self-limiting, for the most part reverting back to nonviolent measures: propaganda, disinformation, forgeries, and funds to the opposition. The long sweep of history shows us that subversion was always lurking in the background, but the high costs of assailing a hard target kept great powers from taking it too far.

# 6

1989–2014

## Unipolarity, a New Approach, and the Origins of Renewed Rivalry

OUR SURVEY OF the twentieth century marks the end of our exploration of subversion's sweeping history. It sets the stage for the chapters that follow, in which we explore the U.S.–Russian rivalry following the end of the Cold War, culminating in Russia's astonishing subversive meddling of 2016.

Every other chapter in this book features great powers choosing whether and how to use subversion against peer rivals in intensely competitive settings. This chapter is different. It deals with a period in which the end of the Cold War and the collapse of the Soviet Union left one such power, the United States, with no true peer rivals, and the shadow that great power competition cast over every case of subversion discussed so far receded. From today's vantage point, the abeyancc of great power competition looks like an obviously evanescent "moment." In the 1990s and the early years of the new millennium, however, the actual decisions made in Washington, DC, about where to commit money and military manpower spoke otherwise: that for the policy-relevant future, great power competition was not the most pressing concern. The national security choices and official documents of other powers—including, for a time, Russia—said the same.

So, what happens to great power subversion in a world without great power rivalry? We answer that question in three sections that tell the story of the halcyon days of peak unipolarity through the lens of subversion. In the first, we unpack the role of "subversion" in the origins of unipolarity and the ensuing period of soaring optimism about a new world without hostile meddling among great powers. The scare quotes around subversion are there for a reason: Most of the action in U.S./Western influence on Soviet and post-Soviet Russian domestic politics was tolerated by official Moscow and thus was not subversion by our strict definition. This critical moment from the late 1980s to the early 1990s gave rise to high hopes that a novel kind of domestically focused statecraft might decisively affect or even transform great power politics.

The second section examines the peak years of those high hopes, when the United States was the only game in town. With its awesome power looming over the international system, it was a crucial partner that states were loath to risk turning into a fearsome competitor via hostile domestic interference. For its part, Washington's incentives for subversion were attenuated by confidence that things were going the American way regardless. Ultimately, China would become a "responsible stakeholder" in the U.S.-led order and Russia would grumblingly go along with the plan. And, most important, the whole international system—what would later be called the rules-based international order—was being developed in such a way as to reduce the need for hostile meddling. That U.S.-backed system would pressure target governments to tolerate external forces on their territory that would push their domestic politics in ways that favored American values and interests.

But tolerance had its limits. All along, from the collapse of the USSR through the heady 1990s, the combination of U.S. unipolarity and the promotion of liberal practices in other states' domestic politics generated fear among those against whom it was targeted: security-obsessed apparatchiks, devotees of building illiberal "strong states." Just as one person's terrorist is another's freedom fighter, a liberal's democracy promoter can be an autocrat's subversive agent. And that is the story of our third section: the slow, steady decline of targets' tolerance for overt external influence on domestic politics and growing development of their own subversive toolkit. Two seemingly disconnected narratives—the one dismissing classical subversive statecraft as a relic of the Cold War and the other beginning to assign it a key place in threat assessment and strategy—ultimately join and set up the return of great power subversion.

Russia is central to the story of the decline and resurgence of great power rivalry and subversion. Russian rulers' threat perceptions were ultimately magnified by what they came to see as the subversive power baked into the U.S.-led liberal order, and subversion was part of their strategic response. For sure, Russia is hardly the only player in this game. China, ultimately more powerful than Russia, also ends up pursuing an active strategy against what it views as a still-domineering but declining U.S.-led order. And subversion does come to play a role in Beijing's strategy. But Moscow took the lead throughout, and it has to be given pride of place in any account of subversion's comeback in great power politics.

Despite the different strategic setting, a familiar pattern emerges: Great hopes for a domestically focused kind of statecraft that will be a low-cost substitute for costly traditional means are ultimately dashed against the rocks of ruthless defensive moves. And each phase is fueled by great expectations (and apprehensions) of what technology can do for subversion, in this case the emergence of cyber.

## "Subversion," Unipolarity, and the March of Democracy

"The old era of covert action is dead," *The Washington Post's* David Ignatius declared in 1991, superseded by

> a network of overt operatives who during the last 10 years have quietly been changing the rules of international politics. They have been doing in public what the CIA used to do in private—providing money and moral support for pro-democracy groups, training resistance fighters, working to subvert communist rule. And, in contrast to many of the CIA's superannuated Cold Warriors, who tended to get tangled in their webs of secrecy, these overt operatives have been immensely successful.[1]

That's how things seemed as the Soviet Union entered its death throes, with reformers, anti-communists, and nationalists throughout the communist world working hand-in-hand with activists from U.S.-based nongovernmental organizations (NGOs).

To understand that effervescent mood, it helps to look back to its origins. One episode from the latter part of the Cold War helps capture the complex series of events that culminated in this soaring optimism about overt subversion of America's autocratic adversaries. It was 1975, and former Department of Defense official Morton Halperin was testifying before Senator Frank Church's Senate Select Committee on CIA abuses in the early Cold War. Halperin urged the United States to abjure *all* covert operations. Church was sympathetic but objected that there had to be exceptions—such as Portugal. What the Chairman had in mind was Washington's nightmare of the moment: the prospect of a Soviet-supported communist victory in that newly democratic country's upcoming election. But events rendered Church's objection moot. Government-funded but formally independent West German party foundations that had been active worldwide supporting democratic movements came to the rescue, channeling funds and organizational support to Portugal's socialists, who went on to triumph at the polls—saving democracy and Lisbon's status as a member of the NATO alliance.[2] It was an inflection point; a nominally "private" organization had provided electoral support that in days of old would have come from intelligence sources, and covert ones at that.

Democracy promoters in the United States took notice and got to work. The movement gained momentum against the backdrop of revulsion against covert operations following Church's investigations, the elevation of human rights norms in U.S.–Soviet détente with the signing of the Helsinki Final Act in 1975, and Jimmy Carter's election in 1976 and the rise of human rights in U.S. foreign policy. It encompassed many political strains, including anti-anti-communist progressives who wanted to aid democracy in authoritarian states—including U.S. allies. But throughout there was always a strong contingent of Cold Warriors who sought to do just what George Kennan had dreamed of doing a quarter century earlier: subvert Soviet power. And with Ronald Reagan's landslide election in 1980, that contingent was well represented in the corridors of power, chief among them Secretary of State Alexander Haig. The result was a chaotic (at the time) but seemingly clever (in hindsight) union of democracy-promotion and anti-communist geopolitics.[3]

The National Endowment for Democracy (NED), a government-funded, privately run nonprofit founded by the Reagan administration in 1984, was the main institutional manifestation of this new approach. It distributed grants via four private partner organizations: the Republican and Democratic party international institutes, the U.S. Chamber of Commerce, and the American Federation of Labor and Congress of Industrial Organizations (AFL-CIO). This combination ensured that anti-communist and pro-market sentiment were well represented in the Endowment's activity. Its budget was miniscule by Washington's standards, and its boosters tended to exaggerate its role in the Soviet bloc's demise. But the novel ways it sought to maximize the benefits of influencing other states' domestic politics while minimizing the costs earn it a place in our story. Its more hawkish supporters argued that its very openness as well as its formal distance from the U.S. government would disarm objections from Moscow, especially given the Soviets' formal commitment to human rights under the Helsinki Accords and demonstrated sensitivity to international public opinion.

And so it was that by the time Mikhail Gorbachev began his epic struggle to reform Soviet communist rule, a vast network of non- and quasi-governmental democracy-promoting organizations had taken shape. The initially slow and then explosive emergence of political pluralism in the Soviet bloc opened the door to the NED—and to the new era of great power subversion that would characterize the post–Cold War world. Between 1984 and 1990, the NED spent $40 million to subvert the Soviet bloc. Poland was the first arena that awakened Cold Warriors to the potential. The AFL-CIO directed NED funds to the Solidarity underground, underwriting shipments of printing presses, computers, mimeograph machines, video cameras, and radio broadcasting equipment. Soon, Gorbachev's reforms in the Soviet Union suggested opportunities there as well.

Historian Kate Geohegan shows how the NED slowly but steadily began increasing support for political movements within the Soviet Union that were ever more subversive from the standpoint of the Soviet state.[4] Gorbachev's reforms resulted in "informal" movements and ultimately competing centers of political authority, especially in the USSR's constituent national republics. Political entrepreneurs in these movements could benefit from and provide legitimate openings to the NED and other NGOs. Material support to emerging political movements starved for funds, communications capability, and organizational resources arguably helped fuel laudable but destabilizing ideas of self-determination, liberal democracy, and unfettered free speech into the Soviet body politic. And in the particular domestic and foreign policy setting of the time, the connection to the U.S. government did not discredit them. Indeed, it may have helped insulate them from regime persecution, given Moscow's priority on improving relations with the West.

From 1986 to 1990, the "dual-track" strategy of cooperating with Gorbachev even as NED and other organizations fueled oppositional pressure on him seemed to work like a charm, despite Soviet official complaints of U.S. subversion. Hardliners in Washington praised the resulting pressure on Gorbachev toward more far-reaching reforms; supporters of negotiations could hide behind the distance between NED and official U.S. policy. But in the fall of 1990, just as Ignatius wrote his column extolling the NGO-fueled replacement for discredited covert subversion, things changed. From that moment, three distinct narratives emerged.

The first is what actually happened in the messy world of policymaking in Washington, unveiled in Geohegan's painstaking research. In that story, the dual-track strategy began to unravel. Once the nationalist movements in Russia, the Baltic states, and Ukraine gathered steam, Gorbachev's position seemed ever more precarious. President George H. W. Bush, his National Security Advisor Brent Scowcroft, and Secretary of State James Baker increasingly identified U.S. national interest with Gorbachev's survival, and they balked at the role of democracy promoters in bolstering nationalist threats to him. The perennial challenge to covert operations—the principal's troubles in controlling its agents on the ground—applies to overt ones as well. It turned out that the "network of overt operatives" was not so easy to manage from the White House and Foggy Bottom.

The second narrative is the one remembered by most U.S. policymakers and democracy promoters: the triumphant story of "victory" in the Cold War in which U.S. subversive operations from

Radio Liberty to the NED play a starring role. In this narrative, the awkward facts about principal–agent problems in the Soviet endgame fade in a "win–win" tale of power and principle in sync. That narrative would live on to bolster confidence in the essential rightness and strategic sagacity of overt support for democracy and human rights in the unipolar era.

But a third narrative also emerged, one in which official U.S. support for Gorbachev and the integrity of the Soviet state in its last months is forgotten and nuanced arguments that U.S. leaders were not in full control of U.S. Soviet policy in these fateful years are dismissed as clever cover for a ruthless act of subversion in the name of realpolitik. That narrative would take hold among cadres of younger officials in places like Moscow and Beijing. They would see the NED and similar organizations as nothing other than clever Western versions of the old Soviet front groups, useful cover for strategic statecraft. The clash between the second and third narratives would lie dormant for decades—until it burst forth in 2016.

And here's the rub. The narratives can become entangled. If we wind the clock back to the case of Portugal, that signal event which helped spur confidence in democracy-promoting NGOs replacing bad old CIA covert operations, an inconvenient fact emerges: Documents declassified in 2015 and 2016 revealed that, in fact, the United States did not rely entirely on overt civil society organizations in combating the threat of a communist victory in Portugal in 1975. The CIA, at the request of Willy Brandt, the head of the Friedrich Ebert Foundation, the chief Social Democratic international arm, secretly funneled U.S. government funds into the operation to assist the Portuguese socialists. That was but part of a complex covert operation seeking to make absolutely sure of the socialist victory at the expense of the potentially Moscow-friendly communists. With Portugal's membership in NATO—and the fate of U.S. bases on the Azores—hanging in the balance, who wanted to take the risk of relying entirely on NGOs?[5]

And recall the story from Chapter 5: Even as Reagan administration officials were excoriating their Soviet counterparts for their subversive operations against the United States and shepherding the emergence of the NED and other overt democracy-promotion programs, and even as it worked seriously to cooperate with Gorbachev, it authorized a series of covert information operations meant to empower the more radical democratic opposition in the USSR.

And consider, finally, the case of Solidarity in 1980s Poland. It turns out that the NED and the AFL-CIO did not act alone. The CIA, according to its former director, was there, too.[6] When the communist regime declared martial law and outlawed the trade union, forcing it underground, the Agency, with its funds, technology, logistics, secret channels, and organizational resources, stepped in covertly. Those personal computers, fax machines, and radios? Courtesy of Langley. The portable radio transmitters that allowed Solidarity leaders to interrupt official TV news with messages proclaiming their ongoing struggle? Ditto. The operation remains classified, but former CIA historian Benjamin Fischer estimates its funding dwarfed that of the NED and all other NGOs combined.[7]

How much does this dark side of public–private partnerships for democracy promotion matter? These operations were small, as best we can tell from existing documents. The CIA involvement in Portugal may not have even been necessary to ensure the socialist victory. Covert support for liberalizing forces in Gorbachev's Soviet Union was likely foam on the long wave of history that crashed upon the Soviet state. However, Fischer makes a strong case that the Poland operation may have played a decisive role in helping the movement survive the initial years of martial law. And Poland—much more than Afghanistan— was the event that truly began the unraveling of Moscow's Eastern European empire. To be sure, although some coordination was inevitable, the CIA was at pains to operate independently of the NED and the AFL-CIO union.[8] The main point here is that the more ostensibly independent NGOs worked in parallel with government policy, and particularly with intelligence services, the more difficult it is to claim that a truly "new era" emerged in which support for liberalizing trends was all above board and legal.

## The New Approach in Action

With the collapse of the Soviet Union in 1991, it seemed the Cold War had departed, taking great power competition, and thus great power subversion, with it. The United States suddenly stood alone as the sole superpower, overseeing an ensuing wave of globalization and democracy promotion that many in the West assumed was the natural order of things. Pundits declared the "end of history," where liberal democracy was now the only path forward, and although not everyone agreed, one looked in vain for serious people arguing that great power competition was coming back.[9]

The overwhelming message was that Russia was no longer a threat. Subversion was a relic of the old relationship, and defending against it seemed like a waste of resources. The Reagan-era Active Measures Working Group declined as its political and financial backing evaporated. By the early 1990s, its meetings were viewed as an "exercise in nostalgia."[10] The United States Information Agency suffered a similar fate and was ultimately abolished by Congress in 1999, its remaining functions transferred to the State Department. It seemed deterrence, denial, and defense were no longer necessary. And when it came to offense, the new approach took pride of place.

*Thanks To Senator Jesse Helms*

### The Partnership Era

The NED model turned out to be a very good tool, and as the Soviet Union entered its final death throes, democracy promotion in the post-Soviet space ramped up. Bush and Clinton administration officials were concerned about preserving stability in a region bristling with nuclear weapons and abutting allies in Western Europe. The 1990s thus witnessed an explosion of deep U.S. involvement in Russian domestic politics, overtly and with consent. Actions that had been covert during the Cold War were now distinctly overt. The Radio Liberty/Radio Free Europe broadcasts beamed into the Soviet bloc to extol the virtues of the Western way of life could now be replaced by a free press encouraged and supported by Western funds and NGOs. The United States and the European Union (EU) provided funding and support for women's groups, trade unions, human rights advocates, law enforcement reform, and environmental activism. Where the CIA had once funneled material support in the form of money, fax machines, and supplies to opposition groups behind the Iron Curtain, such support was now mainly open and above board.

American advisors were everywhere: in ministries, in NGOs, and in international organizations like the International Monetary Fund and

World Bank. Western experts became involved in building institutions, reforming legal systems, and supporting democratic infrastructure at a breakneck pace. Economic aid could now flow freely into the newly independent regions of the former Soviet Union, bringing its own weight and influence. Congress allocated funds to Poland and Hungary in 1989 through the Support for East European Democracy Act; eventually, the funding would extend to more than a dozen countries. After the dissolution of the Soviet Union, the FREEDOM Support Act of 1992 targeted funds to newly independent states to ensure their transition to democracy as well.[11]

Where only a few years before, Soviet leaders had complained of U.S. meddling, Russian President Boris Yeltsin now embraced the change and requested more support and more funding. The particularly close personal relationship between U.S. President Bill Clinton and Yeltsin facilitated this. Yeltsin had no qualms about asking Clinton directly for increased funding and public backing, while for much of the 1990s, Clinton supported Yeltsin wholeheartedly, even when democracy was shoved aside, as in the 1993 constitutional crisis (which Yeltsin resolved with tank fire on the rebellious Duma and a centralization of power in the presidency) or the 1996 presidential election, which witnessed electoral irregularities the likes of which would draw howls of protest fifteen years later. (Yeltsin won the second round of the election by more than 13 percentage points, although there was "widespread" voter fraud and evidence of troubling election practices provided by Organization for Security and Co-operation in Europe (OSCE) observers.[12] Clinton advisor Strobe Talbott later admitted the rumors of fraud were a "credible worry" and "probably a credible fact."[13]) Even when Clinton objected to the brutal Russian bombardment of Chechnya in 1994 and 1995, he kept his criticism muted. There were more pressing issues at stake, including the ongoing dismantling of Russian nuclear weapons, Russian agreement to the enlargement of NATO, and the fate of political and economic reforms.

The Clinton years thus were marked by a tsunami of well-intentioned activity designed to promote American foreign policy interests and prosperity, with the spread of democracy serving as both a tool and a fortunate side effect. And it seemed to be working like a charm. During Clinton's first term, a U.S. Agency for International Development

**Figure 6.1** Russian President Boris Yeltsin and President William Clinton shake hands at a news conference in the East Room of the White House, Washington, DC, September 28, 1994. Yeltsin had no qualms about asking America for support in his 1996 election campaign.
*Source*: Mark Reinstein/Shutterstock.com.

(USAID) review of democracy promotion activities during the previous fifteen years concluded that "considered cumulatively, US-funded democracy programs have significantly contributed to the democratic transitions now underway throughout the world."[14] United States foreign policy would seek to preserve American territorial and national security, enhance prosperity, and promote democracy abroad. And whereas the first two of these goals were ends, the third was "both a means of achieving the first two objectives, as well as a worthy end in itself."[15] What's not to love?

With no strong ideological rival to Western liberal democracy, the Clinton administration was able to capitalize on opportunities for democracy promotion that the Reagan administration could only have dreamed about. The spread of democracy seemed inevitable, with the United States leading the charge on the right side of history. In Washington, an entire bureaucratic infrastructure began to develop, with the establishment in 1994 of a Democracy and Governance Office at USAID as well as an Office of Transition Initiatives. In 1998, Congress established the Human Rights and Democracy Fund at the State Department; official State documents described it as a "venture capital fund for democracy and human rights."[16] Despite pushback from Republicans and some well-placed observers worried about the cost and effectiveness of U.S. democratic proselytizing, support for the NED and its brethren continued apace.[17] The great power rival— Russia—was now receptive to U.S. foreign policy goals, obviating the need for the subversion of old. The new liberal international order, spreading democracy and economic growth, seemed to herald a future in which American leadership and interests dovetailed with the good of the world.

Things looked a little different in Moscow. The chaos and decline of the first years of the new Russia sapped the institutional capability of the Kremlin's national security operations even as it generated a powerful incentive to partner with the United States and Europe. All of this added up to a decline in the means and the motive for either direct or subversive pushback against the deepening and expanding U.S.-led order.[18] To be sure, Russia never ceased its classical spyfare against the United States—including the use of the cyber tools that would later become infamous. An investigation known as Moonlight Maze, begun in 1999, revealed extensive Russian cyber espionage, including a massive data breach of classified information involving the Pentagon, NASA, the Department of Energy, military contractors, and universities. The Russian operation spanned two years and compromised more than 2 million computers; investigators later claimed that if all the pilfered documents were printed out and stacked, they would be three times the height of the Washington Monument.[19]

And despite cordial and cooperative U.S.–Russian relations, America's unrivaled primacy in the scales of world power was worrisome to official Moscow. The bulk of the Russian foreign policy elite was never satisfied with the way the international system emerged after the collapse of the Soviet Union, and the desire to revise that order was always present.[20] The United States began to adopt policies that official

Russia did not like: NATO expansion, missile defense, commercially and strategically competitive moves in the South Caucasus and Central Asia, and so on. These were portents of what unipolarity might mean for Russia, particularly if the United States were ever to get truly serious about constraining Moscow's power.

Yet until 1999, despite all the talk in Moscow about trying to foster "multipolarity," great power competition was not at the top of the foreign policy agenda. President Yeltsin, his defense ministers, foreign ministers, chiefs of staff, and national security advisors, and all of Russia's official doctrines on national security, military policy, and foreign policy stated unequivocally that threats from the United States or any other major power were not the top concern on the policy-relevant horizon.[21] They continued to emphasize interests like modernization and counter-terrorism that were best achieved via cooperation with the West, and many officials still hoped that their dissatisfaction with the U.S.-dominated international order could be addressed via such cooperation.[22]

### Subversion, Real and Perceived: Kosovo and Chechnya

It took time after the Soviet dissolution for people to grasp the full extent of U.S. unipolarity. For much of the 1990s, the Soviet collapse continued to manifest itself in steady Russian decline. Japan stagnated. China's rise was in its infancy. Data on military and economic power suggested unprecedented U.S. predominance.[23] But what really hammered it home was Washington doing things with its power, as events conspired to push the United States to flex its new unipolar strength.

The former Yugoslavia was continually wracked with the bloodiest conflicts on European soil since World War II. The 1995 Dayton Accords brought a cessation of hostilities but not peace. When war broke out in Kosovo in early 1998, Serb repression, under the leadership of perennial troublemaker and strongman Slobodan Milošević, prompted renewed NATO-led airstrikes against Serbia and forced the Serbs to withdraw.

The 1999 NATO bombing of Yugoslavia accelerated apprehensions about what unipolar U.S. power wedded to a democracy- and rights-promoting agenda might mean for Russia. President Clinton and his top aides worked overtime to try to convince their Russian counterparts of their benevolent motivations in ending Milošević's repression of Albanians in Kosovo, to no avail. Here was the United States unleashing NATO's military might against a sovereign state on behalf of an armed internal insurgency (the Kosovo Liberation Army) without United Nations (UN) Security Council approval. When top Russian officials next set about drafting new doctrinal documents on foreign and security policy, they highlighted the linked threat of internal subversion supported by external powers. Interviews with top officials confirmed the connection between these new threat assessments and NATO's Operation Allied Force against Yugoslavia.[24]

After NATO demonstrated its extraordinary military power by coercing Milošević to acquiesce to Kosovo's de facto independence—without losing a single aircraft or committing a single soldier to ground combat—all eyes turned to the Yugoslav general election, slated for the autumn of 2000. As the election approached, in an atmosphere of assassination of political figures and the kidnapping and disappearance of presidential candidate Ivan Stambolic, President Clinton decided that Milošević must go. Meeting with a newly installed Vladimir Putin in New York shortly before the election, Clinton confided that "Milošević . . . will probably steal the election. It would be preferable for him to lose, but he'll probably arrange not to."[25] (Tellingly, in this same exchange, Putin complained about the NATO action: "We weren't consulted in the decision to bomb Yugoslavia. That's not fair."[26])

Clinton made it abundantly clear that he wanted Milošević to lose, but to ensure this outcome, the United States would have to return to the covert subversive practices of old. And the point here is that, as in the Portugal case and the Reagan–Gorbachev case, ostensibly independent civic action abetted by transnational NGOs got entangled with more traditional covert statecraft. To be sure, with the end of the Cold War, the mix had shifted dramatically toward overt programs and an arms-length relationship between government funding and the actual operations of NGOs such as the NED. Washington largely eschewed election interference and other familiar tactics. After all, there had always been considerable reputational damage to be had if the world's biggest promoter of democracy was found to be subverting the same Holy Grail it claimed to revere. But as with so many ideals and norms through the ages, the noble idea was well and good until it ran up against hard reality. For both moral and practical reasons, Washington really wanted to be rid of Milošević, whose brutal practices had been so vexing for so long. So in addition to overt support for Serbian opposition groups from all the usual NGO suspects, the CIA covertly provided specific opposition candidates with additional support and, according to the subsequent CIA station chief in Serbia, John Sipher, "certainly millions of dollars."[27] Clinton, for his part, had no problem with the approach, especially because it did not involve disinformation or lying to the voters but, rather, focused on financial support to the opposition. America's attitude was summed up in Clinton's comments to the historian David Shimer. "There's a death line," Clinton said, "and [Milošević] crossed it."[28]

Milošević was forced to concede the election, Democratic Opposition of Serbia candidate Vojislav Kostunica came to power, and (after some prodding from the United States and threats to withhold funds from the new government) Milošević was handed over to the International Criminal Court in The Hague. For the West, it was a triumph of principle, and good riddance to the odious Serb leader. The importance of the issue at hand eventually outweighed the potential reputational cost to the United States if its covert activities were discovered. The potential damage of appearing un-American was less than the perceived need to remove a "genocidal maniac" from power.[29]

For statist- and national security-minded Russians, however, it was a triumph of amazingly clever statecraft that transformed the politics of an entire region that had been traditionally aligned toward Russia, priming it for incorporation into the security and economic structures dominated by the liberal West. Neuralgia about external support for subversion in its neighborhood and within Russia's own borders thus loomed over the transition to the new millennium in Moscow, especially given the selection of a former KGB officer as president; the beginnings of an authoritarian turn domestically, featuring much more central control over regional governments; and a brutally forceful invasion of Chechnya to forestall what military officials claimed to fear, namely a second Kosovo in the North Caucasus. These moves— especially the horrific assault on Chechnya—predictably elicited strong criticisms from U.S. presidents, which had the equally predictable effect of reinforcing the connection in many Russian official minds between the unipolar U.S.-led liberal order and subversive support for domestic fifth columns.

And there was more. In addition to criticizing the bloody Russian assault on Grozny, the Bush administration advocated for a negotiated settlement, which required recognition of some Chechen resistance leaders as "moderates" who could be engaged diplomatically. Russian officials vehemently rejected such distinctions. Congressional leaders infuriated their Russian counterparts by referring to some of the Chechen rebels as "freedom fighters." And, again, the new public–private approach made an appearance in the form of an NGO, the American Committee for Peace in Chechnya, which received funding from Freedom House, which itself received U.S. government funding and in turn supported NED-linked entities like the International Republican Institute (IRI) and the National Democratic Institute (NDI), both active overseas. A group of distinguished Americans, featuring high-ranking Russia hawks (including former U.S. national security adviser Zbigniew Brzezinski and former Secretary of State Alexander Haig) and neoconservatives (including former CIA head James Woolsey) headlined the outfit, which took a much more forward stance in sympathy with the Chechen cause than the administration. This skated near but did not rise to the level of state-sponsored subversion: There is no open source evidence that the U.S. government materially supported the Chechen resistance.[30] For Russian officials with Kosovo on their minds, however, this combination of official and quasi-official activity hammered home fears that Russia might just be next.[31] And it would end up earning pride of place on Putin's list of grievances against overweening U.S. power.[32]

### The Gathering Storm: Subversion and the Return of Great Power Rivalry

The return of great power subversion is thus both a consequence and a cause of the re-emergence of great power rivalry. It was a Russian strategic reaction to unipolarity that played a leading role in bringing great power rivalry back to the front burner. And the story of that reaction can't be told without Russian official perceptions of the subversive threat inherent in the United States' new approach. Although the

Balkan saga registered particularly strongly, it was but one in a series of events highlighting Russian fears of a new and potentially decisive kind of subversion. After Kosovo, President Yeltsin and Clinton did patch things up, to a degree, and even though he would later complain bitterly about U.S. meddling in Russia's Chechen and larger North Caucasus crises, Putin famously responded to the September 11, 2001, terrorist attacks (9/11) by reaching out to the Bush administration in search of a partnership of equals against terrorism. But the flow of events continued to raise the specter of subversive statecraft.

### Moscow Nightmare: The Freedom Agenda

If the Clinton years had been marked by copious amounts of democracy promotion with a little bit of military muscle, as in Kosovo, the arrival of the Bush administration took it to an entirely new level. After the shock of 9/11, democracy promotion became central to both the war on terror and America's overall grand strategy. American military and political power would now be dedicated to democracy promotion around the globe in a much more forceful way, in an approach variously labeled as "democratic realism," "democratic globalism," "national security realism," or even "messianic universalism."[33] There was a sense of urgency, a recognition that the United States had an unparalleled opportunity to shape the world and make it more secure while it had all the power.

The 2002 National Security Strategy lauded a "moment of opportunity to extend the benefits of freedom across the globe . . . [The United States] will actively work to bring the hope of democracy, development, free markets, and free trade to every corner of the world." This could only happen if the United States were "the sole pillar upholding a liberal world order that is conducive to the principles [the United States] believes in."[34] And other major powers, notably Russia and China, would hardly stand in the way because "Russia is in the midst of a hopeful transition, reaching for its democratic future and a partner in the war on terror. Chinese leaders are discovering that economic freedom is the only source of national wealth."[35]

America was now willing to go it alone, and woe unto the state that stood in the way. George W. Bush's Second Inaugural Address made the case in soaring language:

> We are led, by events and common sense, to one conclusion: The survival of liberty in our land increasingly depends on the success of liberty in other lands. The best hope for peace in our world is the expansion of freedom in all the world. . . . So it is the policy of the United States to seek and support the growth of democratic movements and institutions in every nation and culture, with the ultimate goal of ending tyranny in our world.

This posture was most dramatically illustrated in the U.S. invasion of Iraq in 2003, but the subsequent decade saw a dramatic string of democratic uprisings and regime changes—the so-called color revolutions. In every case, U.S. NGOs were on the ground, aiding the opposition to entrenched or entrenching authoritarians and promoting transparency. And in each, just like in the case of the Kosovo Liberation Army in the late 1990s, the opposition seemed from the Western perspective to represent popular movements for freedom and democracy but were interpreted in Moscow as pro-Western proxies empowered by the United States and its allies to push for regime change favorable to Western geopolitical interests. The Georgian Rose Revolution in November 2003, which resulted in the ouster of President Eduard Shevardnadze, was greatly influenced by the civic youth resistance movement *Kmara* (Enough!), which in turn received training from the Serbian opposition youth group *Otpor*, which had been funded and supported by democracy-promoting NGOs in the 2000 Serbian elections.

A pattern soon emerged. In the 2004 Orange Revolution in Ukraine, election monitoring and civic engagement supported by Western NGOs resulted in a forced vote recount after Russia-leaning presidential candidate Viktor Yanukovych won a fraud-plagued run-off election. Opposition candidate Viktor Yushchenko was the ultimate victor. The ebullience of the times even embraced the unlikely territory of Central Asia. In 2005, disputed parliamentary elections brought protestors into the streets in Kyrgyzstan, leading to the ouster of Kyrgyz President Askar Akayev, who took refuge in Moscow. It was the third time in eighteen months that flawed elections and public protest had toppled a government in the Commonwealth of Independent States, and it seemed to show that even hardline holdouts against the democratic trend would eventually be affected. As a Carnegie Endowment report noted at the time,

> The "Tulip Revolution" (in Kyrgyzstan) could prove to be the most remarkable of all, causing positive reverberations throughout a region that many had written off as lost from the point of view of building democratic societies. If the revolution is unsuccessful, it will not be because the masses in Central Asia failed to make the grade, but because the ruling elite in Kyrgyzstan managed to sabotage the process of political change.[36]

By 2006, there was clear evidence that democracy promotion was creating blowback. In Russia, President Putin signed into law a controversial bill forcing local and foreign NGOs to report, in advance, every project they planned to undertake. This was part of a wider trend. As the Carnegie Endowment's Thomas Carothers noted, "After two decades of the steady expansion of democracy-building programs around the world, a growing number of governments are starting to crack down on such activities within their borders."[37] U.S. officials took note. U.S. Ambassador in Moscow William Burns recalled that the color revolutions

> led Putin to conclude that the Americans were not only undercutting Russia's interests in its sphere of influence, but might eventually aim the same kind of color revolution at his regime. These disappointments were piled on top of his anger over the Iraq war, a symbol of America's predilection for unilateral action in a unipolar world, and President Bush's second inaugural address and its "freedom agenda"— which Putin believed included Russia near the top of the administration's "to-do" list. Democracy promotion, in his eyes, was a Trojan horse designed to further American geopolitical interests at Russia's expense, and ultimately to erode his grip on power in Russia itself.[38]

Putin's now-famous speech at the Munich Security Conference in 2007, in which he called for multipolarity and essentially warned the West that Georgia and Ukraine were within Russia's sphere of influence, laid out his thinking for all to see.

*The Arab Spring and the Russian Elections*

If the turn of the millennium marked the moment when the full scale of unipolarity became apparent, the Great Recession of 2008 inaugurated the period when dissatisfied powers increasingly began to assess that America's power was declining even as it sustained its core approach to the expanding liberal order. The economic setback of 2008, against the backdrop of China's dramatic rise, suggested a weakening of unipolarity and a discrediting of liberalism. Yet the old impulse to press hard for liberalizing trends in other nations' domestic politics remained firmly in place in Washington, as evidenced in the Arab Spring in 2010–2012 and the U.S. response to the massive protests in Russia in 2011. In Moscow, these events propelled the narrative of a subversive threat. As a result, the sense of both threat and the relative power to combat it increased.

With the beginning of the Arab Spring in 2010, commentators ramped up grumbling about the perceived U.S. strategy of fomenting civil unrest to direct the Arab world toward Western-style liberal democracy. And as in Eastern Europe, the NED, IRI, NDI, and others were present and active, assisting but not initiating the protests, providing economic and strategic support. As the Russian government increasingly cracked down on NGOs and the liberal opposition more generally, the U.S. government sought to empower the opposition to subvert regime controls. At Secretary of State Hillary Clinton's initiative, the United States funded programs to train activists in Russia and other repressive regimes to employ cyber tools to protect their anonymity from government surveillance and jump over internet firewalls. By 2011, Clinton noted, "[The United States] had invested more than $45 million in tools to help keep dissidents safe online and trained more than five thousand activists worldwide, who turned around and trained thousands more." She visited one of these workshops in Lithuania just before massive protests rocked the Kremlin.[39] When an OSCE report following the Russian parliamentary elections on December 4 cited electoral irregularities, including ballot box stuffing, fraud, and manipulation, Clinton announced that the United States "had serious concerns" and called publicly for a "full investigation."[40]

To be sure, not all these events fit the Kremlin story about U.S.-supported subversion. After all, the most prominent leader toppled in the Arab Spring was stalwart U.S. ally Hosni Mubarak, and the NATO intervention in Libya occurred with an authorizing UN Security Council resolution on which Russia abstained due to a decision by then-president Dmitry Medvedev. And Clinton's statements concerning the election's integrity were utterly typical for U.S. officials of the time, reflecting settled policy in an organization—the OSCE—of which Moscow was a member. But the mindset building in Moscow ever since Kosovo ignored such nuance. The subsequent appointment as ambassador to Russia of Michael McFaul, a distinguished scholar with a long record of studying and working for democratization in Russia, played directly into this narrative. Putin's later claim that Secretary Clinton's outspoken accusations of electoral fraud had "sent a signal" to protestors was clearly a deliberate exaggeration, but her comments were followed by a mass movement that eventually swelled to stage some of the largest demonstrations in Russia since the 1990s.[41] Most Russia experts take seriously the claim that for many in the leadership, it seemed as if the tide of color revolutions might finally be lapping at Moscow's shores.

**Figure 6.2** Hillary Clinton calling out electoral fraud in the Russian parliamentary elections at an OSCE meeting, December 2011.
*Source*: AP photo/J. Scott Applewhite, pool.

Some English language media inadvertently pushed that narrative by dubbing the protests the "Snow Revolution."

Three processes unfolding simultaneously, whose relative importance will forever be debated by scholars, propelled and enabled ever more pugnacious Russian responses: the continued expansion of the U.S.-led "rules based order," Russia's increasing authoritarianism, and the Kremlin's belief in its increasing capability to push back. The more authoritarian Russia became, the more subversive and threatening U.S.-led democracy promotion seemed, and the more Moscow adopted internal countermeasures against it, eliciting more condemnation from the West, which simply served to reinforce the spiral. The stronger Russia thought it was becoming compared to the United States and the less it thought it had to lose if it ran afoul of the Americans, the more it turned to external subversive operations to undermine the liberal order and the bolder those operations became.

Much of the action was domestically focused, part and parcel of the country's increasing authoritarianism. Feeling under threat by what he perceived as U.S. subversion, Putin responded by hardening the target, just as Elizabeth I had done against the English Catholic resistance. Although we can't settle the debate over whether Russian rulers simply used the fear of subversion as an excuse, many of the regime-protecting measures followed key events that suggested the subversive power of the West, and scholars do see some connection, granting that rulers of a still penetrable autocracy have rational reasons for such fears.[42] Russian authorities sought to combat key aspects of what they viewed as a coherent, organized Western approach with their own system of election monitoring, using regime-friendly right-wing Western confrères, a more explicit conservative state ideology, and a government-sponsored nationalist youth movement (*Nashi* ["Ours"]) as a counter to mass youth opposition.[43]

The color revolutions were immediately followed in Russia by new restrictions on foreign-funded NGOs, limits on free media, and repression of transnational advocacy networks. In response to the 2011 and 2012 demonstrations, the regime organized "anti-Orange" protests, alluding to the Orange Revolution in Ukraine, backed by youth groups such as *Nashi* and Young Guard, the youth branch of Putin's United Russia party. Protests culminated in violent police crackdowns just before Putin's inauguration for a third term as president. Putin immediately moved to tighten further laws against dissent, with strictly enforced boundaries on protests and stiff penalties for unauthorized activities.

But Russia also increasingly turned to external action. There, too, the response sought to mimic, counter, and neuter the clever, concerted Western approach Russian officials imagined emanated from Washington. It began in the information realm. The more authoritarian and nationalist Russia became, the more hostile the global information space dominated by liberal values seemed. From Kosovo to Chechnya to Ukraine, Russian officials fretted that they kept losing the "information war."[44] The first move was to up Moscow's public diplomacy game. *Russia Today* was founded in 2005 and rebranded as *RT* in 2008. Its logo, "Question More," indicated that its aim was less about burnishing Russia's image abroad than it was in sowing discord, dissension, and doubts about the liberal order.

The Arab Spring and the Moscow protests of 2011 and 2012 hammered home the significance of social media and the internet, and the Russian government quickly set about countering the mobilizing power of that medium. Its response at home was partly regulatory, in the classic authoritarian mode, simply replicating for online media and influencers the same kind of repression it used to gain control over traditional media and targeting domestic opposition bloggers. However, it also went on the offensive, deploying newer means more tuned to the new medium, like "troll armies" and bots. By 2013, this newly created apparatus was being tuned up for use abroad. That summer, a new entity registered with the government in St. Petersburg: the Internet Research Agency. Soon thereafter, it unleashed the "translation project," designed to enlist foreign language speakers in its growing army of online trolls and influencers.

Russian subversion (by our definition) against the West—much less the United States—remained limited. Most activity was still aimed at the "Near Abroad," with Estonia the target of cyber-attacks in 2007, and both Estonia and Latvia the subjects of meddling via Russian diasporas. But as with the information strategy, the tools, methods, and relationships for more direct forms of subversion were well underway. At the same time, the more conservative, nationalist, anti-liberal Russian state began to find more willing interlocutors among the growing right-wing nationalist movements in the West.[45]

In February 2013, Russia's top military official, the Chief of the General Staff of the Russian Armed Forces and First Deputy Minister of Defense, General Valery Gerasimov, published an article titled "The Value of Science Is in the Foresight."[46] Commentators in the West would soon seize upon the article as the harbinger of a new Russian approach—a so-called Gerasimov doctrine, a distinctive and novel Russian way of waging "hybrid war"—under which subversive means come to dominate conventional military capability. Those who originally coined the term would later refute it, but the moniker stuck. Meanwhile, the article was setting forth the chief's view of the operational environment and challenges that Russia faced in protecting its own security.[47] Gerasimov was calling attention to a feature of this environment that the Russian security establishment had been obsessing about since Kosovo: the role that subversive transnational action (as seen from Moscow's corridors of power), in concert with U.S. military power, plays in advancing U.S. political objectives to the detriment of Russia. He dwelled not on the major U.S. conventional war against Iraq in 2003, but rather the familiar litany of indirect or "nonlinear" operations: Kosovo, Libya, the Arab Spring, and the color revolutions.

As analyst Michael Kofman insightfully noted, "Gerasimov's description of the various non-military means employed by the West as part of non-linear warfare bears a striking resemblance to Kennan's definition of overt and covert political warfare" at the dawn of the Cold War. If we set aside the distaste any liberal-minded person inevitably has for Russia's ever more autocratic political regime as of 2013, Kofman's parallel is compelling. "Gerasimov's operating environment looks a lot like America's from the late 1940s faced with Soviet chicanery."[48] In Chapter 5, we saw George Kennan arguing that America had to take a page from Stalin's playbook and answer Soviet subversion with political warfare of its own. Gerasimov's essay signaled that the Russian military and security establishment was in the same mood: It was time to respond in kind.

The year 2013 thus opens with Russia thinking it is losing vis-à-vis the United States and the West not because it is weak in conventional military terms but because it is incapable of combatting the amazingly clever set of tools Washington brings to the strategic table. It opens with most of the ingredients that would later be deployed in bold subversive operations against the West and the United States already in place. And it opens with intensifying contestation between Moscow and the West over the fate of one nation—Ukraine.

*Ukraine in the Crosshairs*

Statesmen and pundits can debate "great power status" and "multipolarity" until the cows come home, but in practice such concepts come to have concrete meaning on specific issues in specific places. For the Russian leadership, the place is Ukraine and the issue is that country's geopolitical orientation. Throughout all the years of unipolarity, perceived humiliation, and political turmoil, through the many elections and color revolutions, through the shifting fortunes of Ukrainian political forces more or less deferential to Russia, people in Moscow could always argue that their assumed prerogative of a sphere of influence including Kyiv remained a realistic prospect. The contest between Moscow and the West over Ukraine in 2013 called that assumption into question. And Russia's response released the coiled springs of great power competition and subversion.

The drama of 2013 featured Brussels and Moscow competing to bring Ukraine into their respective economic blocs while presenting the choice as zero-sum.[49] Although his personal and political fortunes generally inclined him toward partnership with Putin, Ukrainian President Viktor Yanukovych sought to maneuver between Brussels and Moscow to get the most favorable deal. In February, Ukraine's parliament voted for an association agreement with the EU. Moscow responded with a combination of diplomatic pressure (big economic carrots on offer for joining its Eurasian Union combined with punishing trade restrictions for the EU dalliance) plus a full-court press of subversion meant to empower Ukrainian political forces that favored the Moscow arrangement and discredit pro-EU forces.[50] This combination—with the traditional statecraft in the driver's seat—met with success in November and December, as Yanukovych pivoted 180 degrees, spurning the EU in favor of the Eurasian Union, reaping a quick pledge of $15 billion from Putin in return.[51]

The celebrations that doubtless followed in Moscow were short-lived, interrupted by the very thing that had been driving Russia's national security managers mad for more than a decade: a color revolution in all but name. Grim Russian apparatchiks surely watched the "revolution of dignity," the tens of thousands marching on Kyiv's Maidan Square protesting Yanukovych's about-face, through the lens of Gerasimov's February article, perceiving events in Ukraine as a ruthless act of Western subversive statecraft. When Yanukovych issued decrees cracking down on the protestors, their numbers swelled to the hundreds of thousands and rioting ensued. An attempt at signing an agreement brokered by the United States, Ukraine, the EU, and Russia to create a temporary coalition government with Yanukovych at its head fizzled when the Russian envoy refused to sign the document. The standoff culminated over three violent days in February 2014, during which a botched government crackdown led to dozens of deaths on the Maidan. His government collapsing, his security forces defecting, and his party's deputies boycotting the parliament, Yanukovych fled to Moscow and the opposition took power in Kyiv.[52] The new government swiftly signaled its intent to turn the ship of the Ukrainian state back on its previous course toward Europe.

U.S. intelligence agencies reported that Putin was furious and determined to avoid what he saw as another U.S.-instigated regime change. In a phone call with British Prime Minister David Cameron to discuss the situation, he was fuming. "This is my backyard," he told the British premier, "The West has repeatedly humiliated me, over Libya, over Syria, etc., for the last ten years."[53] Putin's efforts at economic statecraft, diplomacy, and subtler forms of subversion had failed. It was time for bolder measures. Within a week, "little green men" in unmarked uniforms had seized the Crimean parliament building. By March, a controversial referendum had resulted in Russian annexation of the Crimean peninsula. At the same time, Moscow, in cahoots with pro-Russian oligarchs in Ukraine's eastern regions of Donetsk and Luhansk, mobilized previously fringe elements to propel separatist violence.[54] The aim was to coerce Ukraine's government into agreeing to a federalization scheme that would give the Kremlin a de facto veto on Kyiv's geopolitical orientation.

**Figure 6.3** U.S. Undersecretary of State Victoria Nuland on the Maidan Square, Kyiv, December 11, 2013.
*Source*: Roman Mikhailiuk/Shutterstock.com.

These moves pushed the West's frenzy over "gray zone" subversion to a new pitch. But the reality on the ground was that subversion failed: Moscow ended up with a conventional military intervention. When Ukraine arrested the self-declared governors and mayors of the Donetsk and Luhansk People's Republics, Russia switched to irregular warfare with paramilitaries. That, too, was on the path to failure in the face of a Ukrainian counter-offensive when Russia moved to an outright invasion with regular Russian units, something it had sought to avoid. The aim remained subversive—to keep a dagger at Ukraine's neck to force it to accept a status for the eastern regions that would give Moscow a veto on Kyiv's westward course—but the means had become conventional military power.

This moment—with Russia's effort to attain the sphere of influence over Ukraine stalled in the Donbas—was when the subversion of American democracy began. Putin launched a wide-ranging attack on Western, and especially American, democratic institutions. A "significant intelligence source" inside the Russian government reportedly told a U.S. embassy official exactly how the attack would play out, including cyber-attacks, disinformation, propaganda, and the weaponization of social media. According to journalists Michael Isikoff and David Corn, the source was crystal clear about the extent of Russian penetration of the West. "You have no idea how extensive these networks are in Europe—Germany, Italy, France, and the UK—and in the US," the informant is said to have reported. "Russia has penetrated media organizations, lobbying firms, political parties, governments, and militaries in all these places."[55]

The critical weapons in the coming campaign would include the new technologies developed over the previous two decades.[56] There already had been a significant indication of what was to come. In January 2014, Assistant Secretary of State for European and Eurasian Affairs Victoria Nuland received a call at her Washington home from the U.S. Ambassador to Ukraine, Geoffrey Pyatt, during which they discussed the various attributes of opposition leaders who could join a coalition government with Yanukovych. Exasperated with what she perceived as EU foot-dragging, Nuland commented, "Fuck the EU." Ten days later, an audio file of the conversation appeared on YouTube, where it was picked up and promoted on Twitter by a Russian official and quickly amplified by Russian media. It was a warning sign of Russian capabilities. Nuland saw it for the danger it was: "The Russians had not put a phone call in the street in twenty-five years. . . . It shouldn't have been ignored. We should have formally protested, and we didn't. . . . With Putin, you always need to smack back."[57]

## Conclusion

The U.S.–Russian relationship had come full circle, from Cold War adversaries to tentative new partners and back once again to adversaries. Ostensibly well-meaning, "benevolent" subversion on the part of the United States, guided by a sense that it was helping formerly autocratic countries to become liberally enlightened and democratic, played a role in this arc, one complicated by episodic entanglement with U.S. intelligence services. To be sure, Putin's and the wider Russian national security elite's inflated sense of their country's power and perquisites, as well as Russian suspicions and entrenched attitudes, were also important drivers of the downturn. However one assigns blame, it was clear by 2014 that Moscow was on the offensive.

**Figure 6.4** President Obama convening a National Security Council meeting in the Situation Room of the White House to discuss matters in Ukraine on March 3, 2014, during Russia's annexation of Crimea.
*Source*: World History Archive/Alamy stock photo.

Although Moscow's initial embrace of Western influence in the early 1990s would seem to exclude parts of this episode from our definition of subversion, American democracy promotion was perceived within a decade of the Soviet Union's collapse as an increasingly unwanted force in many former Soviet countries. With the march of democracy reinforced by military measures in Kosovo, Libya, and Iraq, the unipolar era morphed from one of cooperation to one of increasing alarm on the part of autocratic rulers, not only in Russia but also globally, particularly in China. Unipolarity came to mean unilateral action on the part of the United States, and color revolutions that seemed like a good thing in Western eyes were perceived as a subversive wave to those rulers in the crosshairs. In the end, it was an episode of great power on small power subversion—Moscow's propaganda, meddling, and eventual sabotage and covert military invasion in Ukraine—that ramped up the great power rivalry between Russia and the United States. The return of this great power rivalry brought great power subversion once again to the fore.

# 7

## The Return of Great Power Subversion

THE "SIGNIFICANT SOURCE" in the Kremlin who reportedly warned of an impending broad-based campaign of subversion was right.[1] In the spring of 2014, with its quest for multipolarity stalled in Ukraine, Russia would escalate its subversive statecraft both vertically, by employing bolder measures, and horizontally, by spreading operations from countries in Russia's "near abroad" to Western Europe and then the United States.[2] With that escalation and all it entailed, great power subversion would come back with a roar.

### The Attack Begins

America's Western European allies were the first to feel the sting. Russian cyber capabilities and their integration into Moscow's intelligence bureaucracies had been building dramatically since 2008, with lucrative offers to clever young hackers of deals they couldn't refuse in exchange for offering their services to the state.[3] Analysts detected a notable escalation in 2014 of operations containing all the elements that would later appear in the United States: social media-borne disinformation, cyber hacking and doxxing, and election interference.[4]

In the United Kingdom, operatives working on Moscow's behalf targeted the hotly contested Scottish independence referendum vote in September 2014, spreading false information across social media to influence the outcome. When the referendum was narrowly defeated, young hackers at the soon-to-be-infamous Internet Research Agency (IRA) in St. Petersburg exploited the genuine upset of independence voters to push the narrative that the vote was rigged. In the weeks following, baseless allegations of voting fraud began to circulate.[5]

In early 2015, a pro-Russian group brought down parliamentary websites in the German Bundestag during a visit by Ukraine's then Prime Minister Arseniy Yatsenyuk. A few months later, Russian hackers—later attributed to the GRU—were discovered roaming around in the Bundestag's communications systems, even gaining access to a computer in the chancellor's office. They stole a trove of data and raised concerns about its weaponization in the upcoming German elections, scheduled for the autumn of 2017.[6]

At the same time, in April 2015, a powerful cyber-attack nearly destroyed the French network TV5Monde, bringing down its systems and causing twelve channels to go dark. In a typical "false flag" operation, a group calling itself the Cyber Caliphate and touting links to ISIS claimed responsibility. Investigations quickly revealed that it was the same GRU outfit, known as APT 28 or Fancy Bear, that had conducted the attack. The TV5Monde attack ramped up the aggression markedly from the Bundestag hack, using malicious software to destroy the networks and create real-world consequences, not just espionage. Intelligence agencies concluded that it was most likely an attempt to test forms of cyber-weaponry.[7]

Clearly, the availability of cyber tools that could be used for an assault on an election was not new in 2016. What was new was the target.

### America in the Crosshairs

The pieces for a hit on America were all in place. As mentioned in Chapter 6, the 1999 Moonlight Maze investigation had revealed that Russia had been steadily snooping around in American cyber networks since roughly 1996. This was regular espionage, mirroring similar efforts by the United States and other countries with cyber capabilities against their adversaries. Fair game all around. Even when U.S. Central Command was hacked in 2008, in what was considered the worst breach of U.S. military computers in history, the damage was limited to theft (and serious money spent rebuilding the networks).

**Figure 7.1** Police guard the entrance to France's TV5Monde after a debilitating Russian cyber-attack. The GRU used a "false flag" operation to pin the attack on the Islamic State.
*Source*: AP photo/Christophe Ena.

The U.S. presidential election was already in Moscow's sights from early 2014; we know this from intelligence indicating that employees at the IRA began discussing it as a target around that time.[8] The attack would unfold along three separate vectors, each featuring a tool of subversion familiar from the past. The first involved information and propaganda; the second a combination of theft, forgery, and dissemination of embarrassing documents; and the third a stab at probing and intrusion into U.S. states' electoral rolls and infrastructure, a harbinger of potential sabotage. All three were tactics of old, but they were harnessed to a new and poorly understood technology that lent unusual fear to the perceptions of Americans on the receiving end.

The information operation would use both overt and covert methods, combining traditional and social media. Russian news outlets like Sputnik (founded in 2014 and aimed initially at the Eurasian information space) and the television network RT (formerly Russia Today) had already been presenting Kremlin-friendly broadcasts in the United States since 2010. To augment their efforts, gray and black propaganda

**Figure 7.2** The Internet Research Agency building in St. Petersburg, from where much of the 2016 information operation would originate.
*Source*: AP photo/Dmitry Lovetsky.

and disinformation, which made up the vast bulk of the action, would be generated by social media campaigns, leaked documents, and forgeries, then amplified in the same way active measures had operated in the Cold War.

Beginning in March 2014, a series of seemingly unconnected events hinted at what was to come. That month, an odd petition appeared on the White House website calling for signatures to demand that Alaska be returned to Russia. Automated Twitter bots and Facebook pages promoted the petition to the extent that within a short time it had nearly 40,000 signatures.[9] In June, IRA social media propaganda and disinformation operations became focused within a unit known as the Translator Department, which dealt with various social media platforms, analytics, graphics, and information technology (IT). That same month, two IRA employees, Anna Bogacheva and Aleksandra Krylova—the third highest ranking employee at the IRA—obtained visas and entered the United States to conduct reconnaissance for the operation. Back in St. Petersburg, IRA "specialists" busily targeted Facebook, YouTube, Twitter, and other social media platforms with posts crafted to build affinity with unwitting Americans, the first step toward manipulating them.

In the autumn of 2014, a spear phishing campaign gave the Russians access to computers throughout the State Department and U.S. embassies, forcing State to shut down its entire nonclassified global network. The malware then jumped to the White House nonclassified networks, which had to be destroyed and rebuilt from scratch.[10] These and other incidents may have been dramatic, but all were considered to be fair game for rivals, despite the novelty of the cyber dimension. "This was an intelligence operation," President Barack Obama is said to have told his aides, "It's just like we would do to them."[11]

On September 11, 2014, residents of St. Mary Parish, Louisiana, received a barrage of text messages about explosions at a nearby chemical plant. "Toxic fume hazard warning in this area until 1:30 PM," the messages read, "Take Shelter. Check Local Media and columbiachemical. com."[12] Images of the plant in flames popped up on Twitter, while other accounts posted screenshots of a CNN feed purporting to cover the story and linking the attack to ISIS. It was a highly coordinated disinformation campaign involving dozens of fake accounts, and even included functional clones of the websites of Louisiana TV stations.[13] In what was essentially a trial run, the IRA had combined social media manipulation and high-tech fakes in an operation that would have impressed Soviet-era KGB officials. Other shenanigans, including a fake Ebola outbreak, a hoax about a police shooting in Atlanta, and an initial experiment in creating a live event involving a spoof offer of free hot dogs in New York, soon followed.[14]

Throughout 2015, the IRA expanded its efforts, creating fake organizations on Facebook with names like "United Muslims of America" (300,000 followers), "Don't Shoot Us" (250,000 followers), "Being Patriotic" (200,000 followers), and "Secured Borders" (130,000 followers). Just as the KGB had directed entities like the World Peace Council, these new digital movements sought to serve the same purpose, trying to create mass movements to disrupt and distract. Unlike the 1980s, however, Moscow's action did not reveal intent to tweak policy in a desired direction. Disruption was the name of this game. And, in contrast to the late Cold War, the internet allowed the IRA to work with lightning speed and the easiest access across oceans and borders in history.

The Obama administration was aware of what was happening, but it was convinced that freedom of speech and information would ultimately prevail. In 2015, the CIA proposed a covert program to beat the Russians at their own game by creating fake websites to push back against Kremlin propaganda. The National Security Agency (NSA) would be enlisted to neutralize the websites and servers used by the fake Russian personae. But senior Obama aides stuck to their belief, perhaps naively, that the free flow of information would prevail against Russian propaganda. The plan went nowhere.[15]

Despite the somewhat slapdash and clumsy tenor of the messaging, the IRA's reach was impressive; the Mueller investigation later concluded that the IRA's social media accounts reached tens of millions of U.S. citizens. Bolstered by illegally purchased Facebook ads, the posts aimed at first to sow divisions over polarizing topics rather than back any particular candidate, appearing before the primary season had even kicked off.[16] Facebook reported IRA-controlled accounts made more than 80,000 posts before their deactivation in August 2017, and these posts reached at least 29 million U.S. persons and "may have reached an estimated 126 million people."[17] Still, at day's end, reach does not equal impact, and the IRA was a state-affiliated trolling operation whose coordination with Russia's real intelligence professionals remained murky. In cyber expert Thomas Rid's words, the IRA "worked more like a spammy call center than a tight intelligence agency."[18]

As the disinformation campaign evolved, however, the pros were laying the groundwork for something much more serious: hacking, forging, and disseminating information on an epic scale. In the summer of 2015, Dutch intelligence officials informed their U.S. counterparts that hackers from Russia's foreign intelligence service, the SVR, had gained access to servers at the Democratic National Committee (DNC). As with other cyber intrusions, this remained, in former NSA director Michael Hayden's words, "honorable state espionage. . . . If we at NSA could have an insight into . . . Russia through the same techniques, game on."[19] U.S. officials believed that "Russia's cyber activity targeting the DNC fell within the bounds of traditional espionage and was not understood immediately to be a precursor to an active measures campaign."[20]

Yet there were signs that something bigger than just espionage was afoot. As the subversive operations got underway, there seemed to be an ebullient mood in Moscow that the tables were turning on the United States and the collective West in the information space. Remarks at the February 2016 Infoforum, Moscow's major cyber conference, by Andrey Krutskikh, Russia's top cyber diplomat, reflected the mood:

> You think we are living in 2016. No, we are living in 1948. And do you know why? Because in 1949, the Soviet Union had its first atomic bomb test. And if until that moment, the Soviet Union was trying to reach agreement with [President Harry] Truman to ban nuclear weapons, and the Americans were not taking us seriously, in 1949 everything changed and they started talking to us on an equal footing.

Krutskikh continued, "I'm warning you: We are on the verge of having 'something' in the information arena which will allow us to talk to the Americans as equals."[21] Krutskikh's comments contributed to the "Gerasimov doctrine" and "hybrid war" scares animating some Western analysts at the same time.[22]

Yet the issue fell through the cracks for several months. It was not until September that the FBI attempted to warn the DNC, which took no immediate action. DNC staffers eventually managed to make some IT upgrades by April 2016, but it was too little, too late. The previous month, more sophisticated hackers from the GRU's Unit 26165 had joined the effort, launching broad spear phishing attacks on individuals within the DNC as well as the Clinton Campaign and the Democratic Congressional Campaign Committee (DCCC).[23] When the DNC finally had the cybersecurity firm Crowdstrike clean its machines, the investigation revealed both the GRU and the SVR presence—each service apparently unaware of the other's activity.[24]

In a stroke of luck for Moscow, on March 19, GRU hackers from APT 28 successfully spear phished Clinton campaign chair John Podesta. Podesta's credentials opened for the hackers a Pandora's box of sensitive and embarrassing emails and provided links into other parts of the Democratic political network. The Russians now targeted top Clinton advisors and Clinton's personal email, along with that of campaign staffers, some of whom unwittingly clicked on malicious links and allowed the Russians access using a malware, known as X-agent, capable of capturing keystrokes, taking screenshots, gathering documents, harvesting passwords, and even tracking targets as they worked.[25] By summer's end, hackers had sent more than 9,000 malicious links to 4,000 accounts.[26] And hackers exfiltrated thousands of emails from Podesta's account, setting the stage for an October surprise.

### From Espionage to Subversion

In April 2016, the hacking game changed from espionage to subversion. As the overt propaganda and covert social media manipulation continued, GRU intelligence gathering now became an influence operation. A separate GRU unit, 74455 (also known as SANDWORM), registered and set up a website, DCLeaks.com (having first botched attempts to register their preferred moniker, electionleaks.com).[27] In early June, documents from prominent Democrats and anti-Russian figures began to appear on the site, including files from the Open Society Foundation, NATO Supreme Allied Commander General Philip Breedlove, Bill and Hillary Clinton, and even some Republicans.

On June 14, the DNC announced publicly that Russia had hacked its servers. Within days, another online persona appeared, calling itself Guccifer 2.0 and claiming credit for the hack and release. To prove it, Guccifer released another trove of documents, this time in coordination with the website WikiLeaks and its founder, Julian Assange.

The Guccifer leaks caught the White House's attention in a way the hacks had not. National Security Advisor Susan Rice, White House Chief of Staff Denis McDonough, and Homeland Security Advisor Lisa Monaco spearheaded the response. They asked the intelligence community (IC) for clarity on what was happening, alarmed by the odd combination of candidate Donald Trump's pro-Russia comments and now the hack and release. There was a growing sense of dread in both the Clinton campaign and the White House that more leaks were coming. And come they did, sometimes including doctored or forged documents. One file attempted to show a $150 million donation to the

CONSPIRACY TO COMMIT AN OFFENSE AGAINST THE UNITED STATES; FALSE
REGISTRATION OF A DOMAIN NAME; AGGRAVATED IDENTITY THEFT; CONSPIRACY
TO COMMIT MONEY LAUNDERING

# RUSSIAN INTERFERENCE IN 2016 U.S. ELECTIONS

Boris Alekseyevich Antonov | Dmitriy Sergeyevich Badin | Anatoliy Sergeyevich Kovalev | Nikolay Yuryevich Kozachek | Aleksey Viktorovich Lukashev | Artem Andreyevich Malyshev

Sergey Aleksandrovich Morgachev | Aleksandr Vladimirovich Osadchuk | Aleksey Aleksandrovich Potemkin | Ivan Sergeyevich Yermakov | Pavel Vyacheslavovich Yershov

## DETAILS

On July 13, 2018, a federal grand jury sitting in the District of Columbia returned an indictment against 12 Russian military intelligence officers for their alleged roles in interfering with the 2016 United States (U.S.) elections. The indictment charges 11 defendants, Boris Alekseyevich Antonov, Dmitriy Sergeyevich Badin, Nikolay Yuryevich Kozachek, Aleksey Viktorovich Lukashev, Artem Andreyevich Malyshev, Sergey Aleksandrovich Morgachev, Aleksandr Vladimirovich Osadchuk, Aleksey Aleksandrovich Potemkin, Ivan Sergeyevich Yermakov, Pavel Vyacheslavovich Yershov, and Viktor Borisovich Netyksho, with a computer hacking conspiracy involving gaining unauthorized access into the computers of U.S. persons and entities involved in the 2016 U.S. presidential election, stealing documents from those computers, and staging releases of the stolen documents to interfere with the 2016 U.S. presidential election. The indictment also charges these defendants with aggravated identity theft, false registration of a domain name, and conspiracy to commit money laundering. Two defendants, Aleksandr Vladimirovich Osadchuk and Anatoliy Sergeyevich Kovalev, are charged with a separate conspiracy to commit computer crimes, relating to hacking into the computers of U.S. persons and entities responsible for the administration of 2016 U.S. elections, such as state boards of elections, secretaries of state, and U.S. companies that supplied software and other technology related to the administration of U.S. elections. The United States District Court for the District of Columbia in Washington, D.C. issued a federal arrest warrant for each of these defendants upon the grand jury's return of the indictment.

### THESE INDIVIDUALS SHOULD BE CONSIDERED ARMED AND DANGEROUS, AN INTERNATIONAL FLIGHT RISK, AND AN ESCAPE RISK

If you have any information concerning this case, please contact your local FBI office, or the nearest American Embassy or Consulate.

www.fbi.gov

**Figure 7.3** FBI wanted poster for IRA and GRU hackers implicated in the 2016 operation.

Clinton campaign by the Bradley Foundation, which would have been illegal under campaign finance laws.[28]

On July 22, just days before the Democratic National Convention was to begin, WikiLeaks released 20,000 emails from top DNC operatives. The emails showed efforts within the DNC to promote Hillary Clinton over Senator Bernie Sanders, her opponent for the Democratic nomination. The uproar led to the resignation of the DNC chair, Debbie Wasserman Schultz, and provoked fury among Sanders delegates at the convention. Clinton campaign aides tried mightily to bring the conversation back around to the fact that the Russians were trying to influence the election, to no avail.

At the beginning of June, before the DNC's announcement of Russian involvement in the hack, the operation's third vector had gotten quietly underway. GRU hackers began to probe state voter databases for weaknesses, eventually targeting voter registration systems or websites in all 50 states, accessing some state systems and stealing personal information of hundreds of thousands of voters. The voter databases in Illinois were actually breached; other states were subjected to breach attempts. Although U.S. intelligence agencies determined that no votes were altered, the Senate Intelligence Committee found that in two states the GRU was in a position to alter or delete voter registration data, and in Illinois the FBI found that "undetermined amounts" of data had been exfiltrated.[29] This posed a real danger of quantifiable electoral interference far beyond propaganda, disinformation, and a smear campaign. To be sure, actually affecting vote counts in America's decentralized electoral system would be a formidable task, but Obama administration officials quickly gamed out multiple plausible pathways through which the Russians could, if they chose, undermine the perceived integrity of the vote.[30]

In summary, in the spring and summer of 2016, the Russian government was having a field day messing around in U.S. politics, with troll troops spreading disinformation, state hackers running rampant around Democratic Party computer systems and using witting and unwitting accomplices to disseminate the ill-gotten information, and the GRU wielding the credible potential to upend the perceived legitimacy of the vote tally.

Throughout all of this, Moscow benefited from the one attribute that has aided subverters from time immemorial: help on the inside. Philip of Macedon had his supporters in Athens. Pope Pius V had his Catholic priests and diplomats. Bismarck benefited from his Tory supporters in Gladstone's England. Putin, too, faced no shortage of people willing to reap political gains from his subversive efforts. Julian Assange and WikiLeaks were critical assets. The GRU was unable to make a splash with DNC and DCCC materials until it secured the savvy assistance of WikiLeaks—widely seen as a highly credible conduit for leaked insider information.[31] Assange, who was well aware of the provenance of the materials he was disseminating, found eager collaborators in the Trump campaign. The Senate Intelligence Committee report documents how Trump campaign operatives strategically used WikiLeaks dumps even after they knew of their origins.[32] Trump campaign advisor Roger Stone was in direct contact with Assange, as was Donald Trump, Jr.[33] Eventually, Trump himself would play this role, although arguably in jest. "Russia, if you're listening," he intoned at a July 27 press conference, "I hope you're able to find the 30,000 emails that are missing," referring to emails that had been deleted from Clinton's controversial private server.[34] A Department of Justice indictment documents that within hours of this quip, GRU operatives "attempted after hours to spear phish for the first time email accounts at a domain hosted by a third-party provider and used by Clinton's personal office." They also targeted seventy-six email addresses at the domain for the Clinton Campaign for good measure.[35]

Meanwhile, Russia's professional intelligence services in Moscow and its diplomats on the ground in Washington were joined by a dog's breakfast of Russian operators: the gun-loving Maria Butina and her handler Alexander Torshin, Russian oligarch Oleg Deripaska, the Russian–Azerbaijani oligarch Aras Agalarov and his pop star son Emin, the anti-Magnitsky Act lobbyist–lawyer Natalya Vesel'nitskaya, and many others. All were energetically engaging in "entrepreneurial, self-starter subversion," seeking contacts with U.S. political figures in ways they reckoned the Kremlin would like.[36] They encountered a cast of characters in the United States doing their best to use Russia for their own purposes.

Of all the multifarious influence attempts those who followed these events may recall—the negotiations about a Trump Tower in Moscow, the meeting of Trump operatives with Vesel'nitskaya on the false premise of Russian-acquired "dirt" on Clinton, the cultivating of campaign aides George Papadopoulos, Carter Page, and Mike Flynn, and so on—the connection between Paul Manafort and Konstantin Kilimnik stands out. Manafort, appointed Trump campaign manager in March, had a long history of lucrative political work with Russia-favored Ukrainians and a particularly close business relationship with Kilimnik, later assessed by the Mueller investigation and the U.S. intelligence community to be a proxy for Russian military intelligence (and identified by the Senate investigation positively as an intelligence officer).[37] Manafort was feeding Kilimnik confidential campaign polling data. According to the Senate report, "Kilimnik specifically sought to leverage Manafort's contacts with the incoming Trump administration" to advance peace plans for Ukraine that would serve Russia's long-standing aim of subordinating the country by creating an autonomous region in the Donbas.[38] The two met at the beginning of August at the Grand Havana Club cigar bar in Manhattan to discuss the plan, and even after stepping down as campaign director just weeks later, Manafort—along with Kilimnik, Deripaska, and associates—would continue to work the Ukraine issue, in particular by propelling disinformation that Ukraine, not Russia, interfered in 2016.

By the time the election came around, Russia, aided and abetted by the internet, had been pummeling the United States with every subversive tool in the toolkit, barring the violence of sabotage, armed insurgency, and assassination. The scale of the information warfare reached mind-boggling proportions because of a technology that had not existed in prior eras. Similarly, snooping around in computer networks and stealing vast amounts of information so easily were only possible because of new technology rather than spies on the ground. Ditto for the leaks, disinformation, and forgeries. It was a brazen affront, and it touched off a frenzied response in America.

## A Febrile Reaction

The world (and most top U.S. officials) became aware of the DNC hack when the whole affair was reported in *The Washington Post* on June 14, 2016. From that moment, the Obama administration maintained tight security around its deliberations and a muted public response. This was logical. Given the supercharged partisan atmosphere amidst the ongoing presidential campaign, officials naturally wanted to avoid giving the appearance of placing a thumb on the scales, particularly when it was widely assumed that Hillary Clinton would defeat Donald Trump. Caution was the order of the day.

Not so for the media or the presidential candidates. News outlets, both traditional and online, followed up on the *Post* reporting, covering the hacks, the potential Russia connection, and the reactions and recriminations of both the Clinton and Trump campaigns. Then-candidate Trump went so far as to accuse the DNC of hacking itself.[39] The furor drew public focus to the controversy and the contents of the leaked emails, distracting from the story behind why they were leaked in the first place.

With the WikiLeaks dump on July 22, the Democratic party reacted like an ant hill poked with a stick. Congressional Democrats, led by Representative Adam Schiff and Senator Dianne Feinstein, top-ranking Democrats on the House and Senate intelligence committees, demanded publicly that Obama react if the Russians were proven responsible. The Clinton campaign tried on its own to flag the Russian connection to the leaked emails. Clinton campaign manager Robbie Mook, when asked on CNN's *State of the Union* by host Jake Tapper about the emails and tensions surrounding DNC favoritism for Clinton over Sanders, stated bluntly that "experts" were telling the Clinton campaign that the Russians were responsible—and were bent on helping Trump. Yet pushback by Trump associates helped keep the focus on the content of the leaked material instead of the Russia angle.[40]

The White House, meanwhile, continued to downplay the situation as much as possible in the midst of excruciating uncertainty. In late July, the FBI had begun a counter-intelligence investigation—dubbed Crossfire Hurricane—into possible links between Trump associates and Russia. This effort required space, time, and the absolute appearance of neutrality. Obama's request to the IC to find out who was behind the hacks and the Guccifer persona had come back with an indication that Russia was the culprit, but that verdict was not unanimous. Added to this was the fact that hacking itself was nothing new. Director of National Intelligence James Clapper had already warned of potential campaign hacking back in May.[41] Speaking at the Aspen Security Forum as the Democratic National Convention was still ongoing, he dismissed the DNC hack as standard fare. No one should be "hyperventilating," he said.[42]

The hacking, leaking, and social media manipulation were essentially components of a propaganda and disinformation operation whose effect was confusing and distracting, but whose impact was largely confined to the political personalities of the Democratic and Republican camps. But August brought reports revealing the Russians' methodical and extensive infiltration of state electoral systems, which had begun in early June. This upped the stakes significantly. The potential to alter voter rolls and target companies that made voting machines pointed toward sabotage, aimed at the most sacred institution of American democracy. This was a much more aggressive tool of subversion than information warfare. And by this point, the IC knew that Putin was personally invested in the operation. Protecting the electoral infrastructure became the prime concern.

There was another wrinkle as well. On August 13, a mysterious online group calling itself the Shadow Brokers began publishing explosive information about stolen top-secret NSA hacking tools, threatening to auction them off to the highest bidder. The posted list of code names was hair-raising to those in the know; it included exploits so powerful that American hackers described them as "fishing with dynamite."[43] NSA had been finding flaws in commercial software—Windows, Unix/Linux, databases, mobile, and telecom—but keeping the knowledge to itself for its own exploits. The Shadow Brokers now threatened to expose it.[44] No one could say who they were, and no one knew exactly what they had stolen or what they would do with it. To add to the paranoia, posts from the group in late October took a political tone, excoriating Americans who did not vote, suggesting that disruption of the upcoming presidential election would be a good thing, and commenting on America's history of meddling in elections abroad.[45] Even if the somewhat Byzantine nature of state electoral processes provided a degree of protection, it was an uncomfortable state of affairs. Everything was new, and nothing seemed safe.

For the administration, there was little that could be done without making things worse. Obama was deeply concerned about Russia meddling in the election, but a hard-charging public accusation (which was exactly what the Clinton campaign was clamoring for) would make it seem as if the administration was politicizing intelligence in order to help Clinton—in effect meddling with the election as well. The Trump campaign would have a field day and the American public might rightly question the integrity of the election. It was a lose–lose situation.

Some voices in the administration advocated a robust response. As evidence of Russian activities mounted throughout the summer, a group of White House experts, led by cybersecurity coordinator Michael Daniel and NSC Russia expert Celeste Wallander, generated a long list of counter-attack options: sanctions; releasing the IC's own dirt on Putin's finances, his daughters, lifestyle, and dubious associations; louder public announcements; disruptive cyber operations; and so on. Both believed the Russians would only desist if the United States pushed back, hard. But these options were all shut down in late August by National Security Advisor Susan Rice. According to Daniel, Rice and homeland security chief Lisa Monaco feared that if information about any of the potential plans were to leak, it would force Obama's hand. Daniel and Wallander were obliged to stand down.[46]

Operating under uncertainty and perceiving tight constraints, the administration's main response boiled down to warnings—five in all— to the Russians to cease and desist or bear the consequences. On August 4, CIA Director John Brennan, in a regularly scheduled call with Federal Security Service director General Alexander Bortnikov, told the Russian that the United States was aware that Russia was interfering in the election. Brennan warned his Russian counterpart to stop it and threatened unspecified consequences, emphasizing that continued meddling put any hope for cooperation with the United States on other issues, such as Syria, at risk. Secretary of State John Kerry raised the issue with Russian Foreign Minister Sergei Lavrov. Meeting privately at the G20 summit in Hangzou, China, on September 5, Obama warned Putin to knock it off or risk dire consequences. On October 7, National Security Advisor Susan Rice called Russia's Ambassador to the United States, Sergey Kislyak, for a meeting to convey a written warning from Obama to Putin threatening potent economic sanctions. The response was stone-faced denial coupled with accusations of U.S. subversion of Russia via color revolutions.[47] Eight days before the election, the United States sent a warning to the Russians about further hacking into polling or registration systems, or making any further effort to affect the outcome of the election. In this instance, Washington employed the seldom-used hotline connecting the Nuclear Risk Reduction Centers in both countries that had been designated to deal with major cyber incidents.

The Obama administration believed its warnings had been a successful deterrent measure, but critics, including former officials, pooh-poohed it. "The Russians don't care what we say," NSC Russia expert Wallander noted, "They care what we do."[48] The debate can't be settled because the main claim is that there was more the Russians could have done that they chose not to do, which is difficult to verify. What is clear is that Moscow did not fully cease and desist. Although no further hacked information was released, the social media campaigns and electoral systems probing continued. Indeed, information operations escalated as the troll troops learned how to incite Americans to real action via Facebook events pages. One credible investigation found

**Figure 7.4** President Obama and President Putin during a tense meeting on September 5, 2016. Obama warned Putin to knock off the election meddling or risk dire consequences.
*Source*: Alexei Druzhinin/Sputnik, Kremlin pool photo via AP.

that the group ended up spending approximately $80,000 to support 100 U.S. activists, who organized 40 different protests throughout the United States.[49]

The limitation of a government response to warnings reflected the fear within the administration that cyber retaliation might trigger Putin to escalate, possibly even attacking critical infrastructure. Better to focus on building up defenses at home. In late August, other retaliatory scenarios were scrapped, and all attention turned to the election. Obama and his aides decided to reach out to congressional Republicans for a bipartisan message on the importance of allowing the Department of Homeland Security to work with state voting officials to shore up their systems. They needed local officials to work closely with federal officials to protect the infrastructure. But trust was in short supply. Senate Majority Leader Mitch McConnell and House Speaker Paul Ryan demurred on a robust statement, accusing Obama of politicizing the situation to help Clinton. They finally agreed at the end of September to a general statement—with no mention of Russia—on the need to protect electoral infrastructure.

Finally, on October 7, Secretary of Homeland Security Jeh Johnson and Clapper issued a joint statement accusing Russia of the hack and release and noting (but not formally attributing to Moscow) the cyber meddling in election systems. It received scant attention, drowned out only hours later when the *Access Hollywood* scandal broke, turning media focus once again onto Trump, this time over his crude comments about women. The administration's message was lost in the fray. And almost immediately, emails from John Podesta's account began to appear on WikiLeaks, distracting the press corps even further.

The government response to the subversion was undeniably slow, and the four-month gap between the revelation of the DNC hack and Johnson and Clapper's press conference had created a window of ambiguity that allowed the media to cite the leaked materials without adding details about their provenance.[50] Administration officials had only become cognizant of the full scale of all three vectors of the Russian operation toward the end of the summer. President Obama did not ask the IC for a full analysis of everything it knew about the operation until a month after the election.[51] The IC's analysis was submitted on December 30, and a declassified version was released on January 6.

The president had opted for restraint. Why? Aside from standard challenges of uncertainty about attribution, the desire not to compromise sources and methods, and the difficulty of getting the unwieldy and unprepared U.S. government to generate fully fledged policy options quickly, two major constraints stand out.[52] Given the politicized election setting, further publicity might just "do the Russians' dirty work for them," advancing Moscow's objective of undermining the election. The president and his top advisors, moreover, feared that the Russians might escalate in response to U.S. retaliation by interfering just enough in voting systems to generate damaging controversy about the results. Whether that fear was warranted remains a matter of debate. But in the moment, it was real. "Intentionally or not," historian David Shimer notes, "by showing what he might do next, Putin had established escalation dominance in Obama's house."[53]

### Lingering Impact

After a quarter century during which no major power dared to undertake subversion of the United States, 2016 was a major shock. The initial febrile public reaction did not subside after the polls closed and the votes were counted. Indeed, it fed into a sense of the operation's significance and success. As researcher Aaron Erlich of McGill University put it, "The biggest effect of all is the talk about the effect."[54]

The release of the IC's preliminary findings in early January 2017, which concluded that Putin had ordered a campaign to hurt Clinton and help Trump, raised the heat. Ongoing questions about Russian influence, and a series of Russia-focused missteps among Trump officials, including the resignation of National Security Advisor Michael Flynn for misleading Vice President Mike Pence and other White House officials about conversations with Russian Ambassador Sergey Kislyak, made it worse. As 2017 progressed, public outrage and partisan arguments sparked a breathless frenzy of headlines urging America to wake up to the danger. A new organization, the Committee to Investigate Russia, was quickly formed, boasting a who's who of intelligence and security professionals, among them former Director of National Intelligence Clapper and General Hayden. The Committee commissioned a public service video featuring the actor Morgan Freeman declaring, "We are at war." Meanwhile, the Trump administration took every opportunity to brand investigations into the Russia affair a "witch hunt."[55]

The partisan hangover was a testament to the success of the operation. Americans couldn't seem to agree on what had actually happened or where the truth lay. As the Mueller investigation proceeded over the next two years, the bitter fallout of the Russian meddling continued to poison political discourse. In January 2017, a CBS news poll showed that Republicans viewed Russia more favorably than they had before the election. For Democrats, it was the reverse. In 2018, 75% of Republicans believed the Russian interference had no benefit to either political campaign, whereas 74% of Democrats believed it had helped Trump. By 2020, nearly 70% of Americans believed Russia had tried to influence the election, but the breakdown was starkly partisan, with 90% of Biden supporters convinced, versus 48% of Trump supporters.[56] The ripple effect of subversion continued long after the initial operation had concluded.

## Conclusion

It is easy in hindsight to find fault with what some observers have alleged was a "weak and underwhelming" U.S. response.[57] It took the government a long time to definitively identify the threat, and yet more time to decide to publicize its assessment. It ultimately limited its pre-election response to private warnings to the Russians to cease and desist and, particularly, to lay off election systems. Facing a lose–lose situation in which the Russians had achieved escalation dominance, American officials tried to find solutions without making it worse.

The administration's hesitant response and the febrile public reaction both stemmed from the country's lack of intellectual and organizational preparedness. And that was the predictable result of being taken by surprise. 2016 was an instance of subversion analogous to strategic surprises like Operation Barbarossa, Pearl Harbor, or the terrorist attacks of September 11, 2001 (9/11). In those cases and many others, warnings abounded but went unheeded.[58] As Richard Betts argued in his classic study, "The primary problem in major strategic surprises is not intelligence warning but political disbelief."[59] For sure, the CIA was out of practice tracking subversion of the United States by a hostile major power, and it had been many years since the FBI had needed to counter such activity. And after 9/11, there had been other fish to fry. As counter-terrorism expert Clint Watts testified in early 2017, "Our intelligence community has been overfocused on terrorism and the Islamic State and there [weren't many] resources or bandwidth to focus" on the Russians or potential subversion. Still, many intelligence analysts and nongovernmental Russia experts were well aware that Russian leaders viewed themselves as victims of U.S. subversion and were eager for payback. They tracked the build-up of Russia's cyber capabilities; they saw the operations in Europe; they noted the steady escalation. But all the top policymakers involved had made their careers in the peak unipolar years, preoccupied with the global war on terror and the spread of democracy and the rules-based liberal order. They can be forgiven for not having a set of standard operating procedures readily available for dealing with a major power rival meddling on the home front.

Similarly, intelligence pros can be forgiven for expressing grudging admiration for what Russia managed to do to America in 2016. The operation arguably had that "can't lose" quality covert action plotters love. If it remained covert, it could have the subtle and difficult-to-measure social effects of fomenting division and suppressing voter turnout, or possibly ever so slightly turning some groups to vote for Trump instead of Clinton. If it ended up being implausibly deniable, as was probably the intent and expectation, so much the better for sending a signal of pugnacious pushback to Washington. Once the GRU's cover was utterly blown in exquisite detail—right down to the names of the hackers and their bosses—the operation didn't suffer from its exposure. Indeed, it became more impactful. Paranoia rippled through the corridors of power. The Obama administration was limited in its ability to react, partly due to fear of stoking candidate Trump's narrative that the election was rigged, and partly out of fear of what the Russians might be able to do in the electoral infrastructure. The federal government didn't have the capabilities to secure the electoral infrastructure due to the fragmented nature of state electoral systems and distrust on the part of some state election officials.

In some ways, the Russian operation in 2016 was a success similar to the Line X program in the 1980s. Then, the United States, alerted by the "Farewell" dossier to Soviet efforts to steal American technology, managed to dangle faulty technology in front of acquisitive Soviet agents. The operation benefitted from the fact that it would be successful whether it was discovered or not. If it remained covert, more flawed technology would be fed into Soviet systems, creating economic or industrial disruption. If it were discovered, paranoia about the extent of the U.S. operation would breed distrust in all technology pilfered from American sources. It was win–win. In a similar fashion, Russia's goal of fomenting division and stirring up a political hornet's nest with social media and doxxing worked whether it was plausibly deniable or an open secret. Once the Russians were outed, partisan divides provided new oxygen to the operation's aftereffects.

Defending their performance in 2016, intelligence professionals and policymakers stressed the operation's unprecedented nature. The U.S. intelligence community's initial comprehensive analysis concluded that the "manner and aggressiveness of the Russian interference was historically unprecedented" and that it "was [the] boldest yet in the U.S."[60] The bipartisan report of the Senate Select Committee on Intelligence's investigation stressed "unprecedented scale and sophistication" of the Russian operation; President Obama's FBI Deputy Director Andrew McCabe stated that the weaponization of information occurred "in a way that we've never seen before"; and his deputy Secretary of State Antony Blinken recalled that policymakers believed they were in "a new world where information warfare was really the new front line."[61] No less an authority than Michael Hayden, former CIA and NSA director, called it "the most successful covert influence operation in history."[62]

In one sense, this claim is inarguable. The operation was unprecedented for the United States—in the post–Cold War period. And the standard problem of surprise was turbocharged by apprehensions about technology. The initial euphoria of the internet age, in which the free-flowing information bonanza of the new tech was expected to benefit humanity (and democracy), had become a tech panic. The dangers of the internet, exemplified by the proliferation of online scams, unwanted information sharing, or the fear of social media's impact on children's mental health, seemed to be turning that initial optimism into a raft of dystopian anxiety. These free-floating fears easily morphed into neuralgia about the potential dangers of cyber in the hands of an adversary. As noted in Chapter 6, 2016 occurred just as the "hybrid" war scare was reaching a crescendo. Much of this commentary portrayed Putin as a cyber-enabled, three-dimensional chess master whose intelligence services might have found just the right mixture of technology and narrative to secretly sway or disrupt large swathes of the American public.[63]

The wide-eyed U.S. reaction to Russia's subversion is thus understandable. It was a brazen operation, and the U.S. IC was right that cyber-enabled subversion of the United States was unprecedented. Subversion involves reaching across borders, and the internet enables this rapidly and at scale. "Our traditional methods for detecting and counter-intelligence, things like active measures, are based on HUMINTs," Watts testified, "We run spies versus counter-spies. Most of [2016's] influence came online. They essentially duplicated the old active measures system without setting foot inside the United States."[64]

Granting that, however, is not the same as answering the tough questions about 2016's implications for great power subversion. Was it truly unprecedented? Does the episode suggest that we're in a new age of subversion? We take up these questions in Chapter 8.

# 8

## 2016

### A Perfect Storm

WHEN EXPERIENCED INTELLIGENCE hands called the Russian meddling unprecedented, they knew well that such things had occurred before. Nevertheless, the claim was that something about it warranted a new sense of danger. "I saw a lot of bad things in my 50 years in intelligence," former Director of National Intelligence James Clapper recalled, "but nothing got me so viscerally as what the Russians did to us in 2016."[1] Had Moscow really found the secret sauce that would allow it to pose a serious threat to American democracy? What exactly *was* novel about 2016?

The argument for novelty centers on three claims: that subversion assumed a newly salient role in Russian strategy; that the new information environment radically altered the cost–benefit calculations for hostile great power rivals; and that the United States has recently become an especially vulnerable target, again easing the path for subverters.

We examine each of these claims against the backdrop of the centuries of great power subversion we've covered so far. Clapper's "visceral" reaction was understandable. But if by claiming the 2016 operation was "historically unprecedented" and the "boldest yet in the US," the U.S. intelligence community (IC) meant any history before 1991, its claim falls flat.

### Russia's Strategic Calculus

Why did Vladimir Putin escalate? The U.S. intelligence community assessed "with high confidence" that Putin ordered his subversive campaign to "undermine public faith in the US democratic process, denigrate Secretary Hillary Clinton, and harm her electability and potential presidency" and to boost the chances of Donald Trump, for whom "the Russian Government developed a clear preference."[2] The massive multiyear investigations overseen by Robert Mueller and the Senate Select Committee on Intelligence—based on thousands of classified and public documents and hundreds of interviews—ratified that judgment in painstaking detail, showing how the pattern of subversive activities shifted opportunistically from a general campaign of sowing discord to one directed at specific candidates.[3] Subsequent IC assessments added context:

> Russian officials are probably willing to accept some risk in conducting influence operations targeting the US—including against US elections—because they believe Washington meddles similarly in Russia and other countries and that such efforts are endemic to geostrategic competition.[4]

The experience of the 1990s and the color revolutions had convinced Moscow that subversion was (still) a regular, normal tool of statecraft.

Moreover, "Russian officials probably also assess that continued influence operations against the United States pose a manageable risk to Russia's image in Washington because US–Russia relations are already extremely poor."[5] In other words, Moscow had little to lose. The constraint on subversion posed by one state's need for cooperation with its rival was duly weakened because cooperation seemed increasingly fraught, or even out of the question.

These assessments nicely fit our framework, which treats subversion as a cheap and potentially useful adjunct to traditional statecraft and expects that it is most likely to assume bold proportions when levels of hostility between subverter and target are high and thus the downside cost of loss of trust is low. They are also consistent with Chapter 6's portrayal of how Russian officials viewed U.S. policies in the 1990s and early 2000s as threateningly subversive and thus likely framed their own skulduggery as payback: "subverting the subverter" with the kind of realpolitik hardball to be expected in view of the hostile state of the rivalry. What these assessments lack is a larger context of how subversion interacts with other elements of Russian policy and how that role compares with historical precedents.

The strategic setting in which the intrigues of 2016 unfolded was the opposite of that in sixteenth- to nineteenth-century Europe: Rather than preventing the emergence of hegemony by sustaining a balance of power, the lodestar for Russia was to restore balance by cutting an existing hegemonic state, the unipolar United States, down to size. By the 2008 financial crisis, Moscow seemed convinced that the decline of U.S. power was accelerating—but that Washington and its allies were stubbornly continuing to do foreign policy like it was 1996. Not only was the United States not downsizing its global role, but it was also continuing to advance—right into Russia's backyard. The problem was that unlike in previous centuries, the status quo was unipolarity, not balance. The power of inertia and legitimacy lay with the United States and its allies. Restoring balance was a revisionist project.

Scholars who devote their professional lives to the study of Russian foreign policy view 2016 as an extension of the broad strategy the country had been applying to Europe since 2008: "weakening the European Union and NATO, distancing Europe and the United States from each other, and generally creating a political and cultural environment more conducive for Moscow and its interests."[6] The key takeaway from scholars' analyses is that subversion was a handmaiden of Moscow realpolitik, never in the driver's seat. The leitmotif is opportunism. Napoleon's famous adage—*On s'engage partout, et puis l'on voit* ("jump into the fray and then figure out what comes next")—best captures it. Loosely coordinated by Putin's powerful but secretive Presidential Administration, and featuring many disparate Russian bureaucracies and operatives opportunistically responding to regime cues, these operations nonetheless served a strategic purpose.

For starters, meddling in U.S. domestic politics arguably helped advance Russia's overall objective of securing its great power status and ushering in multipolarity. It worked in diffuse and indirect ways to shape the global political environment in a manner that Moscow favored, but it could also be targeted much more directly to seek specific policy changes.

Subversion was part of a larger strategy of imposing costs in combination with other moves to harass and distract Washington. Russia analyst Michael Kofman likened the strategy to the "raiding" and "brigandage" of the late Middle Ages, with Moscow acting not as a mindless "spoiler" but with a defined objective in view:

> The Russian long game is to raid and impose painful costs on the United States, and its allies, until such time as China becomes a stronger and more active contender in the international system. This theory of victory stems from the Russian assumption that the structural balance of power will eventually shift away from the United States towards China and other powers in the international system, resulting in a steady transition to multipolarity. . . . The hope is that a successful campaign of raiding, together with the greater threat from China, will force Washington to compromise and renegotiate the post–Cold War settlement.[7]

Along with policies supporting U.S. adversaries in the Middle East, Africa, and Latin America, subversion helped force Russia onto the U.S. policy agenda and could be dialed down as part of a new deal in which Moscow's great power prerogatives would be accorded greater respect. None of these policies—and certainly not the subversive parts—promised to materially weaken the United States. But they might weaken its political resolve to sustain the post-1991 security order in Europe and Russia's exclusion from it. In official Russia's view, the shift in power away from the United States was a potent underlying trend, headlined by China's meteoric rise and the pressure this would put on U.S. resources. But events since the 2008 financial crisis—when elites in Moscow and Beijing seemed to think unipolarity's days were numbered—showed that Washington and its allies in the collective West had yet to get the memo. From Putin's notorious 2007 speech at the Munich Security Conference, it became clear that he thought the move to multipolarity needed a push. Subverting U.S. allies and then the United States itself might help Washington wake up and smell the multipolar coffee. As Kofman stated, "Throughout history, leading

empires, the superpowers of their time, have had to deal and negotiate settlements with raiders." One had to just keep adding pressure
against the stronger adversary until it realized that the game of standing
athwart Russia's sense of itself as a great power wasn't worth the candle.
In this light, 2016 was a measured horizontal escalation, moving the
subversive activity to the United States in a long-standing campaign of
cost imposition.

The same logic applied to much more targeted aims. Harassing the
United States via subversion might also help strengthen Moscow's hand
in negotiations on governing cyberspace—what Russia calls "information security." Moscow's officialdom thought it was replying to a massively effective U.S. information war aided and abetted by the U.S.-led
liberal information order. It sought to get the Americans to agree to
tacit and explicit rules of the road that would make the world safer
for their undemocratic regime, one based on the principle of internet
sovereignty.[8] As we observed in Chapter 7, the operation against the
United States occurred as Russia's community of information warriors
was feeling its oats. When the Kremlin's top cyber diplomat Andrey
Krutskikh warned that "we are at the verge of having 'something' in
the information arena, which will allow us to talk to the Americans as
equals," the implication was that hitting Washington on the head with
Russia's new capabilities would allow Moscow to come to terms with
the United States on formal and informal rules for information operations that would leave the regime more secure. A baby step toward
multipolarity, perhaps, but one we know Moscow cared a lot about.[9]

Subversion was also part of a more intense, forward-leaning effort
to undermine the legitimacy of Western-style democracy, especially the
presumption baked into the liberal international order that countries
not governed by liberal principles were second-class global citizens, no
matter how great their material power. The enemy here was any idea
supporting the claim that the principle of state sovereignty did not
apply fully to nondemocratic states that, in Western eyes, trampled on
human rights. The more discredited those ideas were, the more secure
Russia's autocratic rulers would feel. The aim was to do in a generalized
way what Russians thought the United States had been doing since
the end of the Cold War, namely establishing an overall narrative that
undercut rivals and forwarded one's own policy. If Russia lacked a

compelling narrative of its own, at least it could undermine the hated liberal one through an all-azimuth campaign of disruption. The main tool was Russia's state media, especially RT, in which Putin invested significant sums and talent. Its content could easily be dialed up or down depending on Moscow's estimate of the probability of the United States coming to the table, with a decided shift toward more edgily subversive content after the first invasion of Ukraine in 2014.[10] The development of deniable online influence campaigns via the Internet Research Agency (IRA)/Project Lakhta, and their eventual deployment in the United States, was a logical infusion of ammunition to this information war.

At the margins, Russia's subversive campaign promised to go beyond the informational realm to help weaken the adversary politically by aiding divisive forces within it. The louder the voices and bolder the actions of anti-liberal political forces within democracies, the weaker the appeal and power of the liberal narrative that so irked Russian officialdom. Hence the suite of policies seeking to boost far right nationalist movements in Europe and the United States.[11] Much of the action here was overt, as in Putin's investments of time and funds in, for example, France's Marine Le Pen, but covert subversion was sometimes a useful complement. It is easy to see how Russian intelligence services, long engaged in this task, sensed opportunity in the unexpected political rise of Donald Trump.

The general all-azimuth strategy of putting the adversary on its back foot and undermining its "soft power" could easily shift to a more directed effort targeted at specific U.S. policies, such as sanctions, democracy promotion, NATO expansion, or, especially, Ukraine. Although it may be only in hindsight that analysts are tempted to view Ukraine as the driving motive behind 2016, there's no doubt that the bargain Moscow wanted to pummel and harass the United States into accepting featured Russia's putative sphere of influence over Kyiv; at the center of the information war and the delegitimization strategy was the aim of undercutting the narrative that Ukraine was a democracy that was freely and properly choosing its geopolitical path; and of all the policies Moscow wanted to change, those that supported Ukraine's westward choice were the main target. Hence, when U.S. politics served up influential figures with seemingly amenable views on Ukraine, Moscow's intelligence services and operatives on the ground in Washington and New York knew what to do.

By the same logic, if presidential candidates or their political parties seemed more or less supportive of policies Moscow loathed, and if opportunities arose to affect their prospects, then the game might be worth the candle. Hence the shift of Russia's effort toward Trump after it became apparent that he would be the candidate. To be fair, Moscow would have probably supported any candidate who opposed Hillary Clinton because she represented everything Moscow was trying to push back against. Intelligence analysts stressed the importance of her stance back in the 2011 and 2012 Russian elections, but that was but an indicator of a deeper and more profound political commitment to the rules-based order and America's leading role in upholding it.

## The Strategy in Perspective

Russian shenanigans up to and including 2016 headlined a lot of rhetoric about the advent of a new world of great power subversion. Ever since the "Gerasimov doctrine" or "hybrid war" bubble took off in 2013, a growing chorus of analysts claimed that subversion promised to do more to advance Russia's strategic goals than it had done for subverting powers of the past. The Russians, in this view, had seized upon new features of the strategic environment that enabled them to escape some of the constraints that had hamstrung their predecessors. Before we unpack those new features, it pays to compare the strategy itself to historical analogs. If the "new world of subversion" claim is right, we should find that subversive tools assume greater importance in Russian strategy than in the strategies of typical subverters in the past. Note that the question isn't about success; it's about subversion's importance relative to other means. Any tool of statecraft can be important even if it is not successful. Success requires a one-sided advantage, offense dominance if you will. If one state makes subversion the very essence of its strategy but the target defends itself adroitly, subversion will have been important to the story even if it did not "succeed" in the sense of substantially advancing one side's interests.

Does the Russian strategy just described suggest a newly important role, a breakout from time-honored constraints? The short answer is no.

What strikes the observer is how familiar, how typical, subversion's role in Russia's strategy for pushing the trend to multipolarity looks, even when we account for the radically different settings of our historical comparisons.

This is most obvious and least surprising when recent events are compared to the ancient and early modern worlds. Little wonder that bribery, propaganda, and manipulation of insiders played a larger role among the ancient world's often much more subvertible polities than anything in recent times. In Thucydides' account, subversion was front and center in Athenian and Spartan strategy, salient enough that the Spartans always had to be vigilant lest their Achilles' heel, the subject Helot population, be transformed into a lethal fifth column. In that multipolar setting, allies were the name of the game, and Thucydides is clear that competitive subversion of the rival's major allies through measures short of war was fundamental to both sides' strategies and was an important cause of the threat perceptions that helped bring about war. That is, it was not just "the rise of Athens" that caused the fear in Sparta that Thucydides mentioned as a prime cause of the great Peloponnesian War. It was what the Athenians were doing with that power: undercutting Sparta's position by meddling in its allies.[12] If this has a familiar ring, it should, for it is the theme of the narrative in Chapters 6 and 7 of the role of subversion in the threat perceptions that drove the rise of the twenty-first-century Russian–U.S. antagonism.

We know what Philip of Macedon wanted to achieve: the conquest of Persia, which required first the subjugation of Greece and ultimately access to Athens' powerful navy. Demosthenes tells us that subversion was a major part of Philip's strategy, playing the lead role in turning many key Greek cities to his cause. Philip then brought the same strategy to Athens, meeting with some success in tweaking the Athenians' policy by persuasive propaganda disseminated by highly credible insiders. But ultimately that democratic polis proved a tough nut to crack because its competitive political institutions proved more difficult to manipulate than those of oligarchic city-states. Although it ended up as an adjunct to rather than a substitute for war, subversion features as a central theme in historians' accounts of Philip's strategy.

The strategic object of Elizabeth's rivals was ultimately nothing short of regime change and the ideological and geopolitical rewards that would follow. When diplomacy failed, they turned to a no-holds-barred subversive campaign that was, for a time, the strategy's main element. Open calls for regime change abetted by subversive agents spreading the word, support for plots of regicide, and empowering armed insurgencies were front and center. Elizabeth's ruthless domestic repressions gave her the security to move to bold support for an insurgency against Philip's empire with the aim of materially sapping his financial and military capabilities. To be sure, in that cutthroat setting, war ultimately supplanted subversion as the chief tool in the protagonists' strategies. But if one were to replay in more modern times the subversive action–reaction spiral narrated in Chapter 3, every case in the nineteenth through twenty-first centuries that we discussed would pale in comparison. To say that Elizabeth's and Philip's strategic use of subversion was bold is, literally, the understatement of the centuries. Subversion's salience in that world dwarfs anything Putin's henchmen were up to in recent times.

Russia's 2016 operation looks more typical when set against nineteenth-century precedents. We detailed episodes in which one of the century's most celebrated statesmen, Otto von Bismarck, placed big bets on subversion: a sustained and intense effort at election interference in France and a campaign designed to undermine and unseat the leader of Great Britain. In both cases, Bismarck faced formidable constraints and yet he persisted, suggesting the strategic importance he placed on subversive statecraft. He sought to weaken France and constrain its options by preventing the restoration of a monarchical government. It's difficult to say for whom the stakes were greater. If for Putin a Clinton presidency promised more of the policies he found irksome if not threatening to his rule, for Bismarck a monarchist victory at the polls threatened his newly won and highly desirable position for Germany as the dominant power in Europe. In keeping with its mastermind's reputation, Bismarck's operation was altogether subtler, more deft, than what Putin, the GRU, and Yevgeny Prigozhin's troll factory got up to in 2016. But it had to be: Bismarck's challenge was that weakening France too much risked drawing other great powers, which needed a capable France for their cherished European equilibrium, to intervene on Paris' behalf. Bearing those constraints in mind, the operation's subtlety can't mask its boldness: Bismarck intrigued to threaten war (in a plausibly deniable way) if French voters elected a government he opposed. Although Putin's operation violated more norms of sovereignty than Bismarck's, the latter was arguably far more extreme.

The tussle between Bismarck and Gladstone is a good reference for the rivalry between Putin and Hillary Clinton. In both cases, the main constraint was alienating the world's greatest power, and in both the subverter was willing to run that risk. In Bismarck's case, the starting point was amicable relations between London and Berlin; in Putin's case, relations had already soured badly before he opted for direct subversion of the unipole. Our framework would thus expect Putin to be willing to lean more heavily on subversion in his overall strategy. Like Bismarck, Putin was pushing back on a rival's liberal policy that he considered misguided and dangerous. Bismarck's goal was to force a foreign policy shift by getting his rival out of elected office; Putin's goal was likely to send a warning shot across his rival's bow, or even to prevent his rival from getting elected in the first place. Bismarck employed a strategy of propaganda through a cunning media campaign; Putin employed a new technology to do the same. Even Randolph Churchill and the Tories celebrated and admired Bismarck in much the same way Donald Trump celebrated and admired Putin. Russia's hack-and-release seems cheekier than Bismarck's efforts to embarrass Gladstone through pushing news stories about setbacks and scandals. The regime security aspect that analysts take seriously in the Putin episode—Moscow's phobia about a "color revolution" in Russia itself—is absent in the nineteenth-century case. Still, placing the two episodes side by side, the comparative importance of subversion hardly supports the claim that the twenty-first century is a dramatically new era.

KGB active measures in the 1960s–1980s are the most frequently invoked precedent for 2016. And that alone is telling us something: As we discussed in Chapter 5, the salience of subversion in the superpowers' overall strategies declined dramatically after the early Cold War years. And even in the dire straits of the late 1940s, the story showed each side ultimately recognizing that the horrendously costly task of building up its own sphere took precedence over subverting the rival's.

If our rendering of Russia's strategy is right, then its emphasis on subversion in the lead-up to 2016 bears no resemblance to the role subversion played in the strategic visions of many top U.S. officials at the Cold War's dawn. Recall that as the Cold War loomed, George Kennan and his fellow political warriors argued that measures short of war might so materially weaken the USSR as to help avoid the need for a standing alliance commitment like NATO. In serious Russian analyses, by contrast, the chief force driving the weakening of the United States and the Western liberal order is actually external to Russia: the rise of China, against the backdrop of the diffusion of power to many other states.[13] Part of that shift is said to be the strengthening of the Russian state. After that comes a raft of non-subversive Russian policies, such as restoring and rebuilding the nuclear shield, reforming and upgrading the military forces, and so on. Then comes a huge range of diplomatic and cost imposition strategies meant to push back against U.S. domination, from supporting thorns in America's side (think Iran, Venezuela, or Cuba) to nurturing new international institutions (e.g., the Eurasian Union and the Shanghai Cooperation Organization) and groups (e.g., BRICS), to efforts to undermine the U.S. dollar's central role. As a factor in achieving the strategic goal, subversion looks like a cheap gamble that might pay off big or might come to nothing. This is an entirely different animal from the deadly serious gambits of the early Cold War.

So, the proper comparison is indeed to subversion in the middle and late Cold War. The Soviet leadership in this era wanted to achieve détente with the United States based on its cherished principle of superpower parity and then, having attained that goal by the early 1970s, to sustain it while continuing to compete for geopolitical gains. Soviet subversion was unquestionably a big deal, entailing large bureaucracies pouring forth propaganda and disinformation, managing front organizations with hundreds of thousands of members, and running elaborately planned active measures that unfolded over years. Scholars lack granular evidence on the relative importance top Soviet leaders placed on these operations. The testimony of former intelligence officials on this matter needs to be taken with a hefty grain of salt. They wouldn't necessarily be privy to that information, and their professional biases would lean toward exaggeration of subversion's importance. The reliable concrete evidence on what these operations sought to achieve indicates a very familiar role: to pressure policy change in target states, to try to make the United States look bad and thus blunt Washington's annoying holier-than-thou human rights rhetoric, to help win friends and influence people in the Third World, and to nudge the United States away from policies it didn't like (e.g., human rights promotion) and toward those it did (e.g., arms control and trade deals on terms as close to Moscow's preferences as possible).

With due regard to the different settings and aims, the similarities are striking, with subversion as a handy, deniable nudge to forces largely driven by conventional policy and power. In both cases, we see circumstantial evidence for "optimism bubbles" during which some officials appear to have been entranced with subversion's potential. But overall the strategy behind Putin's 2016 operation was roughly in the spirit of the skulduggery of Yuri Andropov's KGB.

## Cyber as the Subverter's Force Multiplier

The story so far can be summed up as "meet the new era of subversion, same as the old era." But the comparison to KGB active measures raises a major caveat: The USSR was a peer superpower, and it devoted substantial resources to subversion. CIA estimates place Soviet expenditures on active measures at $3 billion annually in the 1980s, with more than 15,000 KGB officials working on disinformation.[14] It's not clear how the agency came up with those figures, but no one disputes that the Soviet subversive–intelligence complex was a massive, disciplined, hierarchical affair. Russia, as President Obama was wont to stress, was not a peer of the United States. And although estimates of the size of Putin's subversive–intelligence complex are murky, no one thinks its scale resembles that of its Soviet predecessor.

Putin, in short, seems to have gotten a lot more subversive ruckus for his ruble than Brezhnev did. And for many observers, the reason that stands out is the internet: Much that matters politically now happens in local networks of computers linked to a global network that spans national boundaries. Much of the "unprecedented" talk hinges on the internet effect. The technology that allowed the adversary inside the tent without having to set foot on the ground had been in place since the mid-1990s. But Putin's decision to move that capability from espionage to subversion of the world's sole superpower revealed that the subverter's cost–benefit calculation had been transformed.

The problem with this claim is that it's difficult to disentangle the internet effect from other aspects of the case: Much of the ruckus generated in the United States resulted from shock after subversion's long absence from the U.S. scene. It is inarguable that Russia's subversion was a surprise. With a hindsight that is unfair to those in office at the time, it's clear that intellectual and cultural complacency had a role to play in America's lack of preparedness. Attitudes toward Russia as a regional power—the very thing Moscow was pushing back against—meant that something as cheeky as election meddling and disinformation on U.S. soil was not at all expected. Because the democracy promotion of the previous two decades was not perceived by Americans as subversive, it followed that no retaliation was expected. Subversive operations against U.S. allies abroad remained "over there" in the American consciousness. The North Korean hack of Sony Pictures in November 2014 garnered attention, in part because it also involved the leak of embarrassing information via WikiLeaks along with veiled terrorist threats, but the government focus tended to stay on government and military security, not private industry. Knowledge of what the Russians were up to in Ukraine, the Baltic states, and U.S. allies like the United Kingdom and France did not translate into actionable concern about similar attacks on U.S. soil.

And one needs to separate the internet's lasting effects on subversion from the febrile, but arguably short-term, reaction to exposure to the technology's dark side. Fortunately, we are in a position to deal with this complexity, for we can consider the 2016 operation's three key vectors— the social media disinformation campaign, the probing of election systems, and the hack-and-release—against historical precedents.

The best case for an internet-altered ruckus–ruble ratio is Operation Lakhta, the social media campaign. That's not because Yevgeny Prigozhin's troll troops actually affected discourse in a meaningful way; most expert analysis views it as evanescent foam on a giant wave of divisive posts that was overwhelmingly made in the United States.[15] And the themes the IRA's trolls used to stoke discord in the United States were familiar, mirroring KGB Cold War efforts, particularly on the issue of race. This had been a lever to exploit fissures in the

United States since the early days of the Soviet Union. In 1928, for example, the Comintern hatched a plan to recruit Southern Blacks to push for a separate Black state in the South, which the Soviet Union would use as a beachhead for spreading the revolution in America. When the infamous Scottsboro trials began in 1932, the Communist Party of the United States of America (CPUSA) joined the National Association for the Advancement of Colored People in campaigning for an appeal, which the Soviet state amplified at every opportunity.[16] To its everlasting credit, CPUSA stood on the right side of the civil rights struggle throughout the Cold War, but Service A's machinations often took a nasty turn, as in its efforts to stir up racial tensions via disinformation.

The social media vector is nevertheless exhibit A for the internet effect because most intelligence analysis warrants that perceptions do matter in subversion, and Project Lakhta generated by far the most attention. The cost, meanwhile, appears to have been minimal, measured in low single-digit millions to rent offices in St. Petersburg, purchase gear, and pay Clever Young Things to run amok across U.S. social media platforms. Given the overheated U.S. response, it's difficult to find examples of better return on investment. Still, Lakhta's punch benefited from a first-mover advantage. Now that the U.S. body politic has absorbed the blow and normalized the fact that the internet comes with the downside of malicious subversion, the effect will be hard to replicate.

And the Cold War analogy brings up another rarely noted calculation: the costs to each side of defense from what it thinks is subversion. In Chapter 5, we reported U.S. intelligence community estimates of the large sums the Kremlin spent to jam Western radio broadcasts—costs that far outweighed what Washington paid to produce them in the first place. The United States clearly pays a price to defend itself against subversion via social media platforms. But the Russian state's efforts to wall its people off from the free internet are almost certainly relatively far greater. And the same goes for China. These defensive programs may largely succeed, but they impose significant material, political, and opportunity costs. The internet clearly lowered the costs of subversion for Russia in 2016, but overall it remains far more subversive to autocratic rivals than to the United States.

The GRU's probing of electoral machinery follows the same pattern: old tactic, new medium, lower costs. Fiddling with the actual vote tally through ballot box stuffing or ballot destruction was part and parcel of earlier meddling efforts of great powers on smaller ones, but the obstacles to such activity in the United States were too high to contemplate—until cyber opened up a new vulnerability. With poor cybersecurity a chronic feature of states' electoral infrastructure, it seemed there might be the possibility that malign actors could alter voting rolls, which would mean voters might be turned away, or potentially alter votes themselves. Either would affect both the vote and faith in the integrity of the election. Two years previously in Ukraine, the Russians had managed to broadcast fake results, but the effort was quickly taken down, and no change to the real vote tallies took place. But having the subversive actor inside the tent, poised to strike and using that to psychological effect on the target, is not really something America had dealt with before. For a brief moment, cyber offered a subversive power boost to Russia. There is no question that for those months in the fall of 2016, the internet leveled the playing field between Moscow and Washington in a new way. It was a temporary effect—government institutions and private enterprise would move to close the vulnerability gaps—but a powerful one.

If—and it's a big if—Russian meddling affected the 2016 election, the vector most responsible was the hack-and-release.[17] It's impossible to deny the Senate Committee's claim that "there is no historical precedent for the use of cyber intrusions followed by release of stolen information (i.e. hacks and leaks)."[18] That is, as long as the claim encompasses the years leading up to 2016, which included warning signs such as the broadcasting of Victoria Nuland's awkward telephone comment about the European Union on YouTube. Needless to say, there was historical precedent aplenty for theft and leaks *without* cyber. In 1967, for instance, a dated but top-secret American war plan, called Operations Plan 10-1, surfaced in a Norwegian newspaper. The plan detailed, among other things, American use of tactical nuclear weapons on European soil in the event of a hot war with the Soviet Union. The U.S. Department of Defense responded by stonewalling, "neither confirm nor deny." Two years later, the same document was recirculated with a little creative editing from the KGB's Service A in an attempt to embarrass the United States further.[19]

The technology that allowed the adversary inside the tent without having to set foot on the ground had been in place since the mid-1990s. Using it to steal and leak emails and documents from the Democratic National Committee and the Clinton campaign, complete with a few forgeries thrown in, was an old trick enhanced by new technology. Did the new tech transform the subverter's cost–benefit calculation? Stealing secrets had traditionally been a human intelligence realm, populated by spy operations that were difficult to run and expensive to maintain. The internet slashed the costs of such activity, obviating the need for human spies and all the things they require: money, housing, cover documents, travel, and time—lots of time. The somewhat mind-boggling capabilities—copying keystrokes, monitoring online activity in real time, clandestinely recording, and exfiltrating enormous amounts of data—pierced the delusion of privacy for those who assumed their emails and passwords were reasonably safe. One does not need detailed inside information about the 2016 operation to surmise that the GRU's young hackers who spear phished John Podesta were easier and cheaper to manage than a web of human spies.

But the theft of information is the espionage side of the equation. It raised eyebrows in Washington but did not set alarm bells ringing. The decision to release the information to influence is the subversive part. The internet changes the game for stealing information. It's less trans-formational on the subversion side. The idea of using embarrassing in-formation to discredit a candidate was old hat. The KGB's campaign against Ronald Reagan's re-election in 1984 bears striking resemblance to 2016. Classified CIA reports at the time

> definitively concluded that KGB leaders were intervening in the 1984 election with the goal of preventing Reagan's re-election. KGB agents actively sought contacts on the campaign, coordinated with front groups and sympathetic journalists, and searched for compromising material on the incumbent president.[20]

The details of the operation from Chapter 7 make the case: The key challenge for the GRU was disseminating its ill-gotten information in a way that would enter the political sphere with maximum effect. The role WikiLeaks played in overcoming that challenge is one played by hundreds of news and media outlets throughout the years that have uncritically reported material emanating from hostile subverters. Political factions that benefit from foreign interference are a feature of any such operation.

In other words, the success of the most successful vector of the 2016 operation had little to do with the internet and much more to do with the U.S. political setting. Michael Hayden's claim that 2016 was history's most successful influence operation was not about the internet. America didn't have a cyber problem, he insisted, it had a Russia problem. It also had a domestic political problem.[21]

## Domestic Vulnerabilities

Working with allies on the territory of the target has been a hallmark of subversion in all of our examples. Alcibiades and the oligarchs in ancient Athens relied on co-conspirators on the inside to effect their coup in 411. The same held for Philip of Macedon, who had a reputation for overthrowing states by cultivating collaborators within and often winning without a fight. Elizabeth of England supported Protestant rebels on Philip II's territory, and he placed his bets on English Catholics rising up against her. Even the Tories in Gladstone's England welcomed Bismarck's intervention and made their support of him well known, cultivating contacts with Bismarck's son Herbert, the German ambassador to London. Opposition figures in the target state usually have their own agenda for collaborating with a subverting foreign government, and the Trump campaign in 2016 was no different.

2016 was hardly the first time the Kremlin tried to influence elections in the United States. As Chapter 5 recounted, Moscow sought to boost Henry Wallace in 1948. It also reached out to Adlai Stevenson and Hubert Humphrey to aid their presidential campaigns, but it was rebuffed. In 1992, top Republican operatives reportedly advised George H. W. Bush's campaign to ask the Russians to dig up dirt on candidate Bill Clinton, but White House Chief of Staff James Baker indignantly rebuffed the proposal.[22] Those episodes are often featured in essays comparing the good old days with 2016's tawdry spectacle of Donald Trump publicly asking Russia to hack Clinton's server and his son's eagerness to meet a Russian operative promising dirt on her. And widening the insiders' circle a bit gets us to Trump advisors Paul Manafort and Roger Stone, as well as other figures of less importance. This apparent collaboration between a presidential candidate and a foreign government raised hackles and prompted the FBI's Crossfire Hurricane counter-intelligence probe and the Mueller investigation.

The comparison to the principled politicians of the Stevenson, Humphrey, or Baker cast may well be depressingly valid. And lots of political science and historical analysis confirms the claim that the United States is more polarized today than it was in the middle of the twentieth century, which offered Russia openings it would not have been able to exploit in an earlier time.[23] All of this may be so, and yet it doesn't truly put the level of U.S. domestic vulnerability in historical perspective. If we widen the lens from targeted electoral intervention to more general domestic vulnerability to subversion, America's travails in 2016 seem relatively minor. For what was missing in 2016 was something many of the subverters from our other great power examples—Athens, Macedon, Queen Elizabeth's England, the Spanish Hapsburgs, the nineteenth-century great powers, the fascist and Nazi powers of the interwar period, and the Soviet Union—employed as potential or actual levers: fifth columns, those powerful organized political movements in the target. No Helots, no oppressed Catholics or Protestants, no nations like Poland or Ireland wanting desperately to break free and on the prowl for a great power sponsor, no fascists or Nazis or communists ready to respond to the call from a foreign dictator.

That missing element made all the difference. Americans were largely unwitting accomplices to Russia's social media and doxxing shenanigans. This had an impact on the response as well. Fortunately, there was no suspect U.S. population or political movement whose rights as citizens were put at risk, as had so often happened in the past. Although the response from the public and commentariat was frenzied for a time, the government itself was measured—nothing like the ruthless repressions to which prior targets had resorted. No internment camps, no violence, no scapegoating, no equivalent of the McCarthy witchhunt, despite protestations to the contrary from President Trump and some of his supporters.

One of the constraints of subversion, a cost measured in lost trust or heightened antipathy, became abundantly clear once Russia was identified as the culprit and Putin was identified as being personally involved. The U.S.–Russian relationship had already been on the rocks, else the subversion wouldn't have happened in the first place. But the clear attribution to Putin and his intelligence services put pressure on the Obama administration to take retaliatory measures. Sanctions, expulsions, and a deterioration in diplomacy were the result. Yet the need and desire for some modicum of trust was still palpable. In its first year, before Russia's full-scale invasion of Ukraine, the Biden administration, staffed by many of the very officials who still felt the sting of Putin's 2016 slap, nonetheless sought stable and normal relations with Russia.

## The Febrile Response in Perspective

As we've noted, real worry on the part of administration officials and intelligence practitioners was matched by a less-informed but highly agitated public response. Part of this was due to the not uncommon but often ungrounded human fear that the enemy is somehow smarter and more organized. This apprehension that the adversary is an evil genius is understandable. It reflects the human brain's predilection for catastrophizing as a survival technique. It may have been exacerbated in this case by the element of surprise, when the threat suddenly came from a formerly underestimated adversary.

There's plenty of historical precedent for this kind of reaction. Spartan fear of potential Athenian subversion and Athenian fear of Philip of Macedon's diplomatic and military successes created similar neuralgia in ancient Greece. The Red Scare of the 1950s evoked the fear of a communist under every bed. Clearly, there are cases in which the adversary was arguably a much greater threat than Russia was in 2016. After all, those earlier subverters were advocating invasion, overthrow, or the triumph of communism. Even Bismarck during the War in Sight crisis threatened actual war. Russia in this instance made no overt threats at all, saucily sticking to its implausibly deniable line that it had nothing to do with the election meddling. Its presence in the electoral infrastructure was a gun to democracy's head, but no one knew how big the gun was or whether it was loaded. And the reality of the fragmented state-run electoral system in the United States meant that it would have been very difficult to make a significant impact on the actual vote tallies.

This fear of the worst-case-scenario possibilities sparked by the appearance of a startling new technology is also nothing new. Twenty-four hundred years ago, the Greek philosopher Socrates warned against writing instead of memorization and oratory because it would "create forgetfulness in the learners' souls." The influential Swiss scientist Conrad Gessner, who died in 1565, warned of the dangers of information overload after the invention of the printing press led to an explosion of printed material. The Catholic Church took it a step further, writing up an index of prohibited books in 1560 to protect the minds of the faithful and the authority of the Church. In the 1930s, radio programs were thought to be disturbing the balance of young children's minds. A similar backlash occurred against the television, whose opponents "voiced concerns about how television might hurt radio, conversation, reading, and the patterns of family living."[24] Perhaps paranoia about technology is baked into technological progress itself. In this sense, the tech panic surrounding the perceived Russian threat to America had a clear pattern stretching back millennia: The tech was new, the panic was not.

## Conclusion

In many ways, 2016 was a perfect storm. A new technology, boasting unprecedented speed and reach, enabled an increasingly hostile rival to take a stab at propaganda, disinformation, and election meddling in a bid to further a long-standing and stalemated foreign policy agenda. The target state, unaccustomed to great power rivalry or subversion after a quarter century of being top dog, was caught off guard.

These events were historic, but they were not transformative. The United States, although slow to respond, did eventually grasp what was happening and begin to push back. One wonders what the outcome might have been had the Active Measures Working Group still been in play. The crippling partisan divide that got in the way of America perceiving and coping with the Russian operation might have been avoided if it had been flagged and publicized much earlier in the game.

In any event, the criteria by which we seek to judge whether or not 2016 was truly unprecedented show that it wasn't. Subversion did not take on a new leading role in Russian strategy. It was just as opportunistic and utilitarian as subversion in previous eras, and it played the same role of seeking a gain short of war when traditional diplomacy and blandishments weren't delivering. The new information environment did indeed radically alter the cost–benefit calculation, but only for a fleeting moment (hence the perfect storm analogy), and not nearly to the extent and effect that was feared. And as with other technological shocks in the past, the target has moved quickly to harden against them, encouraging an explosion of private enterprise in cybersecurity and creating new organizations to tackle the problem. Finally, America's vulnerability, while aggravating, was not as profound as that which other polities have experienced. The biggest danger facing the U.S. body politic was apathy and ignorance, not a homegrown movement eager to collaborate with Russia. In terms of our long-arc, great-power–centered approach to subversion, 2016 was just the latest episode in a familiar and eternal story.

# 9

## Looking Back

### Reflections on Subversion

THIS BOOK IS based on a novel way of thinking about its subject. First, we distinguished subversion from both espionage and traditional state-craft like diplomacy, balancing, coercion, and war. We defined it as hostile, unwanted activity on the territory of a rival with the intent of seeking effects, specifically to weaken the target or change its foreign policy in some way. We imagined subversion as encompassing every-thing beyond diplomacy but short of war, including overt and covert propaganda, disinformation, bribery, funding opposition on the inside, election meddling, sabotage, regime change, and covert military ac-tion designed to undermine (rather than prop up) a regime. Subversion can be political or physical, words or deeds, or some amalgamation of all of them. The goals are consistent, and the tactics listed above have changed little over the centuries, shaped only by new technologies that expand their reach or speed up their execution.

Second, we narrowed our focus to the dynamics of great power sub-version. What can we learn from observing the greater power of great powers? The symmetry of great powers' enormous resources keeps sig-nificant meddling to a simmer in peacetime. The flip side of this—a power asymmetry with a great power using all kinds of subversion against a weaker rival—serves to reinforce this message. As one moves from power symmetry to power asymmetry, one would expect to see more (and more aggressive) subversion. And this proves to be the case. History is littered with so many instances of great powers having their way with smaller ones that it almost becomes axiomatic that this is the way of the world. The greatest hits of the twentieth century are a case in point: Czechoslovakia in the late 1930s, Italy in 1948, the states of Central Europe from 1945 to 1950, Iran in 1953, Guatemala in 1954, Chile in 1973 and the list goes on. We therefore decided to distinguish subversion among great power peers from the more picayune meddling by the powerful in the domestic affairs of the weak. What we discovered was a story of endless probing and experimentation, a search for the silver bullet that might deliver big results at low cost. But because great power targets have so many resources to dodge, deflect, deter, and defend, we found that constraints usually have had the upper hand over inducements to a greater degree among great powers than between the powerful and the weak. Subversion is always difficult, but it's especially difficult against great powers.

## Constraints Rule

The cases show how the greater power of great powers creates a variety of constraints. Strategically, fear of retaliation and escalation limits great power subversion. If it happens at all, it tends to manifest as overt or covert propaganda and meddling, but rarely violence. This fits with the framework laid out in Chapter 1. We saw England's restraint toward meddling in the Spanish Netherlands in the mid-sixteenth century guided in part by fear of retaliation or worse. Our examples from the nineteenth century feature great powers holding back on subverting one another over the issue of Poland, despite the tempting subversive potential of nascent nations wanting to break free of empires. The daggers of this kind of subversion were kept sheathed out of fear of escalatory consequences—the key exception was the Eastern Question at whose epicenter was an Ottoman Empire sufficiently weak vis-à-vis powerful subverters such as Russia to dampen escalation fears. In a similar vein, the American excitement over the possibilities of rollback in the early Cold War soon gave way to fear of provoking the Soviets into armed response. Restraint was the result. In contrast, against a China too weak to retaliate, U.S. support for armed insurgents after the Chinese communist victory in 1949 continued into the middle of the Cold War.

A second strategic reason great powers keep the gloves on vis-à-vis other great powers also comes straight from our introductory framework: They generally need to maintain a modicum of trust and diplomacy for issues on other fronts. The power of trust as a restraint on subversion is a function of the diplomatic importance of the target. Great powers' influence spreads far beyond their borders and even their geographic regions; hence the downsides of alienating such weighty actors are magnified. Recall that Philip II of Spain refrained from subverting Elizabeth I when he thought there might be a chance of a marriage alliance. Elizabeth did the same vis-à-vis Philip at the outset of the Dutch revolt in the 1560s because she needed a possible alliance with Philip against France. Big subversion was kept small because neither of these actors wanted to ruin what trust existed between them. Once that trust was shattered, subversion—violent subversion at that—quickly spiraled. In 1875, Paris kept the wily Bismarck at bay in part by invoking the other great powers' fear of the balance-of-power implications of a dangerously weak France. Bismarck backed down because he needed cooperation with those other great powers. Sixty years later, Stalin kept the French Communist Party (PCF) on a leash because he needed cooperation with France on other issues more important to Soviet foreign policy goals. In 1987, Secretary of State George Schultz was able to tell Soviet Premier Mikhail Gorbachev in no uncertain terms that the Soviets needed to tone down their active measures—particularly over the AIDS libel—or face a reduction in cooperation with the United States on other fronts. As these examples show, it is the rare case in which carrots are completely off the table.

Yet these strategic imperatives are not the whole story. By magnifying the granular but crucially important *operational* challenges of subversion, we can see that the greater power of great powers also has more prosaic constraining effects. A simple but important constraint bears emphasis: Great powers are tough targets with a home field advantage. By definition, they are usually comparatively strong institutionally, with the wealth and experience to maintain robust domestic intelligence and policing agencies. Great powers usually have an ideological advantage as well: The resources of the government can be marshaled to foster strong in-group feelings—patriotism and nationalism—that counter the efforts of foreign powers to persuade or recruit insiders to their cause. In addition, on their own turf, great powers have a material advantage over even a peer subverter. With few exceptions, it's usually cheaper to crush sedition at home than to fund and inspire it farther afield. In other words, it's often easier for the target to defend than for the subverter to subvert.

These defenses sometimes manifest as tough internal repression. The line between prudent counter-subversion and paranoid hysteria can become blurred. The post-war French government cracked down on PCF-organized strikes with "exceptional brutality" and implemented an elaborate "psychological counteroffensive" against communists.[1] The United States and United Kingdom engaged in what sometimes seemed to be over-the-top surveillance and repression of feared "fifth columns" in the 1930s and 1950s.[2] Each of these cases featured actual subversion with real subversives but also violated the civil rights of too many innocents. And Stalin's deadly, destructive paranoia about subversion was in a class by itself, leading to a frenzied counter-subversive campaign that swept up tens of thousands of innocent people. When an actual threat did appear—as when the United States supported anti-Soviet insurgencies in the early Cold War—the Soviet state was in a position to roll it up with ruthless efficiency. This echoes events under Elizabeth I 500 years earlier, when Catholic priests and disloyal nobles met heavy-handed and often fatal punishments. This in turn mimics the brutality of the ancient world, where potential subverters were massacred by the thousands or crucified on the hill of Golgotha. And with great power subversion's return, we see it in the increasingly punitive restrictions on free speech and dissent in Russia, China, Iran, and other autocracies. The Russian and Chinese governments have raised allegations of invidious foreign meddling to a linchpin of the official ideology.

Contrast this with the defenses of a weaker power—made vulnerable by corruption, poverty, lack of sophistication or resources, institutional disarray, or any number of other factors that leave it open to effective meddling—and it becomes clear why smaller powers are easier targets. The memoirs of General Frantisek Moravec, who as head of Czechoslovakia's military intelligence battled both Nazi and communist subversion, offer a visceral feel for what it's like to be a weak, divided state in the crosshairs of powerful and determined subverters. A great power's military superiority and diplomatic leverage tend to make the target state think twice before venturing a tough response.[3]

Furthermore, the greater power of great powers serves to magnify the standard logistical and organizational barriers to successful covert operations with which intelligence professionals and scholars are familiar. Secrecy works against scale, but to go overt versus a great power risks invoking heavy additional costs. Subversion requires control over agents on the target's territory—never an easy task. It also demands exquisite intelligence on the target and the cultivation of those agents, which works against speed. For example, in the early Cold War, the CIA had to navigate its way through the treacherous shoals of the Ukrainian resistance movement for three years before it could determine whom to support and get operations going.[4]

Our cases illustrate how even the massive intelligence bureaucracies of superpowers still run afoul of these operational constraints. Despite huge resources and lots of potential allies in the target states, conflicts can still develop between the subverting state and its agents on the ground: the so-called principal–agent problem. The KGB had to work overtime to keep the front organizations it supported from adopting too even-handed a stance in the Cold War. Moscow's struggles to get communist parties to toe its line are a leitmotif of Comintern scholarship. The CIA's travails were similarly indicative. Langley's frustrations with the fractious, duplicitous, squabbling, and at times double-crossing Russian exile community are a case in point.[5] The CIA-supported Chinese Nationalist army in Burma in the early 1950s was not only routed by Chinese communist troops when it attempted an invasion but also heavily involved in the drug trade in the infamous Golden Triangle.[6] Mercenaries on the ground can exceed their brief; domestic opposition activists have their own agendas.

## Explaining Variation and Change

The structure and power of all these constraints are clear. Yet sometimes we see the sorts of meddling operations we've highlighted in these pages. Why? The answer lies in temporary shifts, both within a given rivalry and throughout the general international setting. Within a rivalry, shifts in strengths and vulnerabilities can open doors to subversion. Domestic political infighting creates opportunities for a malign actor to stoke the flames of division, as does the chaos following internal rebellion (as in fifth-century BC Sparta) or war (as in nineteenth-century France). Competition stoked by religious or ideological currents also presents opportunities. The existential split of the sort witnessed between Spain and England in the sixteenth century, or between the United States and the Soviet Union in the twentieth century, prompted an eventual throwing of caution to the winds and a turn to violent subversion in both cases. The appearance of technological innovations, particularly in communications, can temporarily facilitate subversive activities. We've seen the impact of the printing press, the radio, and the internet. Each opened up new opportunities for subversion. Those shifts led to a temporary disruption in the great power equilibrium and a corresponding rise in subversion. The operative word here is "temporary"; among great powers, it seems the pendulum always swings back to the status quo.

As a result, we live in a world in which great power leaders are constantly tempted to reach into their subversion bag of tricks for tools that are cheaper, more flexible, and more deniable than warfare. Against lesser rivals, the temptation often gives way to action. But against great power peers, we see time and again evidence of strategic restraint—great powers limiting or refraining from clearly feasible operations to exploit divisions within their opponents. Subversion is deterred or put back in the box by the familiar list of cons holding it at bay, whether it's fear of retaliation, concerns about reputational damage, or the logistical headache of penetrating a really hard target. The strategic (escalation and reputation) and operational (logistical and home field advantage) barriers are interdependent: When subverters find ways around the latter, targets must lean more heavily on the former. All of this fits into a cost–benefit analysis that is strikingly consistent over time.

Yet if our big finding is the constancy of subversion's constraints, incentives, tools, and purposes, we also see large-scale changes through time: In the ancient world, subversion appears to yield bigger results; in early modern Europe, bolder, more violent subversion is easier to find than in later centuries; the nineteenth century's subversive operations look more subtle than what came before or after; the twentieth century saw massive effort devoted to subversion, but it's harder to identify effects than in earlier centuries; and, as noted, there are periods—the first two decades after the Cold War's end being a recent one—when subversion seems to subside. Across our cases, three major factors influence these large-scale shifts.

First is war. For the reasons we identified in Chapter 1, some constraints on subversion weaken when the real fighting starts. When great powers anticipate major war against each other, incentives to build networks on the inside of rivals are magnified. During war, belligerent great powers will try to insert or support armed forces behind enemy lines if they can. Any fissure—political, religious, or ethnic—that can be used, will be. Once the guns fall silent, the legacy of all those wartime subversive operations looms over subsequent great power interactions, in a sort of subversion hangover. The big picture here is that the distinction between war and non-war—and thus between measures short of war and war—weakens when there is constant war.

All of this means that the more frequently wars among great powers occur, the more salient subversion becomes. In our ancient world cases, war was nearly constant: States were fighting, recovering from war, or preparing for war. Subversive operations assumed major proportions and sometimes produced major effects. In the Early Modern cases, too, war was nearly constant, and the brashness and boldness of subversion were similarly notable.

In the nineteenth and twentieth centuries, great power war, while fierce, was far less frequent. The lines between peacetime and wartime were clearer, and thus we observe much less violent subversion among great powers. Each major war reignites subversive behavior, which lingers long after the guns have fallen silent. Violent subversion in the early Cold War thus can be understood in the context of the recent world war and expectations of new war. Constraints kicked back in as expectations of war receded in the face of nuclear deterrence and the rising cost of escalation.

Second is the subvertibility of the major actors. We've already noted that short-term fluctuations in the vulnerability of targets influence choices to subvert. But across our cases, it's difficult to miss a secular strengthening of the state through time. Our sample of cases leads us to argue that viewed over the very long term, the ability of great powers to defend against peer subversion has outpaced their offensive capability to undermine rivals. Hence, the ancient world's arguably more dramatic subversion was in part the result of a double whammy: relatively penetrable states nearly constantly at war. Early modern states were, overall, tougher targets than their ancient forebears, but industrializing and bureaucratizing nineteenth-century states were even more so. It's undeniable that the England of Gladstone was simply a tougher target than the England of Elizabeth I. By the time we get to the twentieth century, we see exceedingly tough totalitarian states, but even the more open democracies boast fearsome counter-subversive institutions. In the arms race between offensive and defensive subversion capability, the latter keeps up. The massive intelligence organizations and huge propaganda and influence agencies, wielding novel technologies like the mass press and radio, ran smack up against the fearsome institutional power of modern industrialized state targets.

Third is the interaction of transnational ideas and sovereignty. Our definition of subversion zeroes in on the idea that rulers of states want to prevent or control the actions of rival rulers on their territory. We stressed that these norms against subversion induce both the subverter and the target regime to regard it as untoward, underhanded, and somehow "bad." That initially suggests that the stronger the norms against unwanted meddling are, the higher the barriers to subversion. As mentioned in Chapter 1, scholars once credited the genesis of these norms to the Peace of Westphalia in 1648, seeing in it the moment when meddling in other states' internal affairs acquired the opprobrium with which it is regarded today.

Yet our investigation supports the recent wave of scholarship upending the old take on Westphalia.[7] It's very clear from our examples that subversion did not abate just because it was considered bad form to violate another state's sovereignty. What's more, our cases from the ancient world show that the concepts of sovereignty and its violation long predated Westphalia. From the Thirty Years' Peace in fifth-century BC Greece to the Congress of Vienna and the United Nations Charter, formally proclaiming fealty to non-intervention has done precious little to make it a reality. In the end, what matters most is rulers' capacity to enforce their sovereign prerogative. As we predicted, norms are a malleable constraint.

Transnational religious, ethnic, or ideological commitments pose a special challenge to sovereignty because they insist on the rightness and propriety of seeking to influence things across borders. The fact that one can find language to this effect in the treaties of Westphalia speaks volumes about the persistence of norms that contradict the idea of sovereignty and provide a warrant for intervention. The stronger the ideas that justify subversion, the more malleable norms of sovereignty are. Political scientist John Owen has shown that during such periods of intense ideological competition, states are more prone to seek forceful regime change, usually while at war.[8] Our investigation reveals how this behavior carries over to measures short of war.

Just as they always look for ways to exploit new technology or the vulnerabilities of rivals for subversive ends, rulers are constantly on the prowl for normative loopholes big enough to run a great power through. When ideas claim strong allegiance across borders, fellow travelers are easier to come by, and support for them abroad is easier to justify. Think about the idea of Greek unity against "barbarian" outsiders in Thucydides' day, or religion in Elizabeth's, nationalism in Bismarck's, communism in Stalin's, or liberal democracy in our own. In each of these periods, we see clever leaders marrying sincere belief with cynical realpolitik in seeking to bend or undermine rivals. The Comintern was a brilliant innovation, exploiting working peoples' transnational solidarity in an institution that Soviet diplomats could, with a straight face, claim to be separate from the government they represented.

More recent transnational ideas are less likely to prompt violent intervention. The human rights enshrined in the Universal Declaration and ultimately in the Helsinki Final Act—which the Soviet Union signed in 1975 in an effort to secure common acceptance of the post–World War II status quo in Europe—offered the U.S. government opportunities to seek to influence Soviet domestic politics in ways that made things awkward for the Kremlin without prompting a call to arms.

## Subversion's Role in Great Power Politics

This book is above all about perspective. We once dubbed subversion "the hyena of international relations" because although people turn their noses up at it, it plays an important role in international

politics.[9] It's clear enough why individual leaders reach for this fur-
tive form of statecraft. The preceding chapters amply demonstrated
all of subversion's appeals, the main one being the chance to nudge a
great power rival's policy in a desired direction when diplomatic forms
of influence alone aren't up to the task and high expected costs deter
measures that raise the risk of war. And it's also clear why great powers
can never eliminate it from their mutual relations. Variation in power
relationships, technology, and ideas/institutions ensures that there are
always some leaders confident that the subversive advantage is tilting
their way. Great powers use diplomacy, defense, and deterrence to keep
subversion in a box. But with some states always seeing subversion as
a force multiplier and hence reluctant to agree to rules that might put
this tool out of reach, consensus policies to repress it further are elusive.

Although power, diplomacy, and war are indeed the chief drivers
of great power politics, subversion is not a sideshow. CIA historian
Michael Warner has noted, "Covert action's dark arts have been with
us at least as long as we have written records, but they have always been
marginal to the larger movements of politics, diplomacy, and war."[10] Yet
"marginal" as it may be in the big geopolitical picture, leaders often find
it indispensable. And backstage shenanigans of the sort we've covered
influence the action on the main stage.

As we conjectured in Chapter 1, subversion can sometimes provide
a safety valve, allowing great powers to try to realize their objectives
without triggering a larger conflict. Subversion, we argued elsewhere,
lets "states avoid the dichotomous choice between war and peace,
allowing them to play out their rivalries in unsettling but perhaps less
dangerous ways."[11] Sometimes it works just as advertised, delivering
results without war. Thanks to subversion, for example, Bismarck
got the French government he wanted without having to reignite
hostilities. If the target proves resilient, the subverter might either back
off and accept the status quo or hope that events might unfold so as
to render moot the issue that sparked the subversion in the first place.
Buying time is a legitimate move. Bismarck took action after action to
subvert Gladstone without actually challenging Britain directly—until
events having little to do with Germany conspired to change London's
government and policy. Likewise, in the early Cold War, as the rivalry
with the Soviet Union gathered steam and diplomacy seemed fruitless,

subversion gave worried U.S. statesmen a sense that they could make progress in realizing their aims in a world in which war was all but unthinkable. By the time it became clear that Stalin's USSR was far too tough a target for "political warfare" to move the needle in the rivalry, U.S. officials had become accustomed to the new Cold War order and learned they could live with it. In these and other cases, by allowing statesmen to delay tough choices and kick the can down the road, subversion may have helped avoid much costlier decisions.

Cardinal Richelieu, the canny genius who served as Louis XIII's chief minister, well understood this point, using subversion to buy time when France was up against its most powerful rival. The scholar Iskander Rehman writes,

> In the decades-long competition with the Habsburgs, Richelieu viewed time as a precious strategic commodity, and opted wherever possible for a strategy of exhaustion and harassment—*la guerre couverte* (covert war)—over one of frontal confrontation. He waged war via a complex constellation of proxies, while his most able diplomats were dispatched to foment internal divisions within both Spain and the Holy Roman Empire.[12]

Kicking the can down the road wasn't just a phenomenon of the nineteenth and twentieth centuries.

Under other conditions, subversion appears not as an exit from but as a way station on the journey to costlier conflict. If the issue of contention is important enough to the subverter and the target defends itself adroitly, the subverter must face a choice: accept the status quo or escalate the subversion and risk a larger conflict. Some of our cases illustrate the latter path. Philip II of Spain tried maximum subversion against England, but Elizabeth and her ministers defended their regime ruthlessly and effectively, ultimately responding by unleashing the dogs of sixteenth-century hybrid war against the Hapsburg Empire. This subversion competition was hardly a substitute for war: Matters were only settled by a major clash of arms. In this case, kicking the can down the road didn't achieve a nonmilitary solution to the problems of the rivalry, but that outcome was not foreordained. In our most recent example, Vladimir Putin increasingly added subversion to his policy mix in his quest to make multipolarity a reality. Initially, he followed a Richelieu-style "strategy of exhaustion and harassment" to undermine America's position and reorder European security, winning now-forgotten plaudits for strategic acumen. In a fine example of an unintended outcome, however, Ukraine proved adept at defense, and efforts to subvert Europe and the United States backfired by stiffening their resistance. His diplomacy and subversive efforts stymied, Putin refused to accept the status quo and escalated from hybrid war to the real thing, albeit with a large subversive element pinned on unwarranted hopes for help from Ukrainian fifth columns.[13] Here, subversion appears to blend into rather than deflect the conflict potential inherent in the strategic setting.

In yet other cases, the fear of subversion appears to exacerbate the underlying sources of conflict. Leaders periodically sense new opportunities for subversion and ramp it up, which leads to new threat perceptions in the target(s) that feed back into and propel the rivalry. Just as subversion can induce internally directed paranoia that can feed repression at home, so can it spark intense fear of rival states. We've covered several such cases, beginning with Thucydides' narrative of the role fears of subversion played in the threat perceptions that helped drive Athens and Sparta to war. In the twentieth century, rapid technological, ideological, and institutional changes fed several cycles featuring Russia and the West. Early Bolshevik leaders reckoned that the global communist movement, organized under the auspices of the Comintern, would substitute for traditional diplomacy, allowing an isolated and relatively weak USSR to revise an unfavorable status quo. That elicited an intense and often repressive response in targets, fed dire threat perceptions in the West, served as a major impediment to diplomacy, and ultimately helped inspire the erstwhile targets to hone their own subversive tools. Similarly, as the Cold War reached its waning years, American officials thought they'd found the secret sauce for successful subversion (although they didn't view it as such): the public–private partnership and promotion of civil society we called the "new approach." That, too, ultimately fed threat perceptions in the target, Russia, which in turn prompted a ruthless domestic crackdown and the counter-subversion that generated the "hybrid war" bubble, a frenzied Western response, and the subversive operation of 2016.

Thus, subversion can contribute to a spiral, serving to exacerbate a rivalry. Despairing over the prospects for traditional statecraft, leaders hope for new opportunities from subversion and ramp it up, which leads to new threat perceptions in the target(s), which responds in kind. We've just experienced one of these cycles. It's not the first, and it won't be the last.

A corollary of this is the observation that paranoia about subversion—either real or imagined—is an indicator of how seriously states regard its potential dangers. As we discussed in Chapter 1, despite its small scale compared to traditional statecraft, subversion carries big risks because it may be (or it may be perceived to be) directed at the security of the target regime. Even if subversion has only marginal effects on the power of the target state, it gets at its rulers' sense of security in an especially direct, visceral way. That jeopardizes the trust governments need to cooperate with each other, and it may generate in the target regime a perception of the subverter's motives as especially threatening.

## Conclusion

Our appraisal of great power subversion through the centuries has shown that it can manifest as all measures short of war, with differing degrees of covertness and violence depending on the situation and the cost–benefit calculation of the subverter. There is a logic to its application. The constraints of escalation fears, trust, and logistical realities tend to keep it to a minimum among great powers unless some shift in vulnerabilities prompts one rival to give it a try against another. In the end, however, the pendulum always seems to swing back toward an equilibrium in which decisive great power meddling is rare.

What's more, we've seen that subversion plays a variety of important roles in international statecraft. When diplomacy is not delivering, subversion can be a useful tool, giving a rival an option for action without resorting to war, helping avert a more catastrophic response to an intractable dispute. Other times, subversion seems to be merely a way station on the road to war, an irritating episode that exacerbates tensions instead of enabling a stalemate. And in a worst-case scenario, sometimes subversion, or even the mere fear of it, sparks a paranoid spiral. We've seen this in the ancient world, we've seen it in U.S.–Russian relations from the late 1990s through 2016, and we will no doubt see it again.

In short, subversion is opportunistic and ever-present, a perennial tool of statecraft to supplement diplomacy, economic pressures, and war as governments seek to achieve their foreign policy goals.

Keeping this in mind, we turn to consider what lies ahead.

# 10

## Looking Forward

### The Future of Great Power Subversion

AMERICA'S FEBRILE REACTION to Russia's 2016 operation will not be the last. If the expert conversation is any guide, the next bout of public neu-ralgia will follow in the wake of another subversive campaign featuring an authoritarian rival such as Russia or China (or both) exploiting fissures in American democracy using new technologies with fright-ening applications.

Having weathered Russia's subversive attacks in 2016 and after, the United States and allied democracies now look on China with fore-boding. U.S. and UK counter-intelligence chiefs have assessed its sub-versive potential as "immense," "breath-taking," and "game-changing."[1] Former MI6 director of operations and intelligence Nigel Inkster has stressed that "China has acquired global economic and diplomatic in-fluence, enabling covert operations that extend well beyond traditional intelligence gathering, are growing in scale, and threaten to overwhelm Western security agencies."[2] Having adjusted to the subversive poten-tial of the internet, officials and experts see much to fear in newer tech-nology, with artificial intelligence (AI) at the forefront. FBI Director Christopher Wray warned that adversaries are "using technology to make their efforts more impactful and less traceable . . . and a deluge of data is overwhelming human capacity to process, exploit, assess, share, and act on it in a timely way."[3] Yet, for many experts, non-democracies seem adept at wielding new technology to their subversive ends. As one warned a Senate panel, "The authoritarian powers . . . have gained confidence that they can both suppress dissent at home and build competing networks of influence abroad, with limited effective resistance from the major democracies."[4]

But the fears that we will inevitably confront in the future—of vulnerability due to democratic dysfunction, of the subversive implications of new technology, of advantages to authoritarian states in the subversion game—are all old news. The long-term perspective we reviewed in Chapter 9 yields three underappreciated lessons for the future of great power subversion. First, diplomacy can still buttress deterrence and defense in a target state's toolkit for managing subversion. Second, history reveals a more nuanced and less fraught assessment of democracies' resilience in the face of subversion than contemporary headlines imply. And third, over the long term, technology is never a game-changer in the complex strategic arena that is great power subversive competition.

## Don't Discount Diplomacy

The evidence presented in this book supports our argument that an important constraint on subversion is the need for rivals to maintain a modicum of trust and diplomacy for dealing with issues on other fronts. In Chapter 9, we stressed that the power of trust as a restraint on subversion is a function of the diplomatic importance of the target. The United States learned this lesson the hard way in 1933, when Franklin Delano Roosevelt (FDR) sat down with Stalin's top diplomat, Maksim Litvinov, to set terms for establishing relations. The Americans had withheld diplomatic recognition in part because of their febrile reaction to communist subversion in the years after the Bolshevik revolution. Now, they made the Soviets a reasonable offer: We'll work with you as a normal country when you stop subverting us by supporting the U.S. Communist Party, formally committed to the destruction of our social and economic order. And FDR got Litvinov to pledge to do just that. "It will be the fixed policy" of the Soviet Union, Litvinov promised,

> to refrain, and to restrain all persons in government service and all organizations of the Government or under its direct or indirect control,

including the organizations in receipt of any financial assistance from it, from any act overt or covert liable in any way whatsoever to injure the tranquility, prosperity, order, or security of the whole or any part of the United States.[5]

The problem was that Stalin honored the agreement in the breach. Things came to a head two years later at the Communist International's 7th World Congress, held in Moscow in an official government building. The Reds gathered to ratify the idea of a popular front against fascism with other, less revolutionary leftist forces. But they were at pains to stress that this meant tabling rather than forswearing their commitment to the revolutionary overthrow of capitalism. Top American communists gave fiery speeches. Seeing such a blatant violation of the FDR–Litvinov deal, U.S. Ambassador William C. Bullitt went ballistic. He fired off a flaming telegram home advocating a harsh reaction to include the closing of Soviet consulates and a major public campaign by the president to expose Soviet duplicity. But he did not advocate breaking off diplomatic relations. "It is difficult to conduct conversations with the Soviet Foreign Office because in that institution the lie is normal and the truth abnormal," he wrote, "But patience and diplomats exist for just that sort of difficulty."[6] For his part, FDR refused even to go as far as Bullitt wanted, settling for a note of protest, to which the Soviets gave a peremptory rebuff.

America, in short, was forced to grin and bear it as another great power openly supported a subversive movement on its territory. Why? For starters, the threat was manageable: FDR knew that FBI Director J. Edgar Hoover had things well in hand. And the other democratic powers had learned to tolerate Bolshevik duplicity. But Roosevelt also needed to work with Moscow—perhaps to counter Japan in Asia and, closer to home, to sign trade deals with large U.S. firms in the depth of the Great Depression. The USSR's diplomatic importance to the United States was high enough that the Americans had to tolerate some meddling. The United States, following a policy that seemed to preclude military involvement in Eurasia's geopolitics, lacked the diplomatic importance to force Moscow to bear the costs of unambiguous distancing from the Comintern. Bullitt reported that Litvinov implied as much in conversations on the matter.[7]

The story of the interweaving of subversion and realpolitik is often presented from the subverter's perspective: the clever state that advances its aims with a subtle mix of subversion and traditional statecraft. Yet as our argument about trust as a constraint expects, the reverse is also true: Diplomacy joins deterrence and defense in the target's toolkit. In the FDR case, Stalin did get the message that the United States was contemplating a breakoff in relations, and America was almost certainly important enough to the Soviets to induce some restraint on subversion.

Leveraging diplomacy to tame subversion may look like a forlorn hope with Russia at war in Ukraine, alleged Russian sabotage operations underway throughout Western Europe, and relations with China becoming ever more rivalrous.[8] But what matters is the expected relative gains of diplomatic bargaining and the ability of the target to establish credible linkage between those gains and restraint on subversion. That dynamic can occur even when rivals' relations have sunk very low. The twenty-first-century United States possesses a level of diplomatic importance unimaginable to pre–World War II Americans. Moscow and, even more, Beijing want and need things only the United States and its allies can give. That is a major and rarely remarked upon potential constraint on subverters. Needless to say, however, it is a constraint that does not act on its own; it must be used. The lesson: Keep defenses up, maintain credible deterrence if rivals take things too far, but keep a weather eye out for ways "patience and diplomats" can tame subversion.

### Democracies Are Less Subvertible Than They Appear

We saw that whenever great powers with relatively open and closed systems competed, people worried that the authoritarians had an unfair advantage. Afterall, one entire category of subversion—election interference—is a threat chiefly to democracies. Since fifth-century BC Athens, the open politics of democracies, subject as they are to the vicissitudes of public opinion and competitive elections for public office, have opened doors to subverters. The argument that democracies are especially subvertible and thus that any international system containing them will feature one-sided contests in subversion is plausible. Consider the case of Poland and the *liberum veto* in the seventeenth and eighteenth centuries. In contrast to the surrounding absolute monarchies, Polish and Lithuanian noblemen represented their regions in a legislative assembly, the *Sejm*. Under this system, all noblemen were considered equal, which meant any one could veto any measure. The result? Foreign powers needed to bribe just one impecunious nobleman to thwart any action by Poland.

Yet overall, democracies do not appear in our study as walk-over targets for subverters. The big picture reveals democracies' inherent toughness, courtesy of their built-in institutions and succession structures. Robust legal systems can prosecute and eventually punish collaborators, and an assassin's bullet may change the leader but not the regime. Cumbersome and slow it may be, but the democratic machinery grinds on. Except for a few cases in which the decisions that a subverter cares about hang on a few votes, the old Polish scenario doesn't often occur. In America, the framers of democracy were well aware of the problem and designed institutions accordingly. James Madison understood that Poland's government was "at the mercy of its powerful neighbors," and Poland appears repeatedly in the *Federalist Papers*, usually as an example of what not to do.[9] The young American republic was founded in the shadow of subversion, with its constituent states ready-made targets for potential great power subverters. Many quirky features of the U.S. political system are partly the result of efforts to ward them off.

Political vulnerability, moreover, is only one variable in the subversion equation. When domestic politics become fractious, opening the door to subverters, a democracy can lean more heavily on those other levers of escalation, defense, and the potential importance to others of having its trust. Given America's particular strengths in those areas, it is in a better position to compensate for political vulnerability than many of history's democratic targets.

Non-democracies, meanwhile, are more subvertible than you might think. True, they can shut their borders to outside influence and thumb their noses at bothersome human rights issues while cracking down on potential subversion. For much of the twentieth century, for example, the USSR seemed to have a decided advantage on this front. Historian Calder Walton's account of the intelligence contest between the Soviet Union and the United States and United Kingdom makes clear that Moscow was just better at human intelligence (HUMINT).[10] And that had implications for subversion, as communist organizational discipline coupled with the KGB's HUMINT chops enabled influence operations the West could never match. But in the big picture, the effects of these operations were minimal, while the Soviet Union eventually turned out to be surprisingly subvertible, proof that autocracies also have vulnerabilities. Ever since the days of Sparta, oligarchies and autocracies have had their own exploitable fissures, usually featuring disaffected, oppressed groups on their territory. Arbitrary law and repression may breed plenty of opportunities for a subversive adversary to find willing accomplices on the inside. Uncertain institutions for the transfer of power open up political Pandora's boxes that outside powers might influence.

The result of these authoritarian vulnerabilities is often a repressive counter-subversive state apparatus that imposes heavy costs. Russia has witnessed a crackdown on dissent, free speech, and the press that was approaching Stalinesque proportions even before the ill-fated invasion of Ukraine. Repressive measures take a toll on Russia's long-term prospects as a great power, prompting the departure of the young and the educated and an increasing nationalistic sclerosis in the society they left behind. In China, a similar atmosphere prevails. From the Great Firewall guarding China's internet ecosystem to the mass internment of Uyghurs and other Turkic Muslims in Xinjiang province, China is intent on stamping out potential vulnerabilities, whether from subversive propaganda or latent fifth columns.

A world in which subversion among great powers is an ever-present possibility weighs down on everyone. The opportunity costs autocracies bear because of their obsession with counter-subversion are difficult to calculate precisely but are certainly large. Most of the measures against interference these governments believe they are obligated to take impede the free flow of information, people, and ideas that feed economic growth and innovation. The shadow of subversion may well sap the wellsprings of authoritarian power more than it undermines democracies. From a ruthless cost–benefit perspective, it could well be that in the long term, it is the democracies that have the unfair advantage.

## Technology Is Not a Game-Changer

We've seen how technological innovations through the ages, from the printing press to the radio to the internet, have created new opportunities for subverters and sparked tech-subversion panics. Yet in our cases, we saw that over time, technology cuts both ways. For one thing, technology that enables subversion frequently gives targets tools with which to combat it. The printing press and the radio offered new opportunities to spread subversive messages across borders, but target governments could use the same means to propagandize their own populations, inducing skepticism about messages from abroad. For another, technology that seems to favor one rival has a funny way of switching sides. The radio was initially thought to be a scary tool in the hands of fascists and Nazis, but ultimately it came to be viewed as one of democracy's strongest subversive weapons against the totalitarian Soviet regime. More recently, the internet was once exhibit A in democracies' innate advantage in undermining autocracies, until the opposite became the conventional wisdom.

These patterns reflect a larger reality supported by the evidence in this book: In international affairs, politics and strategy dominate technology. This lends support to analysts such as Thomas Rid and Gavin Wilde, who warn that panicking about technology can inflict more strategic harm than technology itself.[11]

We did find that windows of opportunity can open as governments that believe they are vulnerable to new technology scramble for responses. But technological determinism is an illusion; the most salient examples in which technology seems to be independently determinative always reflect combinations of political and technological causes. This even applies to one of the most prominent examples of faith in technology's transformative effects: the belief that the internet plus social media would be fatally subversive to authoritarian governments. If we had to fix dates on it, this window opened from about the mid-1990s until roughly 2012 and 2013, when targets pushed back hard. That's a long time, during which leading liberal powers felt both invulnerable to the influence attempts of others and empowered to influence the domestic politics of others.

But bear in mind that great power rivalry was itself in abeyance through most of this period. The reasons China and Russia initially tolerated vulnerability to flows of potentially subversive information across their borders were less helplessness in the face of the implacable force of technology than strategic, political, and economic calculations about the costs of domestic repression and closing themselves off. Eventually, the relative power of the authoritarian challengers seemed to rise and the rivalry heated up, in part driven by the fears and hopes of subversion. As a result, authoritarian powers' calculations shifted, and they became more willing to bear the costs of insulating themselves from the political influence the internet once conveyed from abroad.

The internet radically lowered the costs of getting a message across a border. It made it easier to steal sensitive information and leak it to subversive effect. But it lowered those costs for everybody, not just hostile states. If it was easy for governments to pour out information and disinformation, the same was true for political parties and other movements, and indeed for individuals. The information environment thus changed in ways that made it more difficult for a hostile actor to move the public opinion needle.[12] Furthermore, our research on the events of 2016 ratifies political scientist Lennart Maschmeyer's claim that cyber tools do not offer a clean escape from the "trilemma" posed by the competing needs of speed, control, and scale.[13] As a rule, and at best, you can't get any two of these desired features without sacrificing the third. The upshot is that subversive activity is naturally self-limiting. The tougher the target, the more acute these trade-offs become.

Indeed, the war in Ukraine showed that cyber was not exactly the apocalyptic bugbear we thought it would be. Although it was used for massive disinformation and cyber-attacks on satellites and critical infrastructure, we've witnessed repeated instances of successful countermeasures by Ukraine and the West. It turned out that cyber activities were difficult to keep secret; the trade-offs of the subversion trilemma were iron-clad. Deniability was difficult for the subverter. Russia's cyber operations in Ukraine, Europe, and the United States were in the end traceable, making plausible deniability untenable and robust defense possible. The advent of AI, deep fakes, quantum computing, and as yet unheralded technological innovations may one day defy the strategic, operational, and political logic that has prevailed for centuries, but we wouldn't bet on it.

## Twenty-First-Century Great Power Subversion in Perspective

Not only are these three lessons true, but if you take the long view, two major enablers of subversion—the frequency and severity of great power war and the intensity of transnational ideological competition—are likely to remain at levels below what we have seen in centuries past.

Rising numbers of conflicts and increased great power tension notwithstanding, great power war is increasingly rare. Eighty years have passed since true great power peers engaged in all-out combat. The statesmen whose subversive operations filled Chapters 2–5 could scarcely have conceived of such a situation. We argued in Chapter 1 that major impediments to subversion—notably fear of escalation and the loss of the trust that diplomacy and cooperation require—become less significant in war. The evidence reviewed in Chapter 9 supports this expectation. And while analysts today make much of an expanded "gray zone" that muddles the distinction between measures short of war and war, there is nothing new about gray zones. Intelligence scholars like Rory Cormac have already established that gray zone statecraft was a perennial feature of the Cold War. Indeed, the preceding pages demonstrate that modern gray zone theorists would have little to teach Cardinal Richelieu or Queen Elizabeth I about the subject. What *is* new compared to our earlier historical cases is a clearer distinction between war and peace, something lacking in the eras of near constant great power war covered in Chapters 2 and 3. That helps explain the more violent and consequential subversion of those eras. For many of our forebears, war among great powers was nearly a constant, and subversion was, too.

Yet even as the frequency of great power war receded in more recent centuries, knock-down drag-out slugfests among great powers recurred often enough to foster major subversive actions. As we documented, an underappreciated consequence of such wars is the persistence of bureaucracies, networks, and habits of subversion that lower logistical barriers—a subversion hangover effect. This doesn't operate as strongly when major, prolonged wars don't happen as often. Looking forward, great power war is almost surely more likely in the second quarter of the twenty-first century than it was in the first. But nuclear deterrence lowers its likelihood compared to the historical norm. The shadow cast by the last such war is not as dark or as far-reaching as it often was in past centuries, while the glimmerings of the next are substantially dimmer.

Finally, although his choice of title was hyperbolic, Francis Fukuyama had a point about "the end of history": Transnational ideologies aren't what they used to be.[14] Yes, liberalism is less triumphant than when Fukuyama penned those words. We may have Russia and China stoking new nationalisms, or a resurgence of far-right political groups and ideologies, but we don't face the likes of the Protestant–Catholic conflict, the existential threat of nationalism to empires, or the battle between fascism and communism and democracy witnessed in the twentieth century. One benefit of examining periods like the Thirty Years' War and the nineteenth and twentieth centuries is that it serves as a stark reminder of what subversion in such settings was like. Missing today are true mass movements genuinely inspired by ideas emanating from a great power rival. And that takes a potent temptation and dangerous fear out of the subversion equation. The current rise of authoritarian governments globally is unlikely to win converts with the same zeal that accompanied the religious and ideological movements that added such potential to many of the most dramatic cases of subversion we studied. Barring the rise of some new fervent transnational cause, the likelihood of subversion that has the potential to change the game is likely to remain lower than in those past cases.

These words may ring hollow to people who toil day and night to protect us against new, invidious subversive threats. But one danger we've identified is overreaction, which can feed spirals of mistrust and make great power rivalry even worse than it needs to be. And the danger of such an overreaction is partly the result of the fact that we are coming out of a period of unusually low levels of great power subversion. Subversion among major powers subsided after 1989 because both American power and liberal ideas lacked credible rivals. Now, rising challenges to the United States and its liberal precepts have accompanied the resurgence of great power competition and subversion's dramatic return. The apprehension this creates is understandable. But it is very unlikely that renewed clashes among great powers or their ideas will reach the levels that drove subversion to the scale we saw in the mid-twentieth century, to say nothing of earlier epochs. Subversion in the future may be much worse than it was during the unipolar era, but it's very unlikely to be as bad as it often was in the past.

Subversive statecraft is part and parcel of great power politics. Always has been; always will be. No state is immune to its effects, and no state can escape the temptation to use it when the timing seems right. Yet despite the challenges of new rivals and new technologies, pushback against it in the future will rest on the same bulwarks that contained it in the past: defense, deterrence, and diplomacy. The burden of proof is on those who cast doubt upon the strength of those bulwarks in the twenty-first century.

We began this book by asking a fundamental question: After the tumultuous events of 2016, are we now in a new age of subversion? The answer is no.

# NOTES

## Preface

1. Ali Watkins, "Obama Team Was Warned in 2014 About Russian Interference," *Politico*, August 14, 2017; accessed February 6, 2024, from https://www.politico.com/story/2017/08/14/obama-russia-election-interference-241547.
2. Ibid.

## Chapter 1

1. See Henry Hemming, *Our Man in New York: The British Plot to Bring America into the Second World War* (London: Quercus, 2019); William Stephenson, ed., *British Security Coordination: The Secret History of British Intelligence in the Americas, 1940–1945* (New York: Fromm International, 1999).
2. Laurence W. Beilenson, *Power Through Subversion* (Washington, DC: Public Affairs Press, 1972).
3. Mark Stout and Michael Warner, "Intelligence Is as Intelligence Does," *Intelligence and National Security* 33, no. 4 (2018): 517–26.
4. E.g., Dov Levin, *Meddling in the Ballot Box: The Causes and Effects of Partisan Electoral Interventions* (New York: Oxford University Press, 2020); David Shimer, *Rigged: America, Russia, and One Hundred Years of Covert Electoral Influence* (New York: Knopf, 2020); Phillip Taylor, *Munitions of the Mind: A History of Propaganda*, 3rd ed. (Manchester, UK: Manchester University Press, 2003); Thomas Rid, *Active Measures: The Secret History of Disinformation and Political Warfare* (New York: Macmillan, 2020); Melissa Lee, *Crippling Leviathan: How Foreign Subversion Weakens the State* (Ithaca, NY: Cornell

University Press, 2020); Lindsey O'Rourke, *Covert Regime Change* (Ithaca, NY: Cornell University Press, 2018); Melissa Willard-Foster, *Toppling Foreign Governments: The Logic of Regime Change* (Philadelphia: University of Pennsylvania Press, 2018); Alexander Downes, *Catastrophic Success: Why Foreign-Imposed Regime Change Goes Wrong* (Ithaca, NY: Cornell University Press, 2021).

5. Rory Cormac, *How to Stage a Coup* (London: Atlantic Books, 2022).

6. Loch K. Johnson, "On Drawing a Bright Line for Covert Operations," *American Journal of International Law* 86, no. 2 (1992): 284–309. In a similar spirit, see Richard Cottam, *Competitive Interventions and 20th Century Diplomacy* (Pittsburgh, PA: University of Pittsburgh Press, 1967).

7. Javier Jordan, "International Competition Below the Threshold of War: Toward a Theory of Gray Zone Conflict," *Journal of Strategic Security* 14, no. 1 (2021): 1–24.

8. Forrest E. Morgan et al., *Dangerous Thresholds: Managing Escalation in the 21st Century* (Santa Monica, CA: RAND Corporation, 2008), https://www.rand.org/pubs/monographs/MG614.html.

9. E.g., Michael J. Mazarr, *Mastering the Gray Zone: Understanding a Changing Era of Conflict* (Carlisle, PA: U.S. Army War College Press, 2015).

10. Gregory Treverton, *Covert Action: the CIA and the Limits of American Intervention in the Post-War World* (New York: Basic Books, 1987).

11. Michael Poznansky, "Feigning Compliance: Covert Action and International Law," *International Studies Quarterly* 63, no. 1 (2019): 72–84.

12. Thucydides, *History of the Peloponnesian War*, trans. Rex Warner (London: Penguin, 1972): 1.20.

13. See Bruce D. Berkowitz and Allan E. Goodman, "The Logic of Covert Action," *The National Interest* (March 1, 1998), https://nationalinterest.org/article/the-logic-of-covert-action-333; Rory Cormac and Richard J. Aldrich, "Grey Is the New Black: Covert Action and Implausible Deniability," *International Affairs* 94, no. 3 (2018): 477–94.

14. Austin Carson, *Secret Wars: Covert Conflict in International Politics* (Princeton, NJ: Princeton University Press, 2018).

15. For a related analysis, see Lennart Maschmeyer, "The Subversive Trilemma: Why Cyber Operations Fall Short of Expectations," *International Security* 46, no. 2 (2021): 51–90. Although his analysis is of cyber subversion, the trade-off dilemma he identifies applies to many traditional operations as well.

16. Our discussion of signaling and trust builds on Andrew H. Kydd, *Trust and Mistrust in International Relations* (Princeton, NJ: Princeton University Press, 2005); and our understanding of the distinction between intentions and motivations comes from Charles L. Glaser, *Rational Theory of International Politics: The Logic of Competition and Cooperation* (Princeton, NJ: Princeton University Press, 2010).

17. See William C. Wohlforth, "Realism and Great Power Subversion," *International Relations* 34, no. 4 (2020): 459–481; and Lennart Maschmeyer, "Subversion, Cyber Operations, and Reverse Structural Power in World Politics," *European Journal of International Relations* 29, no. 1 (2023): 79–103.

18. But see Stephen D. Krasner, *Sovereignty: Organized Hypocrisy* (Princeton, NJ: Princeton University Press, 1999); Benjamin de Carvalho, Halvard Leira, and John M. Hobson, "The Big Bangs of IR: The Myths That Your Teachers Still Tell You About 1648 and 1919," *Millennium: Journal of International Studies* 39, no. 3 (2011): 735–58.

19. See Treverton, *Covert Action*; Loch Johnson, *The Third Option: Covert Action and American Foreign Policy* (New York: Oxford University Press, 2022): 170–75.

20. Alex Downes and Lindsey O'Rourke count more than 100 overt foreign-imposed regime change operations since 1816—none of which occurred between great power peers in peacetime. See Alex Downes and Lindsey A. O'Rourke, "You Can't Always Get What You Want," *International Security* 41, no. 2 (2016): 43–89. O'Rourke's data reveal that the United States attempted covert regime change in the Cold War against 54 targets, only 3 of which (France, China, and the USSR) were great powers. See O'Rourke, *Covert Regime Change*. John M. Owen's data show forcible efforts to impose domestic institutions on great power rivals almost exclusively during wars. John M. Owen, "The Foreign Imposition of Domestic Institutions," *International Organization* 56, no. 2 (2002): 375–409. Melissa Lee's cases of subversion via support for armed proxies feature exclusively weak targets. Lee, *Crippling Leviathan*.

## Chapter 2

1. Victoria Hiu, "Toward a Dynamic Theory of International Politics: Insights from Comparing Ancient China and Early Modern Europe," *International Organization* 58, no. 1 (2004): 193, 195.

2. Ilhan Niaz, "Kautilya's *Arthashastra* and Governance as an Element of State Power," *Strategic Studies* 28, nos. 2–3 (2008): 1–17; Christopher Andrew, *The Secret World* (New Haven, CT: Yale University Press, 2018), 60–69.

3. R. Shamasastry, *The Arthashastra* (New Delhi: Penguin, 1992), 689–93, 13.1.21; see also K. S. Vishnu Prabhu, "Kautilya's Views on Espionage and Its Current Relevance," *Research on Humanities and Social Sciences* 5, no. 7 (2015), http://www.iiste.org, ISSN (Paper) 2224-5766; ISSN (Online) 2225-0484.

4. Dan Reiter, "Gulliver Unleashed? International Order, Restraint, and the Case of Ancient Athens," *International Studies Quarterly* 65, no. 3 (September 2021): 582–93.

5. Arthur M. Eckstein, *Mediterranean Anarchy, Interstate War, and the Rise of Rome* (Berkeley: University of California Press, 2006), 150.

6. André Gerolymatos, *Espionage and Treason in Classical Greece: Ancient Spies and Lies* (New York: Lexington Books, 2019), 14.

7. For examples, see Thucydides, *History of the Peloponnesian War*, Trans. Rex Warner (London: Penguin, 1972), 1.24–26 (Epidamnus), 1.113 (Boeotia), 3.34 (Colophon), 4.52 (exiles from Lesbos), 4.66–74 (Megara), 4.75 (exiles from Samos), etc. Special thanks to Professor Hugh Bowden of King's College London for these references and helpful comments.

8. Thucydides, *History of the Peloponnesian War*, 1.115.

9. Gerolymatos, *Espionage*, 49; M. Cary, "Arthmius of Zeleia," *The Classical Quarterly* 29, nos. 3–4 (July–October 1935): 177–80, http://www.jstor.org/stable/636610.

10. Thucydides, *History of the Peloponnesian War*, 8.80.2.

11. Gerolymatos, *Espionage*, 46.

12. Graham Allison, "Thucydides' trap has been sprung in the Pacific," *Financial Times*, August 21, 2012; Graham Allison, *Destined for War: Can America and China Escape Thucydides's Trap?* (New York: Mariner Books, 2017).

13. Thucydides, *History of the Peloponnesian War*, 1.95.

14. Thucydides, *History of the Peloponnesian War*, 1.92.1.

15. Thucydides, *History of the Peloponnesian War*, 1.101.

16. Thucydides, *History of the Peloponnesian War*, 1.101.

17. Donald Kagan, *The Peloponnesian War: Athens and Sparta in Savage Conflict, 431–404 BC* (New York: HarperCollins, 2003), 3.

18. Xenophon, *Hellenica*, trans. Carleton L. Brownson (Cambridge, MA: Harvard University Press, 1921), 3.3.6.

19. Thucydides, *History of the Peloponnesian War*, 4.80.

20. Kagan, *The Peloponnesian War*, 14.

21. Thucydides, *History of the Peloponnesian War*, 1.102.

22. Thucydides, *History of the Peloponnesian War*, 4.55.1.

23. Robert D. Luginbill, "Cimon and Athenian Aid to Sparta: One Expedition or Two?" *Rheinisches Museum für Philologie* 159, no. 2 (2016): 139, http://www.jstor.org/stable/26315588; Aristophanes, *The Lysistrata*, trans. Benjamin Bickley Rogers (London: Heinemann, 1924), 1137–46.

24. Richard Ned Lebow, "Play It Again, Pericles: Agents, Structures, and the Peloponnesian War," *European Journal of International Relations* 2, no. 2 (1996): 252.

25. Dan Reiter, "Gulliver Unleashed?"

26. For background, see David Stuttard, *Nemesis: Alcibiades and the Fall of Athens* (Cambridge, MA: Harvard University Press, 2018).

27. Plutarch, "The Life of Alcibiades," in *Lives, Volume IV: Alcibiades and Coriolanus. Lysander and Sulla*, trans. Bernadotte Perrin (Loeb Classical Library 80; Cambridge, MA: Harvard University Press, 1916), Chapter 25.

28. Thucydides, *History of the Peloponnesian War*, 8.63.

29. Thucydides, *History of the Peloponnesian War*, 8.73. See also Donald Kagan, *The Fall of the Athenian Empire* (Ithaca, NY: Cornell University Press, 1987), 170, http://www.jstor.org/stable/10.7591/j.ctt1xx58s.

30. Kagan, *The Fall*, 59.
31. Xenophon, *Hellenica*, 1.3.16.
32. Lionel Pearson, "Propaganda in the Archidamian War," *Classical Philology* 31, no. 1 (1936): 33–52.
33. George Cawkwell, *Philip of Macedon* (London: Faber & Faber, 1978), 85.
34. Demosthenes, *Speeches*, trans. J. H. Vince et al. (Cambridge, MA: Harvard University Press, 1939), 18.48.
35. Demosthenes, *Speeches*, 18.19.
36. Cawkwell, *Philip of Macedon*, 86.
37. Diodorus Siculus, *Diodorus of Sicily in Twelve Volumes*, Vols. 4–8, trans. C. H. Oldfather (Cambridge, MA: Harvard University Press, 1989), 16.37.4.
38. William Smith, ed., *A Dictionary of Greek and Roman Biography and Mythology* (Ann Arbor: University of Michigan Library, 2005), 18, http://www.perseus.tufts.edu/hopper/text?doc=Perseus%3Atext%3A1999.04.0104%3Aalphabetic+letter%3DP%3Aentry+group%3D18%3Aentry%3Dphalaecus-bio-2.
39. Cawkwell, *Philip of Macedon*, 109.
40. "Pro-Macedonian" refers to support for peace with Philip.
41. Minor Markle, "The Strategy of Philip in 346 B.C.," *The Classical Quarterly* 24, no. 2 (1974): 263.
42. Donald Kagan, "Philip of Macedon: Twilight of the Polis in Ancient Greece," Lecture, December 6, 2007, published on Brewminate, January 29, 2017, https://brewminate.com/philip-of-macedon-twilight-of-the-polis-in-ancient-greece.
43. Cawkwell, *Philip of Macedon*, 126.
44. Demosthenes, *Speeches*, 3.156, 173, 239, 240.
45. Charles Darwin Adams, ed., *The Speeches of Aeschines* (London: Heinemann, 1919), xvi–xvii.
46. Andrew, *The Secret World*, 45.
47. Eckstein, *Mediterranean Anarchy*, 147.
48. Eckstein, *Mediterranean Anarchy*, 157.
49. Eckstein, *Mediterranean Anarchy*, 158.
50. Eckstein, *Mediterranean Anarchy*, 171.
51. Ernst Badian, "Rome, Athens and Mithridates," *American Journal of Ancient History* (1976): 105, et seq. ISSN 0362-8914.

## Chapter 3

1. Edward N. Luttwak, *The Grand Strategy of the Byzantine Empire* (Cambridge, MA: Belknap, 2009).
2. Paul Kennedy, *The Rise and Fall of the Great Powers: Economic Change and Military Conflict from 1500 to 2000* (New York: Random House, 1987), 16.
3. Edward Louis Keenan, Jr., "Muscovy and Kazan: Some Introductory Remarks on the Patterns of Steppe Diplomacy," *Slavic Review* 26, no. 4 (1967): 548–58.

4. Kennedy, *The Rise and Fall*, 15.

5. Kenneth M. Swope, *The Military Collapse of China's Ming Dynasty, 1618–1644* (Abingdon, UK: Routledge, 2014).

6. Geoffrey Parker, *The Grand Strategy of Philip II* (New Haven, CT: Yale University Press, 1998), 147.

7. Parker, *The Grand Strategy*, 3.

8. Marc Trachtenberg, *History and Strategy* (Princeton, NJ: Princeton University Press, 1991), 64–65.

9. The strategy sometimes required the sacrifice of religious principles for realpolitik. In 1542, the Catholic French allied with the Ottoman Turks to attack Habsburg-held Nice. In 1552, French armies moved into Germany in support of the Protestant princes, again to prevent Habsburg gains. Henry III of France (a Catholic) supported Dutch rebels (who were Protestant) against Philip, until it became expedient for Henry to switch sides. Henry of Navare famously became Henry IV of France and converted from Calvinism to Catholicism in 1593 because "Paris is well worth a mass." Parker, *The Grand Strategy*, 108.

10. Parker, *The Grand Strategy*, 8; original quote from AGS Estado (Archivo General de Simancas, Negociación de Estado) 1239/51, marquis of Ayamonte to Philip II, June 16, 1574.

11. Parker, *The Grand Strategy*, 148–49.

12. Kennedy, *The Rise and Fall*, 60.

13. Parker, *The Grand Strategy*, 152.

14. Parker, *The Grand Strategy*, 153.

15. Matthew L. Lubin, "International Aspects of the Ridolfi Plot," Undergraduate Diss., Dartmouth College, January 1, 1997, 6; J. B. Black, *The Reign of Elizabeth 1558–1603* (Oxford, UK: Clarendon Press, 1959), 161.

16. Parker, *The Grand Strategy*, 154.

17. Parker, *The Grand Strategy*, 156–57.

18. Parker, *The Grand Strategy*, 154.

19. Marian Sugden and Ernest Frankl, *Yorkshire Moors and Dales* (Cambridge, UK: Pevensey Press, 1987).

20. Black, *The Reign of Elizabeth*, 166–205.

21. Aislinn Muller, "Transmitting and Translating the Excommunication of Elizabeth I," *Studies in Church History* 53 (2017): 210–22.

22. Muller, "Transmitting," 213.

23. Lubin, "International Aspects of the Ridolfi Plot," 6; Black, *The Reign of Elizabeth*, 169.

24. Mauricio Drelichman and Hans-Joachim Voth, "The Sustainable Debts of Philip II: A Reconstruction of Castile's Fiscal Position, 1566–1596," *Journal of Economic History* 70, no. 4 (2010): 813–42, http://www.jstor.org/stable/40984779.

25. Wallace T. MacCaffrey, *Queen Elizabeth and the Making of Policy, 1572–1588* (Princeton, NJ: Princeton University Press, 1981), 228.

26. Similar English colleges were established at Rome (1579), Valladolid (1589), Seville (1592), and Lisbon (1628).

27. Thomas M. McCoog, S. J., *The Society of Jesus in Ireland, Scotland and England, 1589–1597: Building the Faith of St. Peter upon the King of Spain's Monarchy* (Farnham, UK/Rome: Ashgate/Institutum Historicum Societatis Iesu, 2012), 5–7; Gerard Kilroy, *Edmund Campion: A Scholarly Life* (Farnham, UK: Ashgate, 2015), 171, 176–78, and 191–92; Robert E. Scully, S. J., *Into the Lion's Den: The Jesuit Mission in Elizabethan England and Wales, 1580–1603* (St. Louis. MO: Institute of Jesuit Sources, 2011), 79–81.

28. K. J. Maitland, "People-Smuggling in Tudor and Jacobean Times," April 1, 2021, https://www.historiamag.com/people-smuggling-in-tudor-and-jacobean-times.

29. Maitland, "People-Smuggling."

30. Michael David Lane, " 'Of Whims and Fancies': A Study of English Recusants Under Elizabeth, 1570–1595," Master's Diss., Louisiana State University (2015), 6, https://digitalcommons.lsu.edu/gradschool_theses/4240.

## Chapter 4

1. Ole Feldbæk, "The Foreign Policy of Tsar Paul I, 1800–1801: An Interpretation," *Jahrbücher für Geschichte Osteuropas* 30, no. 1 (1982): 16–36.

2. David Schimmelpenninck van der Oye, "Paul's Great Game: Russia's Plan to Invade British India," *Central Asian Survey* 33, no. 2 (2014): 143–52; 146.

3. James J. Kenney, Jr., "Lord Whitworth and the Conspiracy Against Tsar Paul I: The New Evidence of the Kent Archive," *Slavic Review* 36, no. 2 (1977): 205–19.

4. Kenney, "Lord Whitworth," 210.

5. Kenney, "Lord Whitworth," 210.

6. Kenney, "Lord Whitworth," 205–6.

7. Kenney, "Lord Whitworth," 216.

8. Schimmelpenninck van der Oye, "Paul's Great Game," 147.

9. Ю А. Сорокин, "Заговор и цареубийство 11 марта 1801 года," *Вопросы истории*, no. 4 (2006): 15–29.

10. Надежда Владимировна Коршунова, "Цареубийство 11 марта 1801 г.: свои или чужие?" *УДК* 94, 2016, no. 47: 71.

11. Albert Resis, "Russophobia and the 'Testament' of Peter the Great, 1812–1980," *Slavic Review* 44, no. 4 (1985): 681–93.

12. This tale is told with colorful detail by Schimmelpenninck van der Oye, "Paul's Great Game."

13. Holly Case, *The Age of Questions: Or, A First Attempt at an Aggregate History of the Eastern, Social, Woman, American, Jewish, Polish, Bullion, Tuberculosis, and Many Other Questions over the Nineteenth Century, and Beyond* (Princeton, NJ: Princeton University Press, 2018).

14. Case, *The Age of Questions*, 48.

15. Hermann Wentler, *Zerstörung der Großmacht Russland? Die britischen Kriegsziele im Krimkrieg* (Göttingen, Germany: Vandenhoeck & Ruprecht, 1993).

16. W. E. Mosse, "England and the Polish Insurrection of 1863," *English Historical Review* 71, no. 278 (1956): 35.

17. Quoted in Case, *The Age of Questions*, 104.

18. Veniamin Ciobanu, "International reactions to the Russian Suppression of the Polish Insurrection," *Romanian Journal for Baltic and Nordic Studies* 5, no. 1 (2013): 92.

19. A. J. P. Taylor, *The Struggle for Mastery of Europe: 1848–1918*, Reissue ed. (Oxford, UK: Oxford University Press, 1980), 10.

20. Case, *The Age of Questions*, 104.

21. Taylor, *The Struggle*, 10.

22. Mosse, "England and the Polish Insurrection," 52.

23. Mosse, "England and the Polish Insurrection," 53.

24. Donald Quataert, *The Ottoman Empire: 1700–1922*, 2nd ed. (New York: Cambridge University Press, 2005), 56.

25. Patrick Balfour, Lord Kinross, *The Ottoman Centuries: The Rise and Fall of the Turkish Empire* (New York: Perennial, 1979), 510.

26. Technically, seeking to secure the Ottomans against further Russian encroachment, the British and French tried to upgrade the Porte to great power status after the Crimean War, but subsequent events revealed the difference between a real and declaratory great power.

27. A. L. Macfie, *The Eastern Question 1774–1923*, 2nd ed., rev. (London: Routledge, 2014); M. S. Anderson, *The Eastern Question 1774– 1923: A Study in International Relations* (New York: Macmillan, 1966).

28. James Stone, "Religion, Rivalry or Regime Change? Bismarck, Arnim and the Pastoral Letters Crisis of 1873/4," unpublished manuscript (n.d.).

29. Bismarck to William I. June 1873. Frankreich. 78/2. PAAA. NFA. Vol. 1, 534–37. See James Stone, *The War Scare of 1875—Bismarck and Europe in the Mid-1870s* (Stuttgart, Germany: Steiner, 2010), 69.

30. James Stone, "Bismarck and the Containment of France, 1873–1877," *Canadian Journal of History* 29, no. 2 (1994): 281–304.

31. George T. Kurian, *World Press Encyclopedia* (New York: Facts on File, 1982), 342.

32. Allan Mitchell, *The German Influence in France After 1870: The Formation of the French Republic* (Chapel Hill: University of North Carolina Press, 1979), 162.

33. Mitchell, *The German Influence*, 146.

34. Report by Stolberg to the Foreign Office, August 4, 1877. No. 288. R6486. Frankreich 79. Politisches Archiv des Auswärtigen Amtes. Stolberg. Courtesy of Dr. James Stone.

35. James Stone, "Bismarck ante Portas! Germany and the Seize Mai Crisis of 1877," *Diplomacy & Statecraft* 23, no. 2 (2012): 232.

36. Friedrich von Holstein, *The Holstein Papers: Volume 3, Correspondence 1861–1896: The Memoirs, Diaries and Correspondence of Friedrich von Holstein 1837–1909*, eds. Norman Rich and M. H. Fisher (Cambridge, UK: Cambridge University Press, 1961), 131.

37. James Stone, "Bismarck Versus Gladstone: Regime Change and German Foreign Policy, 1880–1885," *Historische Mitteilungen Der Ranke-Gesellschaft* 23 (2010): 167–200.

38. Paul Kennedy, *The Rise of the Anglo-German Antagonism, 1860–1914* (London: Allen & Unwin, 1980), 166.

39. Kennedy, *The Rise of the Anglo-German Antagonism*, 166.

40. David Stafford, "A Moral Tale: Anglo-German Relations, 1860–1914," *International History Review* 4, no. 2 (1982): 250, http://www.jstor.org/stable/40105201.

41. Vikram Doctor, "First Crimean War: The Indian Connection & Parallels with Current Crimea Conflict," *The Economic Times* (March 9, 2014), https://economictimes.indiatimes.com/news/politics-and-nation/first-crimean-war-the-indian-connection-parallels-with-current-crimea-conflict/articleshow/31683664.cms?utm_source=contentofinterest&utm_medium=text&utm_campaign=cppst.

42. Robert Noell von der Nahmer, *Bismarcks Reptilienfonds: Aus den Geheimakten Preussens und des Deutschen Reiches* (Wiesbaden: v. Hase & Koehler, 1968), 116–118; 186.

## Chapter 5

1. Terry Martin, "The Origins of Soviet Ethnic Cleansing," *Journal of Modern History* 70, no. 4 (1998): 813–61.

2. See, e.g., Hiroaki Kuromiya and Georgres Mamoulia, "Anti-Russian and Anti-Soviet Subversion: The Caucasian–Japanese Nexus, 1904–1945," *Europe-Asia Studies* 61, no. 8 (2009): 1415–40.

3. Claudia Baldoli, *Exporting Fascism: Italian Fascists and Britain's Italians in the 1930s* (Oxford, UK: Oxford University Press, 2003).

4. Bradley W. Hart, *Hitler's American Friends: The Third Reich's Supporters in the United States* (New York: St. Martin's Press, 2018).

5. Tim Tate, *Hitler's Secret Army: A Hidden History of Spies, Saboteurs, and Traitors* (London: Pegasus, 2019).

6. Sander A. Diamond, *The Nazi Movement in the United States 1924–1941* (Ithaca, NY: Cornell University Press, 1974), Chapter 5.

7. Henry Hemming, *Our Man in New York: The Plot to Bring America into the Second World War* (London: Quercus, 2019).

8. Beverley Gage, *G-Man: J. Edgar Hoover and the Making of the American Century* (New York: Simon & Schuster, 2022), Chapter 22.

9. Baldoli, *Exporting Fascism*.

10. Gary Love, " 'What's the Big Idea?' Oswald Mosley, the British Union of Fascists and Generic Fascism," *Journal of Contemporary History* 42, no. 3 (2007): 455.

11. Fridrikh I. Firsov, Harvey Klehr, and John Earl Haynes, *Secret Cables of the Comintern, 1933–1943* (New Haven, CT: Yale University Press, 2014).

12. Marc Lazar, "The French Communist Party," in *The Cambridge History of Communism*, Vol. 2, eds. Norman Naimark, Silvio Pons, and Sophie Quinn-Judge (Cambridge, UK: Cambridge University Press, 2017), 619–641.

13. See Stephen Kotkin, *Stalin, Vol. II: Waiting for Hitler, 1929–1941* (New York: Penguin, 2017); Jonathan Haslam, *The Spectre of War: International Communism and the Origins of World War II* (Princeton, NJ: Princeton University Press, 2021), Chapter 8.

14. Kotkin, *Stalin*, Part III.

15. Haslam, *The Spectre of War*, 381 and Chapters 3 and 5.

16. Firsov, Klehr, and Haynes, *Secret Cables*, Chapter 3.

17. See especially Christian F. Ostermann, *Between Containment and Rollback: The United States and the Cold War in Germany* (Stanford, CA: Stanford University Press, 2021); Gregory Mitrovich, *Undermining the Kremlin: America's Strategy to Subvert the Soviet Bloc, 1947–1956* (Ithaca, NY: Cornell University Press, 2000).

18. Silvio Pons, "Stalin, Togliatti, and the Origins of the Cold War in Europe," *Journal of Cold War Studies* 3, no. 2 (2001): 19.

19. Silvio Pons, *The Global Revolution: A History of International Communism 1917–1991* (New York: Oxford University Press, 2014), Chapter 4.

20. Marie-Catherine Villatoux, "The Fight Against Subversion in France in the Forties and Fifties," *Dans Inflexions* 14, no. 2 (2010): 167.

21. Trachtenberg, "Soviet Policy in 1945: Some Research Notes" (UCLA Department of Political Science, n.d.) walks through sources and sifts the evidence for this from recent studies of Soviet policy in Germany; Ostermann, *Between Containment and Rollback*, tracks the twists and turns in the policy from 1945 to 1953.

22. Harvey Klehr, John Earle Haynes, and F. I. Firsov, *The Secret World of American Communism* (New Haven, CT: Yale University Press, 1995); Andrew Thorpe, *The British Communist Party and Moscow, 1920–43* (Manchester, UK: Manchester University Press, 2000).

23. Benn Steil, *The World That Wasn't: Henry Wallace and the Fate of the American Century* (New York: Avid Reader Press, 2024), Chapter 15.

24. Quoted in Steil, *The World That Wasn't*, 461.

25. Evan Mawdsley, "Anti-German Insurgency and Allied Grand Strategy," *Journal of Strategic Studies* 31, no. 5 (2008): 695–719.

26. National Security Council, "NSC 20/4 Note by the Executive Secretary on U.S. Objectives with Respect to the USSR to Counter Soviet Threats to U.S. Security, November 23, 1948," Document 60 in *Foreign Relations of the United States, 1948, General; the United Nations, Volume I, Part 2*, eds. Neal H. Petersen et al. (Washington, DC: U.S. Government Printing Office, 1976), https://history.state.gov/historicaldocuments/frus1948v01p2/d60.

27. See especially Jeffrey Burds, "The Early Cold War in Soviet West Ukraine, 1944–1948," *The Carl Beck Papers in Russian and East European Studies*, no. 1505 (2001): 73, https://doi.org/10.5195/cbp.2001.116; and the declassified CIA historical account by Kevin C. Ruffrer, "Cold War Allies: The Origins of CIA's Relationship with Ukrainian Nationalists," in *50 Years of the CIA*, eds. Michael Warner and Scott A. Koch (Washington, DC: Center for the Study of Intelligence, 1998), 19–43. For estimates of the size of insurgencies, see Alexander Statiev, *The Soviet Counterinsurgency in the Western Borderlands* (Cambridge, UK: Cambridge University Press, 2010); Melissa Willard-Foster, *Toppling Foreign Governments: The Logic of Regime Change* (Philadelphia: University of Pennsylvania Press, 2018).

28. Harry Rositzke, "America's Secret Operations: A Perspective," *Foreign Affairs* 53, no. 2 (1975): 336.

29. Calder Walton, *Spies: The Epic Intelligence War Between East and West* (London: Hatchette, 2023), 214.

30. Peter Grose, *Rollback: America's Secret War Behind the Iron Curtain* (New York: Houghton Mifflin, 2000), 187.

31. Ruffrer, "Cold War Allies," 43.

32. Sarah Jane Corke, "George Kennan and the Inauguration of Political Warfare," *Journal of Conflict Studies* 26, no. 1 (2006), https://journals.lib.unb.ca/index.php/JCS/article/view/2171; Sarah Jane Corke, *U.S. Covert Operations and Cold War Strategy: Truman, Secret Warfare, and the CIA, 1945–53* (London: Routledge, 2008); Stephen J. K. Long, "Strategic Disorder, the Office of Policy Coordination and the Inauguration of US Political Warfare Against the Soviet Bloc, 1948–50," *Intelligence and National Security* 27, no. 4 (2012): 459–87; Scott Lucas and Kaeten Mistry, "Illusions of Coherence: George F. Kennan, U.S. Strategy and Political Warfare in the Early Cold War, 1946–1950," *Diplomatic History* 33, no. 1 (2009): 39–66; Benjamin Tromly, *Cold War Exiles and the CIA—Plotting to Free Russia* (New York: Oxford University Press, 2019); Rory Cormac, "The Pinprick Approach: Whitehall's Top-Secret Anti-Communist Committee and the Evolution of British Covert Action Strategy," *Journal of Cold War Studies* 16, no. 3 (2014): 5–28.

33. Quoted in Walton, *Spies*, 216.

34. Statiev, *The Soviet Counterinsurgency*; Pavlo Savchenko, "The Insurgent Movement in Ukraine During the 1940s and 1950s: Lessons Learned from the Case Study of the Ukrainian Insurgent Army (OUN-UP)," thesis presented to the faculty of the U.S. Army Command and General Staff College, Fort Leavenworth, Kansas, 2012.

35. "A Review of NSC Policy Toward the Soviet Union Emphasizing US Policy on the Exploitation of Soviet Vulnerabilities," quoted in Corke, *U.S. Covert Operations and Cold War Strategy*, 91.

36. Quotes from NSC 5502/1 "Statement of Policy on US Policy Toward Russian Anti-Soviet Political Activities," January 31, 1955, and NSC 5505/1 "Exploitation of Soviet Vulnerabilities," January 31, 1955, in *Foreign Relations of the United States, 1955–1957, Vol. XXIV, Soviet Union and Eastern Mediterranean*, eds. Ronald D. Landa, Aaron D. Miller, and Charles S. Sampson (Washington, DC: U.S. Government Printing Office, 1989), 16–21.

37. Quoted in Grose, *Rollback*, 98.

38. See John Delury, *Agents of Subversion: The Fate of John T. Downey and the CIA's Covert War in China* (Ithaca, NY: Cornell University Press, 2022); Kenneth Conboy and James Morrison, *The CIA's Secret War in Tibet* (Lawrence: University Press of Kansas, 2011).

39. Ostermann, *Between Containment and Rollback*, Chapter 9.

40. On the ongoing arms-length support for Ukrainian nationalism, see David C. S. Albanese, "'It Takes a Russian to Beat a Russian': The National Union of Labor Solidarists, Nationalism, and Human Intelligence Operations in the Cold War," *Intelligence and National Security* 32, no. 6 (2017): 782–96; David C. S. Albanese, "In Search of a Lesser Evil: Anti-Soviet Nationalism and the Cold War," PhD Diss., Northeastern University, 2015, https://doi.org/10.17760/D20194401; Taras Kuzio, "U.S. Support for Ukraine's Liberation During the Cold War: A Study of Prolog Research and Publishing Corporation," *Communist and Post-Communist Studies* 45, nos. 1–2 (2012): 51–64. For assessments of the radio broadcasts, see A. Ross Johnson and R. Eugene Parta, eds., *Cold War Broadcasting: Impact on the Soviet Union and Eastern Europe: A Collection of Studies and Documents* (Budapest, Hungary: Central European University Press, 2010); Richard H. Cummings, *Cold War Frequencies: CIA Clandestine Radio Broadcasting to the Soviet Union and Eastern Europe* (Jefferson, NC: McFarland, 2021); Michael Nelson, *War of the Black Heavens: The Battles of Western Broadcasting in the Cold War* (Syracuse, NY: Syracuse University Press, 1997); Eugene R. Parta, *Discovering the Hidden Listener: An Assessment of Radio Liberty and Western Broadcasting to the USSR During the Cold War: A Study Based on Audience Research Findings, 1970–1991* (Stanford, CA: Hoover Institution Press, 2007); Ralph A. Uttaro, "The Voices of America in International Radio Propaganda," *Law and Contemporary Problems* 45 (1982): 103–22, https://scholarship.law.duke.edu/lcp/vol45/iss1/6; V. K. Lehtoranta, "Jamming, or Deliberate Interference Against Radio Broadcasting Stations," *Radiomaailma Magazine*, August 1999, https://www.voacap.com/documents/jamming_radio_broadcasting_VKL.pdf; Rimantas Pleikys, "Radio Jamming in the Soviet Union, Poland and Other East European Countries," *Atentop*, January 2006, http://www.antentop.org/008/jamm008.htm; Audra Wolfe, "Project Troy: How Scientists Helped Refine Cold War Psychological Warfare," *The Atlantic*, December 1, 2018, https://www.theatlantic.com/science/archive/2018/12/project-troy-science-cold-war-psychological-warfare/576847; Allan A. Needell, "'Truth Is Our Weapon': Project TROY, Political Warfare, and Government–Academic

Relations in the National Security State," *Diplomatic History* 17, no. 3 (1993): 399–420.

41. See Steve Coll, *Ghost Wars: The Secret History of the CIA, Afghanistan and Bin Laden* (New York: Penguin, 2004), 104–5.

42. Ostermann, *Between Containment and Rollback*, 141.

43. Mitrovich, *Undermining the Kremlin*, 21.

44. The CIA's role was exposed in a 1967 article in *Ramparts* magazine; by the mid-1970s, the State Department picked up the tab. Cummings, *Cold War Frequencies*, Chapter 3.

45. "Memorandum from the President's Assistant for National Security Affairs (Kissinger) to President Nixon," in *Foreign Relations of the United States, 1969–1976, Volume XII, Soviet Union, January 1969–October 1970*, ed. Erin R. Mahan (Washington, DC: U.S. Government Printing Office, 2002), https://history.state.gov/historicaldocuments/frus1969-76v12, Document 149.

46. Richard H. Cummings, *Cold War Radio: The Dangerous History of American Broadcasting in Europe, 1950–1989* (Jefferson, NC: McFarland, 2009), Chapters 1–3.

47. "'Every Story That We Covered Was a Test': James Critchlow on the Creation of Radio Liberty," Radio Free Europe/Radio Liberty interview with James Critchlow, undated, https://about.rferl.org/article/every-story-that-we-covered-was-a-test-james-critchlow-on-the-creation-of-radio-liberty/.

48. "Memorandum from the President's Assistant for National Security Affairs (Kissinger) to President Nixon," *Foreign Relations of the United States, 1969–1976, Volume XII*.

49. Stanislav Lunev, with Ira Winkler, *Through the Eyes of the Enemy: Russia's Highest Ranking Military Defector Reveals Why Russia Is More Dangerous Than Ever* (Washington, DC: Regnery, 1998); James Slate, "How the Soviet Union Helped Shape the Modern Peace Movement," *Medium*, January 29, 2018, https://jameslate.medium.com/how-the-soviet-union-helped-shape-the-modern-peace-movement-d797071d4b2c.; On U.S. and UK estimates, see Walton, *Spies*, 424–25.

50. Best source: Geoffrey Roberts, "Averting Armageddon: The Communist Peace Movement, 1948–1956," in *The Oxford Handbook of the History of Communism*, ed. Stephen A. Smith (New York: Oxford University Press, 2013), 322–38. See also William Styles, "The World Federation of Scientific Workers, a Case Study of a Soviet Front Organisation: 1946–1964," *Intelligence and National Security* 33, no. 1 (2018): 116–29.

51. Roberts, "Averting Armageddon."

52. John Vinocour, "KGB Officers Try to Infiltrate Anti-War Groups," *The New York Times*, July 26, 1983, A1, https://www.nytimes.com/1983/07/26/world/kgb-officers-try-to-infiltrate-antiwar-groups.html.

53. Lee Ferran, "Inside a '$100 Million' Russian Propaganda Operation, 40 Years Ago," InsideHook, March 23, 2018, https://www.insidehook.com/article/military/jimmy-carter-neutron-bomb-russia.

54. Robert M. Gates, *From the Shadows* (New York: Simon & Schuster, 2007), 260.

55. Mark Kramer, "The Soviet Roots of Meddling in U.S. Politics," PONARS Eurasia Policy Memo no. 452, January 2017. See, in particular, Thomas Rid, *Active Measures: The Secret History of Disinformation and Political Warfare* (New York: Macmillan, 2020).

56. Fletcher Schoen and Christopher J. Lamb, *Deception, Disinformation, and Strategic Communications: How One Interagency Group Made a Major Difference* (Washington, DC: Institute for National Security Studies, National Defense University Press, 2012).

57. Walton, *Spies*, 425.

58. Christopher Andrew and Vasiliy Mitrokhnn, *The Sword and the Shield* (New York: Basic Books, 1999).

59. The definitive account is the nearly book-length work by Douglas Selvage, "Operation 'Denver': The East German Ministry of State Security and the KGB's AIDS Disinformation Campaign, 1985–1986, Part 1," *Journal of Cold War Studies* 21, no. 4 (2019): 71–123; and Douglas Selvage, "Operation 'Denver': The East German Ministry for State Security and the KGB's AIDS Disinformation Campaign, 1986–1989, Part 2," *Journal of Cold War Studies* 23, no. 3 (2021): 4–80.

60. Vladislav Zubok, *Failed Empire* (Chapel Hill: University of North Carolina Press, 2009).

61. See Selvage, "Operation 'Denver,' Part 2," 11–14.

62. Quoted in Selvage, "Operation 'Denver,' Part 1," 78.

63. Douglas Selvage and Christopher Nehring, "Operation 'Denver': KGB and Stasi Disinformation Regarding AIDS," Wilson Center, July 22, 2019, https://www.wilsoncenter.org/blog-post/operation-denver-kgb-and-stasi-dis information-regarding-aids.

64. "Wuhan Lab Leak Theory: How Fort Detrick Became a Center for Chinese Conspiracies," BBC News, August 23, 2021, https://www.bbc.co.uk/news/ world-us-canada-58273322. For more on domestic effects of AIDS libel, see Jacob Heller, "Rumors and Realities: Making Sense of HIV/AIDS Conspiracy Narratives and Contemporary Legends," *American Journal of Public Health* 105, no. 1 (2015): e43–e50.

65. Gus W. Weiss, "The Farewell Dossier: Duping the Soviets," *Studies in Intelligence* 39, no. 5: 121–26.

66. See David S. Painter, "Energy and the End of the Evil Empire," in *The Reagan Moment: America and the World in the 1980s*, eds. Jonathan R. Hunt and Simon Miles (Ithaca, NY: Cornell University Press, 2021), 43–63; Thomas Rid, "Cyber War Will Not Take Place," *Journal of Strategic Studies* 35, no. 1 (2012): 10–12.

67. Quoted in Walton, *Spies*, 425.

68. Seth G. Jones, "Russian Meddling in the United States: The Historical Context of the Mueller Report," CSIS Brief, March 27, 2019,

https://www.csis.org/analysis/russian-meddling-united-states-historical-cont
ext-mueller-report.

69. Email from John Lenczowski, July 31, 23.

70. See, in particular, Schoen and Lamb, *Deception, Disinformation, and Strategic Communications.*

71. See Schoen and Lamb, *Deception, Disinformation, and Strategic Communications.*

72. Ibid., 104.

73. Schoen and Lamb, *Deception, Disinformation, and Strategic Communications*, 6; Selvage, "Operation 'Denver,' Part 2," 12–14.

74. Schoen and Lamb, *Deception, Disinformation, and Strategic Communications*, 102 ff.

75. *Foreign Relations of the United States, 1981–1988, Volume VI, Soviet Union, October 1986–January 1989*, ed. James Graham Wilson (Washington, DC: U.S. Government Printing Office, 2016), https://history.state.gov/hist oricaldocuments/frus1981-88v06, Document 93.

76. Ibid., Document 114.

77. Selvage, "Operation 'Denver,' Part 2," 19–20.

## Chapter 6

1. David Ignatius, "Innocence Abroad: The New World of Spyless Coups," *The Washington Post*, September 22, 1991, https://www.washingtonpost.com/arch ive/opinions/1991/09/22/innocence-abroad-the-new-world-of-spyless-coups/ 92bb989a-de6e-4bb8-99b9-462c76b59a16.

2. M. Pinto-Duschinsky, "Foreign Political Aid: The German Foundations and Their US Counterparts," *International Affairs 67*, no. 1 (1991): 33–63.

3. Historian Robert Pee is the indispensable source. See Robert Pee, "The Rise of Political Aid: The National Endowment for Democracy and the Reagan Administration's Cold War Strategy," in *The Reagan Administration, the Cold War, and the Transition to Democracy Promotion*, eds. Robert Pee and William Michael Schmidli (London: Palgrave, 2019), 51–73; Robert Pee, *Democracy Promotion, National Security and Strategy: Foreign Policy Under the Reagan Administration* (Abingdon, UK: Routledge, 2015); Robert Pee, "Containing Revolution: Democracy Promotion, the Cold War and US National Security," *International Politics* 55 (2018): 693–711.

4. Kate Geoghegan, "A Policy in Tension: The National Endowment for Democracy and the U.S. Response to the Collapse of the Soviet Union," *Diplomatic History* 42, no. 5 (2018): 772–801; Kate Geoghegan, "The Specter of Anarchy, the Hope of Transformation: The Role of Non-State Actors in the U.S. Response to Soviet Reform and Disunion, 1981–1996" (PhD diss., University of Virginia, 2015).

5. Cullen Nutt, "Sooner Is Better: Covert Action to Prevent Realignment" (PhD diss., Massachusetts Institute of Technology, 2019); see also Cullen Nutt, "When the Clever See Danger: U.S. Covert Action in Portugal" (Draft

working paper, Notre Dame Emerging Scholars Conference, n.d.), https://11disc.nd.edu/assets/320705/portugal_for_ndisc_nutt_fnl.pdf. The CIA went so far as to offer arms to Portuguese moderates if the country descended into civil war.

6. Robert M. Gates, *From the Shadows* (New York: Simon & Schuster, 2007), 233–41.

7. Benjamin B. Fischer, "Solidarity, the CIA, and Western Technology," *International Journal of Intelligence and CounterIntelligence* 25, no. 3 (2012): 427–69.

8. Gates, *From The Shadows*, 237.

9. See Francis Fukuyama, "The End of History?" *The National Interest*, no. 16 (1989): 3–18, http://www.jstor.org/stable/24027184.

10. Fletcher Schoen and Christopher J. Lamb, *Deception, Disinformation, and Strategic Communications: How One Interagency Group Made a Major Difference* (Washington, DC: Institute for National Security Studies, National Defense University Press, 2012), 96, https://ndupress.ndu.edu/port als/68/documents/stratperspective/inss/strategic-perspectives-11.pdf.

11. "Democracy Promotion: An Objective of US Foreign Assistance," Congressional Research Service, January 4, 2019, https://sgp.fas.org/crs/row/R44858.pdf.

12. Organization for Security and Co-operation in Europe, "Final Statement of the OSCE/ODIHR Observer Mission," July 5, 1997, https://www.osce.org/files/f/documents/a/9/16282.pdf.

13. David Shimer, *Rigged: America, Russia, and One Hundred Years of Covert Electoral Interference* (London: Collins, 2020), 128.

14. "Democracy Promotion Programs Funded by the US Government: A Report to the Senate Foreign Relations Committee and the House Foreign Affairs Committee of the US Congress," U.S. Agency for International Development, n.d., https://pdf.usaid.gov/pdf_docs/Pcaaa756.pdf.

15. "Democracy Promotion," 2.

16. "Democracy Promotion," fn 30.

17. "Examining the Clinton Record on Democracy Promotion," Carnegie Europe, September 12, 2000, https://carnegieeurope.eu/2000/09/12/examin ing-clinton-record-on-democracy-promotion-event-197; Eric T. Hale, "A Quantitative and Qualitative Evaluation of the National Endowment for Democracy" (PhD diss., Louisiana State University, 2003).

18. U.S. Information Agency, *Soviet Active Measures in the 'Post-Cold War' Era, 1988–1991* (June 1992); Mark Galeotti, "Active Measures: Russia's Covert Geopolitical Operations," *Security Insights*, no. 31, George C. Marshall European Center for Security Studies, June 2019; Eugene Rumer, "Disinformation: A Primer in Russian Active Measures and Influence Campaigns," Testimony before the Senate Select Committee on Intelligence, March 30, 2017, https://www.govinfo.gov/content/pkg/CHRG-115shrg25362/html/CHRG-115shrg25362.htm.

19. Paul J. Springer, ed., *Encyclopedia of Cyber Warfare.* (Santa Barbara, CA: ABC-CLIO, 2017), 185–86; "Hack May Have Exposed Deep US Secrets; Damage yet Unknown," *The Independent*, December 15, 2020, https://www.independent.co.uk/news/hack-may-have-exposed-deep-us-secrets-damage-yet-unknown-hackers-hackers-donald-trump-government-us-b1774648.html.

20. William Zimmerman, *The Russian People and Foreign Policy: Russian Elite and Mass Perspectives* (Princeton, NJ: Princeton University Press, 2002); William C. Wohlforth and Vladislav M. Zubok, "An Abiding Antagonism: Realism, Idealism, and the Mirage of US–Russian Partnership in the End of the Cold War," *International Politics* 54, no. 4 (2017): 405–19.

21. "Osnovnye polizheniia voennoi doktriny Rossiskoi Federatsii," *Izvestiia* (November 19, 1993): 1; the debates on doctrine in "Military Doctrine of the Russian Federation (Russia)," *Voennyi Vestnik* 13–14, nos. 139–40 (1992): 2–34; "Russian Military Doctrine Today in Light of the New Realities," *Zarubezhnaya Voennoie Obozrenie* (1994): 2, as translated and reprinted in JPRS-UFM-94-005.

22. For example, regarding NATO, they were trying to "kill (or at least transform) NATO with kindness." See A. A. Sushentsov and William C. Wohlforth, "The Tragedy of US–Russian Relations: NATO Centrality and the Revisionists' Spiral," *International Politics* 57, no. 3 (2020): 427–50.

23. As one of us emphasized at the time: William C. Wohlforth, "The Stability of a Unipolar World," *International Security* 24, no. 1 (1999): 5–41.

24. Stephen J. Blank, "Threats to Russian Security: The View from Moscow," The Strategic Studies Institute, July 2000, https://press.armywarcollege.edu/monographs/134.

25. Shimer, *Rigged*, 111.

26. Quoted in Shimer, *Rigged*, 111.

27. Former CIA operations officer John Sipher, quoted in Shimer, *Rigged*, 113.

28. Shimer, *Rigged*, 115.

29. See comments of Douglas Wise in Shimer, *Rigged*, 115.

30. "Claim (in 2004, 2015 and 2017): The U.S. Government Supported Chechen Separatism," Russia Matters, accessed October 22, 2023, https://www.russiamatters.org/node/20317.

31. Blank, "Threats to Russian Security."

32. An exhaustive analysis of Putin's claims conducted by the "Russia Matters" project at Harvard's Belfer Center for Science and International Affairs determines that they are "partially correct," mainly because of the official and quasi-official actions discussed in this paragraph. The analysis turns up zero evidence crossing the line to subversion as we define it. "Claim (in 2004, 2015 and 2017): The U.S. Government Supported Chechen Separatism," Russia Matters, accessed October 22, 2023, https://www.russia matt ers.org/node/20317.

33. Jonathan Monten, "The Roots of the Bush Doctrine," *International Security* 29, no. 4 (2005): 112.

34. Monten, "The Roots of the Bush Doctrine," 112.

35. The White House, "The National Security Strategy of the United States of America," September 2002, https://georgewbush-whitehouse.archives.gov/nsc/nss/2002/.

36. Martha Brill Olcott, "Kyrgyzstan's 'Tulip Revolution,'" Carnegie Endowment for International Peace, March 28, 2005, https://carnegieendowment.org/2005/03/28/kyrgyzstan-s-tulip-revolution-pub-16710.

37. Thomas Carothers, "The Backlash Against Democracy Promotion," *Foreign Affairs*, March–April 2006, https://www.foreignaffairs.com/united-states/backlash-against-democracy-promotion.

38. William J. Burns, *The Back Channel* (New York: Random House, 2020), 209.

39. Hillary Rodham Clinton, *Hard Choices* (New York: Simon & Schuster, 2014), 549, 545.

40. Elise Labott, "Clinton Cites 'Serious Concerns' About Russian Election," CNN, December 6, 2011, https://www.cnn.com/2011/12/06/world/europe/russia-elections-clinton/index.html.

41. On Putin believing the United States was involved in intervention against him before the election took place in 2011, see Kathy Lally, "Russia Targets US-Linked Election Monitor," *The Washington Post*, November 30, 2011, https://www.washingtonpost.com/world/europe/russia-targets-us-linked-election-monitor/2011/11/30/gIQAlqzcDO_story.html.

42. See, e.g., Evgeny Finkel and Yitzhak M. Brudny, "Russia and the Colour Revolutions," *Democratization* 19, no. 1 (2012), 15–36; Keith A. Darden, "Russian Revanche: External Threats & Regime Reactions," *Daedelus* 142, no. 2 (2017): 128–41. On the election monitors, see Anton Shekhovtsov, *Russia and the Western Far Right: Tango Noir* (Abingdon, UK: Routledge, 2018), Chapter 4. Beyond the Russian case, see Evgeny Finkel and Yitzhak M. Brudny, "No More Colour! Authoritarian Regimes and Colour Revolutions in Eurasia," *Democratization* 19, no. 1 (2012): 1–14; Alexander Cooley, "Authoritarianism Goes Global: Countering Democratic Norms," *Journal of Democracy* 26, no. 3 (2015): 49–63.

43. Finkel and Brudny, "Russia," 15–36.

44. Keir Giles, "Russia's 'New' Tools for Confronting the West: Continuity and Innovation in Moscow's Exercise of Power," Research paper, Chatham House, March 2016, https://www.chathamhouse.org/2016/03/russias-new-tools-confronting-west-continuity-and-innovation-moscows-exercise-power.

45. Shekhovtsov, *Russia and the Western Far Right*.

46. Valery Gerasimov, "The Value of Science Is in the Foresight: New Challenges Demand Rethinking the Forms and Methods of Carrying out Combat Operations," *Military Review* (January–February 2016): 23–29.

47. Charles K. Bartles, "Getting Gerasimov Right," *Military Review*, January–February 2016, 30–38.

48. Michael Kofman, "Russian Hybrid Warfare and Other Dark Arts," *War on the Rocks*, March 11, 2016, https://warontherocks.com/2016/03/russian-hybrid-warfare-and-other-dark-arts/.

49. Samuel Charap and Timothy J. Colton, *Everyone Loses: The Ukraine Crisis and the Ruinous Contest for Post-Soviet Russia* (Abingdon, UK: Routledge, 2017), 17–18.

50. A document leaked to the Ukrainian press discussed the campaign in detail: see Maschmeyer, "Trilemma," 69.

51. Sanshiro Hosaka, "The Kremlin's Active Measures Failed in 2013: That's When Russia Remembered Its Last Resort—Crimea," *Demokratizatsiya: The Journal of Post-Soviet Democratization* 26, no. 3 (2018): 321–64.

52. Charap and Colton, *Everyone Loses*, 17–18.

53. Anthony Seldon and Peter Snowdon, *Cameron at 10: The Inside Story* (Glasgow, Scotland: Collins, 2016), quoted in Michael Isikoff and David Corn, *Russian Roulette: The Inside Story of Putin's War on America and the Election of Donald Trump* (New York: Twelve, 2018), 48.

54. Jesse Driscoll and Dominique Arel, *Ukraine's Unnamed War: Before the Russian Invasion of 2022* (Cambridge, UK: Cambridge University Press, 2023), Chapters 6 and 7.

55. Quoted in Isikoff and Corn, *Russian Roulette*, 51.

56. Isikoff and Corn, *Russian Roulette*, 46.

57. Isikoff and Corn, *Russian Roulette*, 46.

## Chapter 7

1. Michael Isikoff and David Corn, *Russian Roulette: The Inside Story of Putin's War on America and the Election of Donald Trump* (New York: Twelve, 2018), 52; This was likely the same source who provided details of Putin's role in ordering the operation and who had to be exfiltrated in 2017. Julian E. Barnes, Adam Goldman, and David E. Sanger, "C.I.A. Informant Extracted from Russia Had Sent Secrets to U.S. for Decades," *The New York Times*, September 9, 2019, https://www.nytimes.com/2019/09/09/us/politics/cia-informant-russia.html.

2. Eugene Kondratov and Elisabeth Johansson-Nogués, "Russia's Hybrid Interference Campaigns in France, Germany and the UK: A Challenge Against Trust in Liberal Democracies?" *Geopolitics* (2022): 1–31.

3. Andrei Soldatov and Irina Borogan, "Russian Cyberwarfare: Unpacking the Kremlin's Capabilities," Center for European Policy Analysis, September 8, 2022, https://cepa.org/comprehensive-reports/russian-cyberwarfare-unpacking-the-kremlins-capabilities/.

4. Kondratov and Johansson-Nogués, "Russia's Hybrid Interference."

5. Luke Harding, *Shadow State: Murder, Mayhem, and Russia's Remaking of the West* (London: Guardian Faber, 2020); John Bowden, "UK Intelligence Report Says Russia Meddled in Scottish Independence Referendum," *The Hill*, July 21, 2020, https://thehill.com/policy/national-security/508266-uk-intelligence-report-says-russia-meddled-in-scottish-independence/; Chris McCall, "Russia Meddled in 2014 Scottish Independence Referendum, Explosive New Book Claims," *The Daily Record*, July 6, 2020,

https://www.dailyrecord.co.uk/news/politics/russia-meddled-2014-scottish-independence-22308246.

6. Janosch Delker, "Germany Fears Russia Stole Information to Disrupt Election," *Politico*, March 20, 2017, https://www.politico.eu/article/hacked-information-bomb-under-germanys-election/.

7. Gordon Corera, "How France's TV5 Was Almost Destroyed by 'Russian Hackers,'" BBC, October 10, 2016, https://www.bbc.co.uk/news/technology-37590375#:~:text=A%20powerful%20cyber%2Dattack%20came,Islamic%20St ate%2C%20first%20claimed%20responsibility.

8. "U.S. Department of Justice, Office of Public Affairs, "Russian Project Lakhta Member Charged with Wire Fraud Conspiracy," September 10, 2020, https://www.justice.gov/opa/pr/russian-project-lakhta-member-char ged-wire-fraud-conspiracy, https://www.justice.gov/opa/press-release/file/1315 491/download; Ben Buchanan, *The Hacker and the State: Cyber Attacks and the New Normal of Geopolitics* (Cambridge, MA: Harvard University Press, 2020), 231.

9. Isikoff and Corn, *Russian Roulette*, 203–4.

10. Isikoff and Corn, *Russian Roulette*, 59.

11. Isikoff and Corn, *Russian Roulette*, 60.

12. Adrian Chen, "The Agency," *The New York Times Magazine*, June 2, 2015, https://www.nytimes.com/2015/06/07/magazine/the-agency.html?; Andy Szal, "Report: Russian 'Internet Trolls' Behind Louisiana Chemical Explosion Hoax," Manufacturing.net, https://www.manufacturing.net/ope rations/news/13099148/report-russian-internet-trolls-behind-louisiana-chemi cal-explosion-hoax.

13. Clint Watts, "Statement Prepared for the U.S. Senate Select Committee on Intelligence Hearing 'Disinformation: A Primer in Russian Active Measures and Influence Campaigns,'" March 30, 2017, https://www.intelligence.sen ate.gov/sites/default/files/documents/os-cwatts-033017.pdf.

14. "Report of the Select Committee on Intelligence, United States Senate, on Russian Active Measures Campaigns and Interference in the 2016 U.S. Election, Volume 2: Russia's Use of Social Media with Additional Views," Select Committee on Intelligence, October 2019 (hereinafter SSCI report), 46.

15. Isikoff and Corn, *Russian Roulette*, 204.

16. Darren Samuelsohn, "Facebook: Russian-Linked Accounts Bought $150,000 in Ads During 2016 Race," *Politico*, September 6, 2017, https://www.politico. com/story/2017/09/06/facebook-ads-russia-linked-accounts-242401.

17. Robert Mueller, "Report on the Investigation into Russian Interference in the 2016 Presidential Election," U.S. Department of Justice, 2018, Vol. I, 26.

18. Thomas Rid, *Active Measures: The Secret History of Disinformation and Political Warfare* (New York: Farrar, Strauss & Giroux, 2020), 409.

19. Julia Munslow, "Ex-CIA Director Hayden: Russia Election Meddling Was 'Most Successful Covert Operation in History,'" *Yahoo News*, July 21, 2017, accessed October 22, 2023, https://www.yahoo.com/news/ex-cia-director-hay den-russia-election-meddling-successful-covert-operation-history-212056 443.html.

20. SSCI report, Vol. 3, 5.

21. David Ignatius, "Russia's Radical New Strategy for Information Warfare," *The Washington Post*, January 18, 2017, https://www.washingtonpost.com/ blogs/post-partisan/wp/2017/01/18/russias-radical-new-strategy-for-informat ion-warfare. The quote is from notes taken by a participant.

22. Soldatov and Borogan, "Russian Cyberwarfare."

23. Rid, *Active Measures*, Chapter 28; Buchanan, *The Hacker*, Chapter 10.

24. Rid, *Active Measures*, 385.

25. Buchanan, *The Hacker*, 220.

26. Buchanan, *The Hacker*, 219.

27. Buchanan, *The Hacker*, 221.

28. Buchanan, *The Hacker*, 226.

29. SSCI report, Vol. 1, 6, 22.

30. SSCI report, Vol. 1, 37.

31. Rid, *Active Measures*, Chapter 14.

32. SSCI report, Vol. 5, 170–256.

33. Buchanan, *The Hacker*, 226.

34. Buchanan, *The Hacker*, 227.

35. *United States of America v. Viktor Borisovich Netyksho, et al.* (18 U.S.C. §§ 2, 371, 1030, 1028A, 1956, NETYKSHO, * and 3551 et seq, 7–8), United States District Court for the District of Columbia, July 13, 2018.

36. The felicitous quoted phrase is from Mark Galeotti, "What Exactly Are 'Kremlin Ties'?" *The Atlantic*, July 12, 2017, https://www.theatlantic.com/ international/archive/2017/07/russia-trump-putin-clinton/533370. For more on this, see Stephen Kotkin, "American Hustle: What Mueller Found—and Didn't Find—About Trump and Russia," *Foreign Affairs*, July–August, 2019, https://www.foreignaffairs.com/united-states/american-hustle. Details in SSCI report, Vol. 5, Section III.

37. SSCI report, Vol. 5, vi.

38. SSCI report, Vol. 5, 98. See Jim Rutenberg, "The Untold Story of 'Russiagate' and the Road to War in Ukraine," *The New York Times Magazine*, November 2, 2022, https://www.nytimes.com/2022/11/02/magaz ine/russiagate-paul-manafort-ukraine-war.html.

39. Eric Bradner, "Trump: DNC Hacked Itself," CNN, June 15, 2016, https:// edition.cnn.com/2016/06/15/politics/dnc-hack-donald-trump/index.html.

40. Isikoff and Corn, *Russian Roulette*, 178–79.

41. "Presidential Candidates May Be Vulnerable to Foreign Hackers, US Says," *The Guardian*, May 18, 2016, https://www.theguardian.com/us-news/2016/ may/18/presidential-candidates-hacking-spying-trump-clinton.

42. Isikoff and Corn, *Russian Roulette*, 181.

43. Buchanan, *The Hacker*, 1.

44. Rid, *Active Measures*, Chapter 31; Buchanan, *The Hacker*, Chapter 11.

45. Buchanan, *The Hacker*, 246.

46. Isikoff and Corn, *Russian Roulette*, 195–96.

47. SSCI report, Vol. 3, 26.

48. David Corn and Michael Isikoff, "'Why the Hell Are We Standing Down?' The Secret Story of Obama's Response to Putin's Attack on the 2016 Election," *Mother Jones*, March 9, 2018, https://www.motherjones.com/polit ics/2018/03/why-the-hell-are-we-standing-down.

49. SSCI report, Vol. 2, 47; see also *United States of America v. Viktor Borisovich Netyksho, et al.*

50. On the IC's challenges in coming up to speed on the hack, see SSCI report, Vol. 3, 6–8, and Vol. 5, 822–45.

51. Director Clapper told the Senate Intelligence Committee, "I don't think we would have mounted the effort we did, probably, to be honest, in the absence of presidential direction, because that kind of cleared the way on sharing all the accesses." SSCI report, Vol. 4, 26.

52. See SSCI report, Vol. 3.

53. David Shimer, *Rigged: America, Russia, and One Hundred Years of Covert Electoral Interference* (London: Collins, 2020), 180.

54. Question and answer session at a January 19, 2023, event at George Washington University. See https://www.gwhatchet.com/2023/01/23/mcgill-university-professor-discusses-pro-kremlin-propaganda-in-ukraine.

55. The group behind Morgan Freeman's "We Are at War" public service video, the Committee to Investigate Russia, boasted an advisory board with a who's who of intelligence and security professionals. For a further sampling of the zeitgeist, see Ignatius, "Russia's Radical New Strategy"; Emanuel Adler and Alena Drieschova, "The Epistemological Challenge of Truth Subversion to the Liberal International Order," *International Organization 75*, no. 2 (2021): 359–86; Javier Solana and Strobe Talbott, "Opinion: The Decline of the West and How to Stop It," *The New York Times*, October 20, 2016, https://www.nytimes.com/2016/10/20/opinion/the-decline-of-the-west-and-how-to-stop-it.html; Keir Giles, "Russia's 'New' Tools for Confronting the West: Continuity and Innovation in Moscow's Exercise of Power," Chatham House, March 21, 2016, https://www.chathamhouse.org/2016/03/russias-new-tools-confronting-west-continuity-and-innovation-moscows-exercise-power; "Actor Morgan Freeman Says the US Is 'at War' with Russia," BBC, September 21, 2017, https://www.bbc.co.uk/news/av/world-europe-41345249.

56. "Americans Split on Relationship with Russia," AP-NORC Center for Public Affairs Research, October 2, 2020, https://apnorc.org/projects/americans-split-on-relationship-with-russia; "Public Confidence in Mueller's Investigation Remains Steady," Pew Research Center, March 15, 2018, https://www.pewresearch.org/politics/2018/03/15/public-confidence-in-muell

ers-investigation-remains-steady; "Most Americans Think Russia
Tried to Interfere in Presidential Election," CBS-SSRS, January 18, 2017,
https://www.cbsnews.com/news/most-americans-think-russia-
tried-to-interfere-in-presidential-election.

57. Benjamin Haddad and Alina Polyakova, "Don't Rehabilitate Obama on
Russia," *The American Interest*, February 28, 2018, https://www.the-american-
interest.com/2018/02/28/dont-rehabilitate-obama-russia/; see also Michael
Isikoff and David Corn, "'Stand Down': How the Obama Team Blew the
Response to Russian Meddling," huffpost.com, March 9, 2018, https://www.
huffpost.com/entry/stand-down-how-the-obama-team-blew-the-response-to-
russian-meddling_n_5aa29a97e4b086698a9d1112.

58. Richard Betts, "Analysis, War, and Decision: Why Intelligence Failures Are
Inevitable," *World Politics* 21, no. 1 (1978): 61–89.

59. Richard Betts, *Surprise Attack: Lessons for Defense Planning* (Washington,
DC: Brookings Institution, 1982), 4.

60. SSCI report, Vol. 5, 7.

61. SSCI report, Vol. 3, 10.

62. Munslow, "Ex-CIA Director Hayden."

63. See Gavin Wilde, "From Panic to Policy: The Limits of Propaganda and the
Foundations of an Effective Response," *Texas National Security Review*, 7, no.
2 (2024): 42–55.

64. Watts, "Statement."

## Chapter 8

1. Calder Walton, *Spies: The Epic Intelligence War Between East and West*
(London: Abacus, 2023), 504.

2. Office of the Director of National Intelligence, Intelligence Community
Assessment, "Background to Assessing Russian Activities and Intentions in
Recent US Elections: The Analytic Process and Cyber Incident Attribution,"
January 6, 2017, https://www.dni.gov/files/documents/ICA_2017_01.pdf.
Confidence in this assessment was based in part on the human source
extracted in 2017. See Julian E. Barnes, Adam Goldman, and David E.
Sanger, "C.I.A. Informant Extracted from Russia Had Sent Secrets to U.S. for
Decades," *The New York Times*, September 9, 2019, https://www.nytimes.com/
2019/09/09/us/politics/cia-informant-russia.html.

3. Robert Mueller, "Report on the Investigation into Russian Interference in
the 2016 Presidential Election," U.S. Department of Justice, 2019; Senate
Select Committee on Intelligence, S. Rep. No. 116-290, 116th Cong., 2d Sess.
(2020).

4. National Intelligence Council, "Foreign Threats to the 2020 US Federal
Elections," ICA 2020-000778D, March 10, 2021, p. 5, https://www.dni.gov/
files/ODNI/documents/assessments/ICA-declass-16MAR21.pdf.

5. National Intelligence Council, "Foreign Threats to the 2020 US Federal
Elections."

6. Mark Galeotti, "Controlling Chaos: How Russia Manages Its Political War in Europe," policy brief, European Council on Foreign Relations, August 2017. https://ecfr.eu/wp-content/uploads/ECFR228_-_CONTROLLING_CHAOS1.pdf.

7. Michael Kofman, "Raiding and International Brigandry: Russia's Strategy for Great Power Competition," *War on the Rocks*, June 14, 2018, https://waront herocks.com/2018/06/raiding-and-international-brigandry-russias-strategy-for-great-power-competition.

8. Henry Farrell and Abraham L. Newman, "The Janus Face of the Liberal International Information Order: When Global Institutions Are Self-Undermining," *International Organization* 75, no. 2 (2021): 333–58.

9. As Julian Nocetti notes, "The Russian leadership has come to consider the foreign policy of the internet as the establishment of a new US-led hegemonic framework that Washington would use to subvert other sovereign states with its own world views and values." Julian Nocetti, "Contest and Conquest: Russia and Global Internet Governance," *International Affairs* 91, no. 1 (2015): 111.

10. Mona Elswah and Philip N. Howard, "'Anything That Causes Chaos': The Organizational Behavior of Russia Today (RT)," *Journal of Communication* 70, no. 5 (2020): 623–45. On an earlier shift to a softer line during the Obama "reset," see Julia Ioffe, "What Is Russia Today?" *Columbia Journalism Review*, September–October 2010. https://archives.cjr.org/feature/what_is_russia_today.php.

11. Anton Shekhovtsov, *Russia and the Western Far Right: Tango Noir* (Abingdon, UK: Routledge, 2018); on the United Kingdom, see Rachel Ellehuus, "Mind the Gaps: Assessing Russian Influence in the United Kingdom," Center for Strategic and International Studies, July 2020, https://csis-website-prod.s3.amazonaws.com/s3fs-public/publication/20720_Ellehuus_GEC_FullR eport_FINAL.pdf.

12. Donald Kagan, *The Peloponnesian War: Athens and Sparta in Savage Conflict, 431–404 BC* (New York: HarperCollins, 2003), 13–18; Richard Ned Lebow, "Play It Again, Pericles: Agents, Structures, and the Peloponnesian War," *European Journal of International Relations* 2, no. 2 (1996): 252; Dan Reiter, "Gulliver Unleashed? International Order, Restraint, and the Case of Ancient Athens," *International Studies Quarterly* 65, no. 3 (2021): 582–93, https://doi.org/10.1093/isq/sqab061.

13. See, for example, the assessment based on extensive reviews of Russian official documents compiled by Michael Kofman et al., *Russian Approaches to Competition* (Washington, DC; Center for Naval Analysis, 2021), 42–48.

14. Walton, *Spies*, 425.

15. For the best summary of this research, see Gavin Wilde, "From Panic to Policy: The Limits of Foreign Propaganda and the Foundations of an Effective Response," *Texas National Security Review* 7, no. 2 (2024): 42–55.

16. Julia Ioffe, "The History of Russian Involvement in America's Race Wars," *The Atlantic*, October 21, 2017, https://www.theatlantic.com/international/archive/2017/10/russia-facebook-race/542796.

17. See Kathleen Hall Jamieson, *Cyberwar: How Russian Hackers and Trolls Helped Elect a President: What We Don't, Can't, and Do Know* (New York: Oxford University Press, 2018); Dov H. Levin, *Meddling in the Ballot Box: The Causes and Effects of Partisan Electoral Interventions* (New York: Oxford University Press, 2020). Reasons to doubt these claims are detailed in, e.g., Justin Grimmer, "Review of *Cyberwar: How Russian Hackers and Trolls Helped Elect a President—What We Don't, Can't, and Do Know*, by Kathleen Hall Jamison," *Public Opinion Quarterly* 83, no. 1 (2019): 159–63, https://doi.org/10.1093/poq/nfy049; John Sides, Michael Tesle, and Lynn Vavreck, *Identity Crisis: The 2016 Presidential Campaign and the Battle for the Meaning of America* (Princeton, NJ: Princeton University Press, 2018).

18. "Report of the Select Committee on Intelligence, United States Senate, on Russian Active Measures Campaigns and Interference in the 2016 U.S. Election, Volume 2: Russia's Use of Social Media with Additional Views," Select Committee on Intelligence, October 2019, 111.

19. Thomas Rid, *Active Measures: The Secret History of Disinformation and Political Warfare* (New York: Macmillan, 2020), 180–93.

20. Seth G. Jones, "Russian Meddling in the United States: The Historical Context of the Mueller Report," CSIS Brief, Center for Strategic and International Studies, March 27, 2019, https://www.csis.org/analysis/russian-meddling-united-states-historical-context-mueller-report.

21. Michael Hayden, "Interview with Charlie Rose," *CBS Mornings*, January 17, 2017, https://www.youtube.com/watch?v=CwElxbmr2YU.

22. Peter Baker, " 'We Absolutely Could Not Do That': When Seeking Foreign Help Was out of the Question," *The New York Times*, October 6, 2019, https://www.nytimes.com/2019/10/06/us/politics/trump-foreign-influence.html.

23. E.g., Steven Levitsky and Daniel Ziblatt, *How Democracies Die: What History Reveals About Our Future* (New York: Penguin, 2019); or, more alarming, Barbara Walter, *How Civil Wars Start and How to Stop Them* (New York: Random House, 2022).

24. Vaughan Bell, "Don't Touch That Dial! A History of Media Technology Scares from the Printing Press to Facebook," *Slate*, February 15, 2010, https://slate.com/technology/2010/02/a-history-of-media-technology-scares-from-the-printing-press-to-facebook.html.

## Chapter 9

1. Marie-Catherine Villatoux, "The Fight Against Subversion in France in the Forties and Fifties," *Dans Inflexions* 14, no. 2 (2010): 167.

2. Matthew Gerth, "British McCarthyism: The Anti-Communist Politics of Lord Vansittart and Sir Waldron Smithers," *History* 107, no. 378 (2022): 813–964.

3. Frantisek Moravec, *Master of Spies* (New York: Doubleday, 1975).

4. See the declassified CIA historical account in Kevin C. Ruffrer, "Cold War Allies: The Origins of CIA's Relationship with Ukrainian Nationalists," in *50 Years of the CIA*, eds. Michael Warner and Scott A. Koch (Washington, DC: Center for the Study of Intelligence, 1998), 19–43.

5. Benjamin Tromly, *Cold War Exiles and the CIA—Plotting to Free Russia* (New York: Oxford University Press, 2019).

6. Richard Michael Gibson and Wen H. Chen, *The Secret Army: Chiang Kai-shek and the Drug Warlords of the Golden Triangle* (Hoboken, NJ: Wiley, 2011); author's interview with Ambassador William J. vanden Heuvel, New York City, July 2019.

7. The bottom line of a huge literature: European polities had more aspects of sovereignty before Westphalia and fewer after—and non-European polities had more aspects of sovereignty—than the old view allowed. See, e.g., Stephen D. Krasner, *Sovereignty: Organized Hypocrisy* (Princeton, NJ: Princeton University Press, 1999); Andreas Osiander, "Sovereignty, International Relations, and the Westphalian Myth," *International Organization* 55, no. 2 (2001): 251–87; Peter Stirk, "The Westphalian Model and Sovereign Equality," *Review of International Studies* 38, no. 3 (2012): 641–60; Ayşe Zarakol, *Before the West: The Rise and Fall of Eastern World Orders* (Cambridge, UK: Cambridge University Press, 2022), Chapter 1.

8. John M. Owen, IV, *The Clash of Ideas in World Politics: Transnational Networks, States, and Regime Change, 1510–2010* (Princeton, NJ: Princeton University Press, 2010).

9. Jill Kastner and William C. Wohlforth, "A Measure Short of War: The Return of Great Power Subversion," *Foreign Affairs*, July–August (2021): 123.

10. Michael Warner, "A Matter of Trust: Covert Action Reconsidered," *Studies in Intelligence* 63, no. 4 (2019): 33.

11. Kastner and Wohlforth, "A Measure Short of War," 123.

12. Iskander Rehman, "Raison d'Etat: Richelieu's Grand Strategy During the Thirty Years' War," *Texas National Security Review* 2, no. 3 (2019): 41, http://dx.doi.org/10.26153/tsw/2928.

13. Mykhaylo Zabrodskyi et al., "Preliminary Lessons in Conventional Warfighting from Russia's Invasion of Ukraine: February–July 2022," Royal United Services Institute, November 30, 2022, https://www.rusi.org/explore-our-research/publications/special-resources/preliminary-lessons-conventional-warfighting-russias-invasion-ukraine-february-july-2022.

## Chapter 10

1. Gordon Corera, "MI5 and FBI Heads Warn of 'Immense' Threat," BBC News, July 7, 2022, https://www.bbc.com/news/world-asia-china-62064506

2. Nigel Inkster, "China Is Running Covert Operations That Could Seriously Overwhelm Us," *The New York Times*, September 14, 2022, https://www.nytimes.com/2022/09/14/opinion/international-world/china-espionage.html.

3. Director Wray's remarks at the Intelligence and National Security Alliance Leadership Breakfast, McLean, VA, February 29, 2024, https://www.fbi.gov/news/speeches/director-wray-s-remarks-at-the-intelligence-and-national-security-alliance-leadership-breakfast.

4. Jessica Brandt, "Propaganda, Foreign Interference, and Generative AI," testimony submitted to the Senate Artificial Intelligence Insight Forum on November 8, 2023.

5. The Soviet Commissar for Foreign Affairs (Litvinov) to President Roosevelt Washington, November 16, 1933. *Foreign Relations of the United States, Diplomatic Papers, 1933, the British Commonwealth, Europe, Near East and Africa, Volume II, The Soviet Union, 1933–1939*, eds. Daniel J. Lawler and Erin R. Mahan (Washington, DC: U.S. Government Printing Office, 2010), Document 25, accessed October 30, 2023, https://history.state.gov/historicaldocuments/frus1933-39/d301.

6. Ibid., Document 301.

7. Ibid., Document 275.

8. Julian E. Barnes, "Russia Steps Up a Covert Sabotage Campaign Aimed at Europe," The New York Times, May 26, 2024, https://www.nytimes.com/2024/05/26/us/politics/russia-sabotage-campaign-ukraine.html.

9. James Madison, Federalist No. 14, at 152; Federalist No. 19, at 180; Federalist No. 39, at 280; in Alexander Hamilton, James Madison, and John Jay, *The Federalist Papers*, ed. Clinton Rossiter (New York: New American Library, 1961); cited in Rett R. Ludwikowski, "Two Firsts: A Comparative Study of the American and the Polish Constitutions," *Michigan Journal of International Law* 8, no. 1 (1987): 117–56.

10. Calder Walton, *Spies: The Epic Intelligence War Between East and West* (London: Abacus, 2023).

11. Gavin Wilde, "From Panic to Policy: The Limits of Foreign Propaganda and the Foundations of an Effective Response," *Texas National Security Review* 7, no. 2 (2024): 42–55; Thomas Rid, *Cyber War Will Not Take Place* (London: Hurst, 2013).

12. See Wilde, "From Panic to Policy."

13. Lennart Maschmeyer, "The Subversive Trilemma: Why Cyber Operations Fall Short of Expectations," *International Security* 46, no. 2 (2021): 51–90.

14. Francis Fukuyama, "The End of History?" *The National Interest*, no. 16 (1989): 3–18, http://www.jstor.org/stable/24027184.

# BIBLIOGRAPHY

## Books

Adams, Charles Darwin, ed. *The Speeches of Aeschines.*
London: Heinemann, 1919.

Allison, Graham. *Destined for War: Can America and China Escape Thucydides's Trap?* New York: Mariner Books, 2017.

Anderson, M. S. *The Eastern Question 1774–1923: A Study in International Relations.* New York: Macmillan, 1966.

Andrew, Christopher. *The Secret World: A History of Intelligence.* New Haven, CT: Yale University Press, 2018.

Andrew, Christopher, and Vasiliy Mitrokhnn. *The Sword and the Shield: The Mitrokhin Archive and the Secret History of the KGB.* New York: Basic Books, 1999.

Aristophanes. *The Lysistrata.* Translated by Benjamin Bickley Rogers. London: Heinemann, 1924.

Baldoli, Claudia. *Exporting Fascism: Italian Fascists and Britain's Italians in the 1930s.* Oxford, UK: Oxford University Press, 2003.

Balfour, Patrick, Lord Kinross. *The Ottoman Centuries: The Rise and Fall of the Turkish Empire.* New York: Perennial, 1979.

Beilenson, Lawrence H. *Power Through Subversion.* Washington, DC: Public Affairs Press, 1972.

Betts, Richard. *Surprise Attack: Lessons for Defense Planning.* Washington, DC: Brookings Institution, 1982.

Безруков, Андрей и Андрей Сушенцов, ред. *Россия и мир в 2020 году: Контуры тревожного будущего.* Москва: ЭКСМО, 2015.

Black, J. B. *The Reign of Elizabeth, 1558–1603.* Oxford, UK: Clarendon, 1959.

Buchanan, Ben. *The Hacker and the State: Cyber Attacks and the New Normal of Geopolitics*. Cambridge, MA: Harvard University Press, 2020.

Burns, William J. *The Back Channel*. New York: Random House, 2020.

Carson, Austin. *Secret Wars: Covert Conflict in International Politics*. Princeton, NJ: Princeton University Press, 2018.

Case, Holly. *The Age of Questions: Or, A First Attempt at an Aggregate History of the Eastern, Social, Woman, American, Jewish, Polish, Bullion, Tuberculosis, and Many Other Questions over the Nineteenth Century, and Beyond*. Princeton, NJ: Princeton University Press, 2018.

Cawkwell, George. *Philip of Macedon*. London: Faber & Faber, 1978.

Charap, Samuel, and Timothy J. Colton. *Everyone Loses: The Ukraine Crisis and the Ruinous Contest for Post-Soviet Eurasia*. Abingdon, UK: Routledge, 2017.

Clinton, Hillary Rodham. *Hard Choices*. New York: Simon & Schuster, 2014.

Coll, Steve. *Ghost Wars: The Secret History of the CIA, Afghanistan and Bin Laden*. New York: Penguin, 2004.

Conboy, Kenneth, and James Morrison. *The CIA's Secret War in Tibet*. Lawrence: University Press of Kansas, 2011.

Corke, Sarah Jane. *U.S. Covert Operations and Cold War Strategy: Truman, Secret Warfare, and the CIA, 1945–53*. Abingdon, UK: Routledge, 2008.

Cormac, Rory. *How to Stage a Coup and Ten Other Lessons from the World of Secret Statecraft*. London: Atlantic Books, 2022.

Cottam, Richard. *Competitive Interventions and 20th Century Diplomacy*. Pittsburgh, Pennsylvania: University of Pittsburgh Press, 1967.

Cummings, Richard H. *Cold War Radio: The Dangerous History of American Broadcasting in Europe, 1950–1989*. Jefferson, NC: McFarland, 2009.

Cummings, Richard H. *Cold War Frequencies: CIA Clandestine Radio Broadcasting to the Soviet Union and Eastern Europe*. Jefferson, NC: McFarland, 2021.

Dehio, Ludwig. *The Precarious Balance: Four Centuries of the European Power Struggle*. Translated by Charles Fullman. New York: Knopf, 1962.

Delury, John. *Agents of Subversion: The Fate of John T. Downey and the CIA's Covert War in China*. Ithaca, NY: Cornell University Press, 2022.

Demosthenes. *Speeches*. Translated by J. H. Vince, C. A. Vince, A. T. Murray, N. W. DeWitt, and N .J. DeWitt. Cambridge, MA: Harvard University Press, 1939.

Diamond, Sander A. *The Nazi Movement in the United States 1924–1941*. Ithaca, NY: Cornell University Press, 1974.

Diodorus Siculus. *Diodorus of Sicily in Twelve Volumes*. Translated by C. H. Oldfather. Vols. 4–8. Cambridge, MA: Harvard University Press, 1989.

Downes, Alexander. *Catastrophic Success: Why Foreign-Imposed Regime Change Goes Wrong*. Ithaca, NY: Cornell University Press, 2021.

Driscoll, Jesse, and Dominique Arel. *Ukraine's Unnamed War: Before the Russian Invasion of 2022*. Cambridge, UK: Cambridge University Press, 2023.

Eckstein, Arthur M. *Mediterranean Anarchy, Interstate War, and the Rise of Rome.*
    Berkeley: University of California Press, 2006.
Ferguson, Everett. *Backgrounds of Early Christianity.* Grand Rapids,
    MI: Eerdmans, 2003.
Firsov, Fridrikh I., Harvey Klehr, and John Earl Haynes. *Secret Cables of the
    Comintern, 1933–1943.* New Haven, CT: Yale University Press, 2014.
*Foreign Relations of the United States, 1948, General: The United Nations, Volume I,
    Part 2*, edited by Neal H. Petersen et al. Washington, DC: U.S. Government
    Printing Office, 1976.
*Foreign Relations of the United States, 1955–1957, Vol. XXIV, Soviet Union and
    Eastern Mediterranean*, edited by Ronald D. Landa, Aaron D. Miller, Charles
    S. Sampson. Washington, DC: U.S. Government Printing Office, 1989.
*Foreign Relations of the United States, 1969–1976, Volume XII, Soviet Union,
    January 1969–October 1970*, edited by Erin R. Mahan. Washington, DC: U.S.
    Government Printing Office, 2002.
*Foreign Relations of the United States, 1981–1988, Volume VI, Soviet Union, October
    1986–January 1989*, edited by James Graham Wilson. Washington, DC: U.S.
    Government Printing Office, 2016.
*Foreign Relations of the United States, Diplomatic Papers, 1933, the British
    Commonwealth, Europe, Near East and Africa, Volume II, The Soviet Union,
    1933–1939*, edited by Daniel J. Lawler and Erin R. Mahan. Washington,
    DC: U.S. Government Printing Office, 2010. Accessed October 30, 2023.
    https://history.state.gov/historicaldocuments/frus1933-39/d301.
Gage, Beverly. *G-Man: J. Edgar Hoover and the Making of the American Century.*
    New York: Simon & Schuster, 2022.
Gates, Robert M. *From the Shadows.* New York: Simon & Schuster, 2007.
Gerolymatos, André. *Espionage and Treason in Classical Greece: Ancient Spies and
    Lies.* New York: Lexington Books, 2019.
Gibson, Richard Michael, and Wen H. Chen. *The Secret Army: Chiang Kai-shek
    and the Drug Warlords of the Golden Triangle.* Hoboken, NJ: Wiley, 2011.
Glaser, Charles L. *Rational Theory of International Politics: The Logic of
    Competition and Cooperation.* Princeton, NJ: Princeton University Press, 2010.
Grose, Peter. *Rollback: America's Secret War Behind the Iron Curtain.*
    New York: Houghton Mifflin, 2000.
Hamilton, Alexander, James Madison, and John Jay. *The Federalist Papers*, edited
    by Clinton Rossiter. New York: New American Library, 1961.
Harding, Luke. *Shadow State: Murder, Mayhem, and Russia's Remaking of the
    West.* London: Guardian Faber, 2020.
Hart, Bradley W. *Hitler's American Friends: The Third Reich's Supporters in the
    United States.* New York: St. Martin's Press, 2018.
Haslam, Jonathan. *The Spectre of War: International Communism and the Origins
    of World War II.* Princeton, NJ: Princeton University Press, 2021.
Hemming, Henry. *Our Man in New York: The British Plot to Bring America into
    the Second World War.* London: Quercus, 2019.

Hill, Fiona, and Clifford Gaddy. *Mr. Putin: Operative in the Kremlin.* Washington, DC: Brookings Institution Press, 2013.

Hunt, Peter. *War, Peace, and Alliance in Demosthenes' Athens.* Cambridge, UK: Cambridge University Press, 2010.

Isikoff, Michael, and David Corn. *Russian Roulette: The Inside Story of Putin's War on America and the Election of Donald Trump.* New York: Twelve, 2018.

Jamieson, Kathleen Hall. *Cyberwar: How Russian Hackers and Trolls Helped Elect a President: What We Don't, Can't, and Do Know.* New York: Oxford University Press, 2018.

Johnson, A. Ross, and R. Eugene Parta, eds. *Cold War Broadcasting: Impact on the Soviet Union and Eastern Europe: A Collection of Studies and Documents.* Budapest, Hungary: Central European University Press, 2010.

Johnson, Loch. *The Third Option: Covert Action and American Foreign Policy.* New York: Oxford University Press, 2022.

Juršėnas, Alfonsas, Kasparas Karlauskas, Eimantas Ledinauskas, Gediminas Maskeliunas, Donatas Rondomanskas, and Julius Ruseckas. *The Role of AI in the Battle Against Disinformation.* Riga, Latvia: NATO Stratcom Center of Excellence, February 2022.

Kagan, Donald. *The Fall of the Athenian Empire.* Ithaca, NY: Cornell University Press, 1987.

Kagan, Donald. *The Peloponnesian War: Athens and Sparta in Savage Conflict, 431–404 BC.* New York: HarperCollins, 2003.

Kennedy, Paul. *The Rise and Fall of the Great Powers: Economic Change and Military Conflict from 1500 to 2000.* New York: Random House, 1987.

Kilroy, Gerard. *Edmund Campion: A Scholarly Life.* Farnham, UK: Ashgate, 2015.

Klehr, Harvey, John Earle Haynes, and F. I. Firsov. *The Secret World of American Communism.* New Haven, CT: Yale University Press, 1995.

Kofman, Michael, Dimitry Gorenburg, Mary Chestnut, Paul Saunders, Kasey Strictlin, and Julian Waller. *Russian Approaches to Competition.* Washington, DC: Center for Naval Analysis, 2021.

Kotkin, Stephen. *Stalin, Vol. II: Waiting for Hitler, 1929–1941.* New York: Penguin, 2017: Part III.

Krasner, Stephen D. *Sovereignty: Organized Hypocrisy.* Princeton, NJ: Princeton University Press, 1999.

Kurian, George T. *World Press Encyclopedia.* New York: Facts on File, 1982.

Kydd, Andrew H. *Trust and Mistrust in International Relations.* Princeton, NJ: Princeton University Press, 2005.

Lazar, Marc. "The French Communist Party." In *The Cambridge History of Communism*, edited by Norman Naimark, Silvio Pons, and Sophie Quinn-Judge, Vol. 2, 619–641. Cambridge, UK: Cambridge University Press, 2017.

Lee, Melissa. *Crippling Leviathan: How Foreign Subversion Weakens the State.* Ithaca, NY: Cornell University Press, 2020.

Levin, Dov. *Meddling in the Ballot Box: The Causes and Effects of Partisan Electoral Interventions.* New York: Oxford University Press, 2020.

Levitsky, Steven, and Daniel Ziblatt. *How Democracies Die: What History Reveals About Our Future.* New York: Penguin, 2018.

Lunev, Stanislav, with Ira Winkler. *Through the Eyes of the Enemy: Russia's Highest Ranking Military Defector Reveals Why Russia Is More Dangerous Than Ever.* Washington, DC: Regnery, 1998.

Luttwak, Edward N. *The Grand Strategy of the Byzantine Empire.* Cambridge, MA: Belknap, 2009.

MacCaffrey, Wallace T. *Queen Elizabeth and the Making of Policy, 1572–1588.* Princeton, NJ: Princeton University Press, 1981.

Macfie, A. L. *The Eastern Question 1774–1923*, 2nd ed. Abingdon, UK: Routledge, 2014.

Mazarr, Michael J. *Mastering the Gray Zone: Understanding a Changing Era of Conflict.* Carlisle, PA: U.S. Army War College Press, 2015.

McCoog, Thomas M. *The Society of Jesus in Ireland, Scotland and England, 1589–1597: Building the Faith of St. Peter upon the King of Spain's Monarchy.* Farnham, UK/Rome: Ashgate/Institutum Historicum Societatis Iesu, 2012.

Mitchell, Allan. *The German Influence in France After 1870: The Formation of the French Republic.* Chapel Hill: University of North Carolina Press, 1979.

Mitrovich, Gregory. *Undermining the Kremlin: America's Strategy to Subvert the Soviet Bloc, 1947–1956.* Ithaca, NY: Cornell University Press, 2000.

Moravec, Frantisek. *Master of Spies.* New York: Doubleday, 1975.

Morgan, Forrest E., Karl P. Mueller, Evan S. Medeiros, Kevin L. Pollpeter, and Roger Cliff. *Dangerous Thresholds: Managing Escalation in the 21st Century.* Santa Monica, CA: RAND Corporation, 2008. https://www.rand.org/pubs/monographs/MG614.html.

Nelson, Michael. *War of the Black Heavens: The Battles of Western Broadcasting in the Cold War.* Syracuse, NY: Syracuse University Press, 1997.

O'Rourke, Lindsey A. *Covert Regime Change: America's Secret Cold War.* Ithaca, NY: Cornell University Press, 2018.

Ostermann, Christian F. *Between Containment and Rollback: The United States and the Cold War in Germany.* Stanford, CA: Stanford University Press, 2021.

Owen, John M., IV. *The Clash of Ideas in World Politics: Transnational Networks, States, and Regime Change, 1510–2010.* Princeton, NJ: Princeton University Press, 2010.

Painter, David S. "Energy and the End of the Evil Empire." In *The Reagan Moment: America and the World in the 1980s*, edited by Jonathan R. Hunt and Simon Miles, 43–63. Ithaca, NY: Cornell University Press, 2021.

Parker, Geoffrey. *The Grand Strategy of Philip II.* New Haven, CT: Yale University Press, 1998.

Parta, Eugene R. *Discovering the Hidden Listener: An Assessment of Radio Liberty and Western Broadcasting to the USSR During the Cold War: A Study Based on Audience Research Findings, 1970–1991.* Stanford, CA: Hoover Institution Press, 2007.

Pee, Robert. *Democracy Promotion, National Security and Strategy: Foreign Policy Under the Reagan Administration.* Abingdon, UK: Routledge, 2015.

Pee, Robert. "The Rise of Political Aid: The National Endowment for Democracy and the Reagan Administration's Cold War Strategy." In *The Reagan Administration, the Cold War, and the Transition to Democracy Promotion,* edited by Robert Pee and William Michael Schmidli, 51–73. London: Palgrave Macmillan, 2019.

Pinker, Steven. *The Better Angels of Our Nature: Why Violence Has Declined.* London: Penguin, 2011.

Pipes, Richard. *Russia Under the Old Regime.* New York: Macmillan, 1974.

Plutarch. *Lives, Volume IV: Alcibiades and Coriolanus. Lysander and Sulla.* Translated by Bernadotte Perrin. Loeb Classical Library 80. Cambridge, MA: Harvard University Press, 1916.

Pons, Silvio. *The Global Revolution: A History of International Communism, 1917–1991.* New York: Oxford University Press, 2014.

Quataert, Donald. *The Ottoman Empire: 1700–1922.* 2nd ed. New York: Cambridge University Press, 2005.

Rid, Thomas. *Cyber War Will Not Take Place.* London: Hurst, 2013.

Rid, Thomas. *Active Measures: The Secret History of Disinformation and Political Warfare.* New York: Macmillan, 2020.

Roberts, Geoffrey. "Averting Armageddon: The Communist Peace Movement, 1948–1956." In *The Oxford Handbook of the History of Communism,* edited by Stephen A. Smith, 322–38. New York: Oxford University Press, 2013.

Ruffrer, Keven C. "Cold War Allies: The Origins of CIA's Relationship with Ukrainian Nationalists." In *50 Years of the CIA,* edited by Michael Warner and Scott A. Koch, 19–43. Washington, DC: Center for the Study of Intelligence, 1998.

Schoen, Fletcher, and Christopher J. Lamb. *Deception, Disinformation, and Strategic Communications: How One Interagency Group Made a Major Difference.* Washington, DC: Institute for National Security Studies, National Defense University Press, 2012.

Scully, Robert E. *Into the Lion's Den: The Jesuit Mission in Elizabethan England and Wales, 1580–1603.* St. Louis, MO: Institute of Jesuit Sources, 2011.

Seldon, Anthony, and Peter Snowdon. *Cameron at 10: The Inside Story.* Glasgow, Scotland: Collins, 2016.

Shamasastry, R. *The Arthashastra.* New Delhi, India: Penguin, 1992.

Shekhovtsov, Anton. *Russia and the Western Far Right: Tango Noir.* Abingdon, UK: Routledge, 2018.

Shimer, David. *Rigged: America, Russia, and One Hundred Years of Covert Electoral Interference.* London: Collins, 2020.

Sides, John, Michael Tesle, and Lynn Vavreck. *Identity Crisis: The 2016 Presidential Campaign and the Battle for the Meaning of America.* Princeton, NJ: Princeton University Press, 2018.

Simms, Brendan. *Europe: The Struggle for Supremacy, 1453 to the Present.* London: Penguin, 2014.

Smith, William, ed. *A Dictionary of Greek and Roman Biography and Mythology.* Ann Arbor: University of Michigan Library, 2005.

Springer, Paul J., ed. *Encyclopedia of Cyber Warfare.* Santa Barbara, CA: ABC-CLIO, 2017.

Statiev, Alexander. *The Soviet Counterinsurgency in the Western Borderlands.* Cambridge, UK: Cambridge University Press, 2010.

Steil, Benn. *The World That Wasn't: Henry Wallace and the Fate of the American Century.* New York: Avid Reader Press, 2024.

Stephenson, William, ed. *British Security Coordination: The Secret History of British Intelligence in the Americas, 1940–1945.* New York: Fromm International, 1999.

Stone, James. *The War Scare of 1875: Bismarck and Europe in the Mid-1870s.* Stuttgart, Germany: Steiner, 2010.

Stuttard, David. *Nemesis: Alcibiades and the Fall of Athens.* Cambridge, MA: Harvard University Press, 2018.

Sugden, Marian, and Ernest Frankl. *Yorkshire Moors and Dales.* Cambridge, UK: Pevensey Press, 1987.

Swope, Kenneth M. *The Military Collapse of China's Ming Dynasty, 1618–1644.* Abingdon, UK: Routledge, 2014.

Tate, Tim. *Hitler's Secret Army: A Hidden History of Spies, Saboteurs, and Traitors.* London: Pegasus, 2019.

Taylor, A. J. P. *The Struggle for Mastery of Europe: 1848–1918.* Reissue ed. Oxford, UK: Oxford University Press, 1980.

Taylor, Phillip. *Munitions of the Mind: A History of Propaganda.* 3rd ed. Manchester, UK: Manchester University Press, 2003.

Thorpe, Andrew. *The British Communist Party and Moscow, 1920–43.* Manchester, UK: Manchester University Press, 2000.

Thucydides. *History of the Peloponnesian War.* Translated by Rex Warner. London: Penguin, 1972.

Trachtenberg, Marc. *History and Strategy.* Princeton, NJ: Princeton University Press, 1991.

Treverton, Gregory. *Covert Action: The CIA and the Limits of American Intervention in the Post-War World.* New York: Basic Books, 1987.

Tromly, Benjamin. *Cold War Exiles and the CIA: Plotting to Free Russia.* New York: Oxford University Press, 2019.

Von der Nahmer, Robert Noell. *Bismarcks Reptilienfonds: Aus den Geheimakten Preussens und des Deutschen Reiches.* Wiesbaden: v. Hase & Koehler, 1968.

Von Holstein, Friedrich. *The Holstein Papers: Volume 3, Correspondence 1861–1896: The Memoirs, Diaries and Correspondence of Friedrich von Holstein 1837–1909*, edited by Norman Rich and M. H. Fisher. Cambridge, UK: Cambridge University Press, 1961.

Walter, Barbara. *How Civil Wars Start and How to Stop Them.*
New York: Random House, 2022.

Walton, Calder. *Spies: The Epic Intelligence War Between East and West.*
London: Abacus, 2023.

Wentler, Hermann. *Zerstörung der Großmacht Russland? Die britischen Kriegsziele im Krimkrieg.* Göttigen, Germany: Vandenhoeck & Ruprecht, 1993.

Wilken, Robert L. *The Christians as the Romans Saw Them.* New Haven, CT: Yale University Press, 1984.

Willard-Foster, Melissa. *Toppling Foreign Governments: The Logic of Regime Change.* Philadelphia: University of Pennsylvania Press, 2018.

Xenophon. *Hellenica.* Translated by Carleton L. Brownson. Cambridge, MA: Harvard University Press, 1921.

Zarakol, Ayşe. *Before the West: The Rise and Fall of Eastern World Orders* Cambridge, UK: Cambridge University Press, 2022.

Zimmerman, William. *The Russian People and Foreign Policy: Russian Elite and Mass Perspectives.* Princeton, NJ: Princeton University Press, 2002.

Zubok, Vladislav. *Failed Empire.* Chapel Hill: University of North Carolina Press, 2009.

Zygar, Mikhail. *All the Kremlin's Men: Inside the Court of Vladimir Putin.*
Washington, DC: Public Affairs Press, 2016.

## Journal and Newspaper Articles

"Actor Morgan Freeman Says the US Is 'at War' with Russia." BBC, September 21, 2017. https://www.bbc.co.uk/news/av/world-europe-41345249.

Adler, Emanuel, and Alena Drieschova. "The Epistemological Challenge of Truth Subversion to the Liberal International Order." *International Organization* 75, no. 2 (2021): 359–86. doi:10.1017/S0020818320000533.

Albanese, David C. S. "'It Takes a Russian to Beat a Russian': The National Union of Labor Solidarists, Nationalism, and Human Intelligence Operations in the Cold War." *Intelligence and National Security* 32, no. 6 (2017): 782–96.

Allison, Graham. "Thucydides' Trap Has Been Sprung in the Pacific." *Financial Times*, August 21, 2012. https://www.ft.com/content/5d695b5a-ead3-11e1-984b-00144feab49a.

Arbeitman, Y. "The Suffix of Iscariot." *Journal of Biblical Literature* 99 (1980): 122–24.

Badian, Ernst. "Rome, Athens and Mithridates." *American Journal of Ancient History* (1976): 105 et seq. ISSN 0362-8914.

Baker, Peter. "'We Absolutely Could Not Do That': When Seeking Foreign Help Was Out of the Question." *The New York Times*, October 6, 2019. https://www.nytimes.com/2019/10/06/us/politics/trump-foreign-influence.html.

Barnes, Julian E. "Russia Steps Up a Covert Sabotage Campaign Aimed at Europe." *The New York Times*, May 26, 2024. https://www.nytimes.com/2024/05/26/us/politics/russia-sabotage-campaign-ukraine.html

Barnes, Julian E., Adam Goldman, and David E. Sanger. "C.I.A. Informant Extracted from Russia Had Sent Secrets to U.S. for Decades." *The New York Times*. September 9, 2019. https://www.nytimes.com/2019/09/09/us/politics/cia-informant-russia.html.

Bartles, Charles K. "Getting Gerasimov Right." *Military Review*, January–February 2016, 30–38. https://www.armyupress.army.mil/Portals/7/military-review/Archives/English/MilitaryReview_20160228_art009.pdf.

Bell, Vaughan. "Don't Touch That Dial!: A History of Media Technology Scares from the Printing Press to Facebook." *Slate*, February 15, 2010. https://slate.com/technology/2010/02/a-history-of-media-technology-scares-from-the-printing-press-to-facebook.html.

Berkowitz, Bruce D., and Allan E. Goodman. "The Logic of Covert Action." *The National Interest*, March 1, 1998. https://nationalinterest.org/article/the-logic-of-covert-action-333.

Betts, Richard. "Analysis, War, and Decision: Why Intelligence Failures Are Inevitable." *World Politics* 21, no. 1 (1978): 61–89.

Blank, Stephen J. "Threats to Russian Security: The View from Moscow." Strategic Studies Institute, July 2000. https://press.armywarcollege.edu/monographs/134.

Borghardt, Thomas. "Operation INFEKTION: Soviet Bloc Intelligence and Its AIDS Disinformation Campaign." *Studies in Intelligence* 53, no. 4 (December 2009). https://digitallibrary.tsu.ge/book/2019/september/books/Soviet-Bloc-Intelligence-and-Its-AIDS.pdf.

Bowden, John. "UK intelligence report says Russia meddled in Scottish independence referendum." *The Hill*, July 21, 2020. https://thehill.com/policy/national-security/508266-uk-intelligence-report-says-russia-meddled-in-scottish-independence.

Bradner, Eric. "Trump: DNC Hacked Itself." CNN, June 15, 2016. https://edition.cnn.com/2016/06/15/politics/dnc-hack-donald-trump/index.html.

Brodsky, Sascha. "How the US Government Is Trying to Protect You from Quantum Computing Hacks." *Lifewire*, January 4, 2023. https://www.lifewire.com/how-the-us-government-is-trying-to-protect-you-from-quantum-computing-hacks-7090899.

Burds, Jeffrey. "The Early Cold War in Soviet West Ukraine, 1944–1948." *The Carl Beck Papers in Russian and East European Studies*, no. 1505 (2001). https://doi.org/10.5195/cbp.2001.116.

Cai, Sophie. "House Committee on China Becoming an Oasis of Bipartisanship." *Axios*, February 16, 2023. https://www.axios.com/2023/02/17/china-select-committee-bipartisanship.

Carothers, Thomas. "The Backlash Against Democracy Promotion." *Foreign Affairs*, March–April 2006. https://www.foreignaffairs.com/united-states/backlash-against-democracy-promotion.

Cary, M. "Arthmius of Zeleia." *The Classical Quarterly* 29, nos. 3–4 (1935): 177–80. http://www.jstor.org/stable/636610.

Chen, Adrian. "The Agency." *The New York Times Magazine*, June 2, 2015. https://www.nytimes.com/2015/06/07/magazine/the-agency.html?.

Ciobanu, Veniamin. "International Reactions to the Russian Suppression of the Polish Insurrection." *Romanian Journal for Baltic and Nordic Studies* 5, no. 1 (2013): 87–114.

"Claim (in 2004, 2015 and 2017): The U.S. Government Supported Chechen Separatism." Russia Matters. Accessed October 22, 2023. https://www.russia matters.org/node/20317.

Conrad, Jennifer. "China's WeChat Is a Hot New Venue for US Election Misinformation." *WIRED*, October 18, 2022. https://www.wired.com/story/ chinese-american-misinformation-midterm-elections-wechat.

Cooley, Alexander. "Authoritarianism Goes Global: Countering Democratic Norms." *Journal of Democracy* 26, no. 3 (2015): 49–63.

Сорокин, Ю А. "Заговор и цареубийство 11 марта 1801 года." Вопросы истории, no. 4 (2006): 15–29.

Corera, Gordon. "How France's TV5 Was Almost Destroyed by 'Russian hackers.'" BBC, October 10, 2016. https://www.bbc.co.uk/news/technology-37590375#:~:text=A%20powerful%20cyber%2Dattack%20came,Islamic%20St ate%2C%20first%20claimed%20responsibility.

Corera, Gordon. "MI5 and FBI Heads Warn of 'Immense' Threat." BBC News, July 7, 2022. https://www.bbc.com/news/world-asia-china-62064506.

Corke, Sarah-Jane. "George Kennan and the Inauguration of Political Warfare." *Journal of Conflict Studies* 26, no. 1 (2006). https://journals.lib.unb.ca/index. php/JCS/article/view/2171.

Cormac, Rory. "Can We Brainwash Our Enemies? The New Cyber Strategy Just Rehashes Old Espionage Techniques." *The Spectator*, April 5, 2023. https:// www.spectator.co.uk/article/can-we-brainwash-our-enemies.

Cormac, Rory. "The Pinprick Approach: Whitehall's Top-Secret Anti-Communist Committee and the Evolution of British Covert Action Strategy." *Journal of Cold War Studies* 16, no. 3 (2014): 5–28.

Cormac, Rory, and Richard J. Aldrich. "Grey Is the New Black: Covert Action and Implausible Deniability." *International Affairs* 94, no. 3 (2018): 477–94.

Corn, David, and Michael Isikoff. "'Why the Hell Are We Standing Down?' The Secret Story of Obama's Response to Putin's Attack on the 2016 Election." *Mother Jones*, March 9, 2018. https://www.motherjones.com/politics/2018/03/ why-the-hell-are-we-standing-down.

Corn, David, and Michael Isikoff. "'Stand Down': How the Obama Team Blew the Response to Russian Meddling." huffpost.com, March 9, 2018. https:// www.huffpost.com/entry/stand-down-how-the-obama-team-blew-the-respo nse-to-russian-meddling_n_5aa29a97e4b086698a9d1112.

Darden, Keith A. "Russian Revanche: External Threats & Regime Reactions." *Daedelus* 142, no. 2 (2017): 128–41.

Davis, Julia. "Russian State Media Airs Its Ultimate 'Revenge Plan' for 2024 U.S. Presidential Elections." *The Daily Beast*, April 11, 2022. https://www.thedai

lybeast.com/russian-state-media-airs-its-ultimate-revenge-plan-for-2024-us-presidential-elections.

De Carvalho, Benjamin, Halvard Leira, and John M. Hobson. "The Big Bangs of IR: The Myths That Your Teachers Still Tell You About 1648 and 1919." *Millennium: Journal of International Studies* 39, no. 3 (2011): 735–58.

Delker, Janosch. "Germany Fears Russia Stole Information to Disrupt Election." *Politico*, March 20, 2017. https://www.politico.eu/article/hacked-information-bomb-under-germanys-election.

Doctor, Vikram. "First Crimean War: The Indian Connection & Parallels with Current Crimea Conflict." *The Economic Times,* March 9, 2014. https://economictimes.indiatimes.com/news/politics-and-nation/first-crimean-war-the-indian-connection-parallels-with-current-crimea-conflict/articleshow/31683664.cms.

Doshi, Rush, and Robert D. Williams. "Commentary: Is China Interfering in American Politics?" Brookings Institution, October 2, 2018. https://www.brookings.edu/articles/is-china-interfering-in-american-politics.

Downes, Alex, and Lindsey A. O'Rourke. "You Can't Always Get What You Want." *Quarterly Journal of International Security* 41, no. 2 (2016): 43–89.

Drelichman, Mauricio, and Hans-Joachim Voth. "The Sustainable Debts of Philip II: A Reconstruction of Castile's Fiscal Position, 1566–1596." *Journal of Economic History* 70, no. 4 (2010): 813–42. http://www.jstor.org/stable/40984779.

Ehrman, A. "Judas Iscariot and Abba Saqqara." *Journal of Biblical Literature* 97 (1978): 72–73.

Elswah, Mona E., and Philip N. Howard. "'Anything That Causes Chaos': The Organizational Behavior of Russia Today (RT)." *Journal of Communication* 70, no. 5 (2020): 623–45.

"'Every Story That We Covered Was a Test': James Critchlow on the Creation of Radio Liberty." Radio Free Europe/Radio Liberty interview with James Critchlow, undated. https://about.rferl.org/article/every-story-that-we-covered-was-a-test-james-critchlow-on-the-creation-of-radio-liberty/.

Farrell, Henry, and Abraham L. Newman. "The Janus Face of the Liberal International Information Order: When Global Institutions Are Self-Undermining." *International Organization* 75, no. 2 (2021): 333–58.

Feldbæk, Ole. "The Foreign Policy of Tsar Paul I, 1800–1801: An Interpretation." *Jahrbücher für Geschichte Osteuropas* 30, no. 1 (1982): 16–36.

Ferguson, Niall. "We Need AI Arms Control to Keep the New Cold War from Turning Hot." Bloomberg, August 27, 2023. https://www.bloomberg.com/opinion/articles/2023-08-27/ai-arms-control-can-keep-the-new-cold-war-from-turning-hot?srnd=undefined.

Ferran, Lee. "Inside a '$100 Million' Russian Propaganda Operation, 40 Years Ago." InsideHook, March 23, 2018. https://www.insidehook.com/article/military/jimmy-carter-neutron-bomb-russia.

Finkel, Evgeny, and Yitzhak M. Brudny. "Russia and the Colour Revolutions."
    *Democratization* 19, no. 1 (2012): 15–36.

Finkel, Evgeny, and Yitzhak M. Brudny. "No More Colour! Authoritarian
    Regimes and Colour Revolutions in Eurasia." *Democratization* 19, no. 1
    (2012): 1–14.

Fischer, Benjamin B. "Solidarity, the CIA, and Western Technology." *International
    Journal of Intelligence and CounterIntelligence* 25, no. 3 (2012): 427–69.

Fukuyama, Francis. "The End of History?" *The National Interest*, no. 16
    (1989): 3–18. http://www.jstor.org/stable/24027184.

Galeotti, Mark. "What Exactly Are 'Kremlin Ties'?" *The Atlantic*, July 12, 2017.
    https://www.theatlantic.com/international/archive/2017/07/russia-trump-
    putin-clinton/533370.

Galeotti, Mark. "Active Measures: Russia's Covert Geopolitical Operations."
    *Security Insights*, no. 31, George C. Marshall European Center for Security
    Studies, June 2019.

Geoghegan, Kate. "A Policy in Tension: The National Endowment for
    Democracy and the U.S. Response to the Collapse of the Soviet Union."
    *Diplomatic History* 42, no. 5 (2018): 772–801.

Gerasimov, Valery. "The Value of Science Is in the Foresight: New Challenges
    Demand Rethinking the Forms and Methods of Carrying Out Combat
    Operations." *Military Review*, January–February 2016, 23–9. https://www.
    armyupress.army.mil/Portals/7/military-review/Archives/English/MilitaryRev
    iew_20160228_art008.pdf.

Gerth, Matthew. "British McCarthyism: The Anti-Communist Politics of Lord
    Vansittart and Sir Waldron Smithers." *History* 107, no. 378 (2022): 813–964.

Giles, Keir. "Russia's 'New' Tools for Confronting the West: Continuity and
    Innovation in Moscow's Exercise of Power." Research paper. Chatham House,
    March 2016. https://www.chathamhouse.org/2016/03/russias-new-tools-conf
    ronting-west-continuity-and-innovation-moscows-exercise-power.

Gorman, Siobhan, and Julian E. Barnes. "Cyber Combat: Act of War, Pentagon
    Sets Stage for U.S. to Respond to Computer Sabotage with Military
    Force." *The Wall Street Journal*, May 31, 2011. https://www.wsj.com/articles/
    SB10001424052702304563104576355623135782718.

Grimmer, Justin. "Review of *Cyberwar: How Russian Hackers and Trolls Helped
    Elect a President—What We Don't, Can't, and Do Know*, by Kathleen Hall
    Jamison." *Public Opinion Quarterly* 83, no. 1 (2019): 159–63. https://doi.org/
    10.1093/poq/nfy049.

"Hack May Have Exposed Deep US Secrets; Damage yet Unknown." *The
    Independent*, December 15, 2020. https://www.independent.co.uk/news/
    hack-may-have-exposed-deep-us-secrets-damage-yet-unknown-hackers-hack
    ers-donald-trump-government-us-b1774648.html.

Haddad, Benjamin, and Alina Polyakova. "Don't Rehabilitate Obama on
    Russia." *The American Interest*, February 28, 2018. https://www.the-american-
    interest.com/2018/02/28/dont-rehabilitate-obama-russia.

Heller, Jacob. "Rumors and Realities: Making Sense of HIV/AIDS Conspiracy Narratives and Contemporary Legends." *American Journal of Public Health* 105, no. 1 (2015): e43–e50.

Hosaka, Sanshiro. "The Kremlin's Active Measures Failed in 2013: That's When Russia Remembered Its Last Resort—Crimea." *Demokratizatsiya: The Journal of Post-Soviet Democratization* 26, no. 3 (2018): 321–64.

Hui, Victoria. "Toward a Dynamic Theory of International Politics: Insights from Comparing Ancient China and Early Modern Europe." *International Organization* 58, no. 1 (2004): 175–205.

Ignatius, David. "Innocence Abroad: The New World of Spyless Coups." *The Washington Post*, September 22, 1991. https://www.washingtonpost.com/arch ive/opinions/1991/09/22/innocence-abroad-the-new-world-of-spyless-coups/ 92bb989a-de6e-4bb8-99b9-462c76b59a16.

Ignatius, David. "Russia's Radical New Strategy for Information Warfare." *The Washington Post*, January 18, 2017. https://www.washingtonpost.com/blogs/ post-partisan/wp/2017/01/18/russias-radical-new-strategy-for-information-warfare.

Inkster, Nigel. "China Is Running Covert Operations That Could Seriously Overwhelm Us." *The New York Times,* September 14, 2022. https://www.nyti mes.com/2022/09/14/opinion/international-world/china-espionage.html.

Ioffe, Julia. "What Is Russia Today?" *Columbia Journalism Review*, September–October 2010. https://archives.cjr.org/feature/what_is_russia_today.php.

Ioffe, Julia. "The History of Russian Involvement in America's Race Wars." *The Atlantic*, October 21, 2017. https://www.theatlantic.com/international/arch ive/2017/10/russia-facebook-race/542796.

Johnson, Loch K. "On Drawing a Bright Line for Covert Operations." *American Journal of International Law* 86, no. 2 (1992): 284–309.

Jones, David. "US Is Making Headway on Securing Cyber Infrastructure, Commission Says." *Cybersecurity Dive*, September 2, 2023. Accessed October 30, 2023. https://www.cybersecuritydive.com/news/us-securing-cyber-inf rastructure/694226/?utm_source=Sailthru&utm_medium=email&utm_ campaign=Issue:%202023-09-20%20Cybersecurity%20Dive%20%5Bis sue:54706%5D&utm_term=Cybersecurity%20Dive.

Jordan, Javier. "International Competition Below the Threshold of War: Toward a Theory of Gray Zone Conflict." *Journal of Strategic Security* 14 (2021): 1–24.

Kastner, Jill, and William C. Wohlforth. "A Measure Short of War: The Return of Great Power Subversion." *Foreign Affairs* (July–August 2021): 118–31.

Keenan, Edward Louis, Jr. "Muscovy and Kazan: Some Introductory Remarks on the Patterns of Steppe Diplomacy." *Slavic Review* 26, no. 4 (1967): 548–58.

Kenney, James J., Jr. "Lord Whitworth and the Conspiracy Against Tsar Paul I: The New Evidence of the Kent Archive." *Slavic Review* 36, no. 2 (1977): 205–19.

Kipling, Rudyard. *Kim*. London: Macmillan, 1960.

Kofman, Michael. "Russian Hybrid Warfare and Other Dark Arts." *War on the Rocks*, March 11, 2016. https://warontherocks.com/2016/03/russian-hybrid-warfare-and-other-dark-arts.

Kofman, Michael. "Raiding and International Brigandry: Russia's Strategy for Great Power Competition." *War on the Rocks*, June 14, 2018. https://waront herocks.com/2018/06/raiding-and-international-brigandry-russias-strategy-for-great-power-competition.

Kondratov, Eugene, and Elisabeth Johansson-Nogués. "Russia's Hybrid Interference Campaigns in France, Germany and the UK: A Challenge Against Trust in Liberal Democracies?" *Geopolitics* (2022): 1–31. doi:10.1080/14650045.2022.2129012.

Коршунова, Надежда Владимировна. "Цареубийство 11 марта 1801 г.: свои или чужие?" УДК 94, no. 47 (2016): 71.

Kotkin, Stephen. "American Hustle: What Mueller Found—and Didn't Find—About Trump and Russia." *Foreign Affairs*, July–August, 2019. https://www.foreignaffairs.com/united-states/american-hustle.

Kuromiya, Hiroaki, and Georges Mamoulia. "Anti-Russian and Anti-Soviet Subversion: The Caucasian–Japanese Nexus, 1904–1945." *Europe–Asia Studies* 61, no. 8 (2009): 1415–40.

Kuzio, Taras. "U.S. Support for Ukraine's Liberation During the Cold War: A Study of Prolog Research and Publishing Corporation." *Communist and Post-Communist Studies* 45, nos. 1–2 (2012): 51–64.

Labott, Elise. "Clinton Cites 'Serious Concerns' About Russian Election." CNN, December 6, 2011. https://www.cnn.com/2011/12/06/world/europe/russia-elections-clinton/index.html.

Lally, Kathy. "Russia Targets U.S.-Linked Election Monitor." *The Washington Post*, November 30, 2011. https://www.washingtonpost.com/world/europe/rus sia-targets-us-linked-election-monitor/2011/11/30/gIQAlqzcDO_story.html.

Landay, Jonathan, and Mark Hosenball. "Russia, China, Iran Sought to Influence U.S. 2018 Elections: U.S. Spy Chief." Reuters, December 21, 2018. https://www.reuters.com/article/us-usa-election-interference/russia-china-iran-sought-to-influence-u-s-2018-elections-u-s-spy-chief-idUSKCN1OK2FS.

Lebow, Richard Ned. "Play It Again, Pericles: Agents, Structures, and the Peloponnesian War." *European Journal of International Relations* 2, no. 2 (1996): 231–58.

Lehtoranta, V. K. " Jamming, or Deliberate Interference Against Radio Broadcasting Stations." *Radiomaailma Magazine*, August 1999. https://www.voacap.com/2023/documents/jamming_radio_broadcasting_VKL.pdf.

Long, Stephen J. K. "Strategic Disorder, the Office of Policy Coordination and the Inauguration of US Political Warfare Against the Soviet Bloc, 1948–50." *Intelligence and National Security* 27, no. 4 (2012): 459–87.

Love, Gary. "'What's the Big Idea?' Oswald Mosley, the British Union of Fascists and Generic Fascism." *Journal of Contemporary History* 42, no. 3 (2007): 447–68.

Lucas, Scott, and Kaeten Mistry. "Illusions of Coherence: George F. Kennan, U.S. Strategy and Political Warfare in the Early Cold War, 1946–1950." *Diplomatic History* 33, no. 1 (2009): 39–66.

Ludwikowski, Rett R. "Two Firsts: A Comparative Study of the American and the Polish Constitutions." *Michigan Journal of International Law* 8, no. 1 (1987): 117–156.

Luginbill, Robert D. "Cimon and Athenian Aid to Sparta: One Expedition or Two?" *Rheinisches Museum für Philologie* 159, no. 2 (2016): 135–55. http://www.jstor.org/stable/26315588.

Maitland, K. J. "People-Smuggling in Tudor and Jacobean Times." *Historia*, April 1, 2021. https://www.historiamag.com/people-smuggling-in-tudor-and-jacobean-times.

Markle, Minor. "The Strategy of Philip in 346 B.C." *The Classical Quarterly* 24, no. 2 (1974): 253–68.

Martin, Terry. "The Origins of Soviet Ethnic Cleansing." *Journal of Modern History* 70, no. 4 (1998): 813–61.

Maschmeyer, Lennart. "The Subversive Trilemma: Why Cyber Operations Fall Short of Expectations." *International Security* 46, no. 2 (2021): 51–90.

Maschmeyer, Lennart. "Subversion, Cyber Operations, and Reverse Structural Power in World Politics." *European Journal of International Relations* 29, no. 1 (2023): 79–103.

Mawdsley, Evan. "Anti-German Insurgency and Allied Grand Strategy." *Journal of Strategic Studies* 31, no. 5 (2008): 695–719.

McCall, Chris. "Russia Meddled in 2014 Scottish Independence Referendum, Explosive New Book Claims." *The Daily Record*, July 6, 2020. https://www.dailyrecord.co.uk/news/politics/russia-meddled-2014-scottish-independence-22308246.

Merchant, Nomaan. "Intel: Putin May Cite Ukraine War to Meddle in US Politics." Associated Press, April 9, 2022. https://apnews.com/article/russia-ukraine-putin-2022-midterm-elections-congress-presidential-elections-7d24ef5ab29a74fb26eb1742982da133.

Merchant, Nomaan, and Matthew Lee. "US Sees China Propaganda Efforts Becoming More Like Russia's." Associated Press, March 7, 2023. https://apnews.com/article/china-russia-intelligence-foreign-influence-propaganda-0476f41aa932cd4850627a7b8984baa2.

"Military Doctrine of the Russian Federation (Russia)." *Voennyi Vestnik* 13–14, nos. 139–140 (1992): 2–34.

Monten, Jonathan. "The Roots of the Bush Doctrine." *International Security* 29, no. 4 (2005): 112–56.

Mosse, W. E. "England and the Polish Insurrection of 1863." *English Historical Review* 71, no. 278 (1956): 28–55.

Muller, Aislinn. "Transmitting and Translating the Excommunication of Elizabeth I." *Studies in Church History* 53 (2017): 210–22.

Munslow, Julia. "Ex-CIA Director Hayden: Russia Election Meddling Was 'Most Successful Covert Operation in History.'" Yahoo News. July 21, 2017. Accessed October 22, 2023. https://www.yahoo.com/news/ex-cia-director-hayden-russia-election-meddling-successful-covert-operation-history-212056443.html.

Myers, Steven Lee, and Sheera Frenkel. "G.O.P. Targets Researchers Who Study Disinformation Ahead of 2024 Election." *The New York Times*, June 19, 2023. https://www.nytimes.com/2023/06/19/technology/gop-disinformation-researchers-2024-election.html.

Needell, Allan A. "'Truth Is Our Weapon': Project TROY, Political Warfare, and Government–Academic Relations in the National Security State." *Diplomatic History* 17, no. 3 (1993): 399–420.

Nerkar, Santul. "When It Comes to China, Biden Sounds a Lot Like Trump." FiveThirtyEight, September 28, 2021. https://fivethirtyeight.com/features/when-it-comes-to-china-biden-sounds-a-lot-like-trump/.

Niaz, Ilhan. "Kautilya's *Arthashastra* and Governance as an Element of State Power." *Strategic Studies* 28, nos. 2–3 (2008): 1–17.

Nocetti, Julian. "Contest and Conquest: Russia and Global Internet Governance." *International Affairs* 91, no. 1 (2015): 111–30.

Nye, Joseph S., Jr. "The End of Cyber-Anarchy? How to Build a New Digital Order." *Foreign Affairs*, January–February 2022. https://www.foreignaffairs.com/articles/russian-federation/2021-12-14/end-cyber-anarchy.

Office of the Director of National Intelligence. "Foreign Malign Influence Center." n.d. Accessed October 23, 2023. https://www.dni.gov/index.php/nctc-who-we-are/director-nctc/340-about/organization/foreign-malign-influence-center.

Olcott, Martha Brill. "Kyrgyzstan's 'Tulip Revolution.'" Carnegie Endowment for International Peace, March 28, 2005. https://carnegieendowment.org/2005/03/28/kyrgyzstan-s-tulip-revolution-pub-16710.

Onishi, Norimitsu. "Canadian Politicians Who Criticize China Become Its Targets." *The New York Times*, July 15, 2023. https://www.nytimes.com/2023/07/15/world/americas/canada-china-election-interference.html.

Osiander, Andreas. "Sovereignty, International Relations, and the Westphalian Myth." *International Organization* 55, no. 2 (2001): 251–87.

"Osnovnye polizheniia voennoi doktriny Rossiskoi Federatsii." *Izvestiia*, November 19, 1993: 1.

Owen, John M. "The Foreign Imposition of Domestic Institutions." *International Organization* 56, no. 2 (2002): 375–409.

Pearson, Lionel. "Propaganda in the Archidamian War." *Classical Philology* 31, no. 1 (1936): 33–52.

Pee, Robert. "Containing Revolution: Democracy Promotion, the Cold War and US National Security." *International Politics* 55 (2018): 693–711.

Pflitsch, Markus. "Quantum Computers Could Make Today's Encryption Defenseless." *Forbes*, May 4, 2023. https://www.forbes.com/sites/forbestech

council/2023/05/04/quantum-computers-could-make-todays-encryption-defe
nseless/?sh=7f5a47478556.

Pinto-Duschinsky, M. "Foreign Political Aid: The German Foundations and
Their US Counterparts." International Affairs 67, no. 1 (1991): 33–63.

Pleikys, Rimantas. "Radio Jamming in the Soviet Union, Poland and Other East
European Countries." Atentop, January 2006. http://www.antentop.org/008/
jamm008.htm.

Pons, Silvio. "Stalin, Togliatti, and the Origins of the Cold War in Europe."
Journal of Cold War Studies 3, no. 2 (2001): 3–27.

Poznansky, Michael. "Feigning Compliance: Covert Action and International
Law." International Studies Quarterly 63, no. 1 (2019): 72–84. https://doi.org/
10.1093/isq/sqy054.

Prabhu, K. S. Vishnu. "Kautilya's Views on Espionage and Its Current
Relevance." Research on Humanities and Social Sciences 5, no.7 (2015): ISSN
(Paper) 2224-5766; ISSN (Online) 2225-0484. https://www.iiste.org.

"Presidential Candidates May Be Vulnerable to Foreign Hackers, US Says." The
Guardian, May 18, 2016. https://www.theguardian.com/us-news/2016/may/
18/presidential-candidates-hacking-spying-trump-clinton.

Rehman, Iskander. "Raison d'Etat: Richelieu's Grand Strategy During the
Thirty Years' War." Texas National Security Review 2, no. 3 (2019): 38–75.
http://dx.doi.org/10.26153/tsw/2928.

Reiter, Dan. "Gulliver Unleashed? International Order, Restraint, and the Case
of Ancient Athens." International Studies Quarterly 65, no. 3 (2021): 582–93.
https://doi.org/10.1093/isq/sqab061.

Resis, Albert. "Russophobia and the 'Testament' of Peter the Great, 1812-1980."
Slavic Review, Winter, 1985, Vol. 44, No. 4 (Winter, 1985): 681–93.

Rid, Thomas. "Cyber War Will Not Take Place." Journal of Strategic Studies 35,
no. 1 (2012): 5–32.

Root, Danielle, and Liz Kennedy. "9 Solutions to Secure America's Elections."
Americanprogress.org, August 16, 2017. Accessed October 30, 2023. https://
www.americanprogress.org/article/9-solutions-secure-americas-elections.

Rositzke, Harry. "America's Secret Operations: A Perspective." Foreign Affairs 53,
no. 2 (1975): 334–51.

"Russian Military Doctrine Today in Light of the New Realities." Zarubezhnaya
Voennoie Obozrenie (1994): 2, as translated and reprinted in JPRS-UFM-94-
005; and, for the recent version, "Voennaia Doktrina Rossiskoy Federatsii."
www.scrf.gov.ru.

Rutenberg, Jim. "The Untold Story of 'Russiagate' and the Road to War in
Ukraine." The New York Times Magazine, November 2, 2022. https://www.
nytimes.com/2022/11/02/magazine/russiagate-paul-manafort-ukraine-
war.html.

Samuelsohn, Darren. "Facebook: Russian-Linked Accounts Bought $150,000 in
Ads During 2016 Race." Politico, September 6, 2017. https://www.politico.
com/story/2017/09/06/facebook-ads-russia-linked-accounts-242401.

Schimmelpenninck van der Oye, David. "Paul's Great Game: Russia's Plan to Invade British India." *Central Asian Survey* 33, no. 2 (2014): 143–52.

Schneier, Bruce. "AI Disinformation Is a Threat to Elections: Learning to Spot Russian, Chinese and Iranian Meddling in Other Countries Can Help the US Prepare for 2024." *The Conversation*, September 29, 2023. https://theconve rsation.com/ai-disinformation-is-a-threat-to-elections-learning-to-spot-russ ian-chinese-and-iranian-meddling-in-other-countries-can-help-the-us-prep are-for-2024-214358.

Selvage, Douglas. "Operation 'Denver': The East German Ministry of State Security and the KGB's AIDS Disinformation Campaign, 1985–1986: Part 1." *Journal of Cold War Studies* 21, no. 4 (2019): 71–123.

Selvage, Douglas. "Operation 'Denver': The East German Ministry for State Security and the KGB's AIDS Disinformation Campaign, 1986–1989: Part 2." *Journal of Cold War Studies* 23, no. 3 (2021): 4–80.

Sheldon, Rose Mary. "Jesus as a Security Risk: Insurgency in First Century Palestine?" *Small Wars & Insurgencies* 9, no. 2 (1998): 1–37.

Sheldon, Rose Mary. "Jesus as a Security Risk." *War on the Rocks*, February 10, 2016. Accessed October 21, 2023. https://warontherocks.com/2016/02/jesus-as-a-security-risk-intelligence-and-repression-in-the-roman-empire.

Singleton, Craig. "Chinese Election Meddling Hits the Midterms." *Foreign Policy*, November 4, 2022. https://foreignpolicy.com/2022/11/04/china-us-midterm-election-interference-meddling-social-media-cybersecurity-disinfo rmation.

Slate, James. "How the Soviet Union Helped Shape the Modern Peace Movement." *Medium*, January 29, 2018. https://jameslate.medium.com/how-the-soviet-union-helped-shape-the-modern-peace-movement-d797071d4b2c.

Solana, Javier, and Strobe Talbott. "Opinion: The Decline of the West and How to Stop It." *The New York Times*, October 20, 2016. https://www.nytimes.com/2016/10/20/opinion/the-decline-of-the-west-and-how-to-stop-it.html.

Soldatov, Andrei, and Irina Borogan. "Russian Cyberwarfare: Unpacking the Kremlin's Capabilities." Center for European Policy Analysis, September 8, 2022. https://cepa.org/comprehensive-reports/russian-cyberwarfare-unpack ing-the-kremlins-capabilities.

Stafford, David. "A Moral Tale: Anglo-German Relations, 1860–1914." *International History Review* 4, no. 2 (1982): 249–63. http://www.jstor.org/sta ble/40105201.

Stirk, Peter. "The Westphalian Model and Sovereign Equality." *Review of International Studies* 38, no. 3 (2012): 641–60.

Stone, James. "Bismarck Versus Gladstone: Regime Change and German Foreign Policy, 1880–1885." *Historische Mitteilungen Der Ranke-Gesellschaft* 23 (2010): 167–200.

Stone, James. "Bismarck ante Portas! Germany and the Seize Mai Crisis of 1877." *Diplomacy & Statecraft* 23, no. 2 (2012): 209–35.

Stout, Mark, and Michael Warner. "Intelligence Is as Intelligence Does." *Intelligence and National Security* 33, no. 4 (2018): 517–26.

Styles, William. "The World Federation of Scientific Workers, a Case Study of a Soviet Front Organisation: 1946–1964." *Intelligence and National Security* 33, no. 1 (2018): 116–29.

Sushentsov, A. A., and William C. Wohlforth. "The Tragedy of US–Russian Relations: NATO Centrality and the Revisionists' Spiral." *International Politics* 57, no. 3 (2020): 427–50.

Szal, Andy. "Report: Russian 'Internet Trolls' Behind Louisiana Chemical Explosion Hoax." *Manufacturing.net*, June 3, 2015. https://www.manufactur ing.net/operations/news/13099148/report-russian-internet-trolls-behind-louisi ana-chemical-explosion-hoax.

Tatlow, Didi Kirsten. "Exclusive: 600 U.S. Groups Linked to Chinese Communist Party Influence Effort with Ambition Beyond Election." *Newsweek*, October 26, 2020. https://www.newsweek.com/2020/11/13/exclus ive-600-us-groups-linked-to-chinese-communist-party-influence-effort-ambit ion-beyond-1541624.html.

Tucker, Eric, and Nomaan Merchant. "US Warns About Foreign Efforts to Sway American Voters." Associated Press, October 3, 2022. https://apnews.com/arti cle/2022-midterm-elections-russia-ukraine-campaigns-presidential-ea913f2b3 b81865ia9db1327adaa330a.

U.S. Department of Justice, Office of Public Affairs. "Russian Project Lakhta Member Charged with Wire Fraud Conspiracy." September 10, 2020. https://www.justice.gov/opa/pr/russian-project-lakhta-member-charged-wire-fraud-conspiracy.

U.S. Department of Justice, Office of Public Affairs. "Two Iranian Nationals Charged for Cyber-Enabled Disinformation and Threat Campaign Designed to Influence the 2020 U.S. Presidential Election." November 18, 2021. https://www.justice.gov/opa/pr/two-iranian-nationals-charged-cyber-enabled-disinformation-and-threat-campaign-designed.

Uttaro, Ralph A. "The Voices of America in International Radio Propaganda." *Law and Contemporary Problems* 45 (1982): 103–22. https://scholarship.law. duke.edu/lcp/vol45/iss1/6.

Villatoux, Marie-Catherine. "The Fight Against Subversion in France in the Forties and Fifties." *Dans Inflexions* 14, no. 2 (2010): 165–72.

Vincent, Isabel. "New Yorker Yan Xiong Reveals What It's Like to Be Spied on by Chinese Police in US." *New York Post*, November 1, 2022. https://nypost.com/2022/11/01/new-yorker-yan-xiong-reve als-what-its-like-to-be-spied-on-by-china-in-us.

Vinocour, John. "KGB Officers Try to Infiltrate Anti-War Groups." *The New York Times*, July 26, 1983: A1. https://www.nytimes.com/1983/07/26/ world/kgb-officers-try-to-infiltrate-antiwar-groups.html.

"Warlord Killed in Chechnya Was Ex-U.S. Marine." *Ria Novosti*, March 24, 2005. Accessed October 22, 2023. https://www.globalsecurity.org.

Warner, Michael. "A Matter of Trust: Covert Action Reconsidered." *Studies in Intelligence* 63, no. 4 (2019): 33–41.

Watkins, Ali. "Obama Team Was Warned in 2014 About Russian Interference." *Politico*, August 14, 2017. Accessed February 6, 2024. https://www.politico.com/story/2017/08/14/obama-russia-election-interference-241547.

Weiss, Gus W. "The Farewell Dossier: Duping the Soviets." *Studies in Intelligence* 39, no. 5 (1996): 121–26.

Wilde, Gavin. "From Panic to Policy: The Limits of Foreign Propaganda and the Foundations of an Effective Response." *Texas National Security Review* 7, no. 2 (2024): 42–55.

Williams, Pete, Andrew Blankstein, and Jonathan Dienst. "Justice Department Accuses Chinese Agents of Trying to Intimidate Critics in the U.S." NBC News, March 16, 2022. https://www.nbcnews.com/politics/national-security/justice-department-accuses-chinese-agents-trying-intimate-critics-us-rcna20306.

Wohlforth, William C. "The Stability of a Unipolar World." *International Security* 24, no. 1 (1999): 5–41.

Wohlforth, William C. "Realism and Great Power Subversion." *International Relations* 34, no. 4 (2020): 459–81.

Wohlforth, William C., and Vladislav M. Zubok. "An Abiding Antagonism: Realism, Idealism, and the Mirage of US–Russian Partnership in the End of the Cold War." *International Politics* 54, no. 4 (2017): 405–19.

Wolfe, Audra. "Project Troy: How Scientists Helped Refine Cold War Psychological Warfare." *The Atlantic*, December 1, 2018. https://www.theatlantic.com/science/archive/2018/12/project-troy-science-cold-war-psychological-warfare/576847.

"Wuhan Lab Leak Theory: How Fort Detrick Became a Centre for Chinese Conspiracies." BBC News, August 23, 2021. Accessed November 2, 2023. https://www.bbc.co.uk/news/world-us-canada-58273322

Zabrodskyi, Mykhaylo, Jack Watling, Oleksandr Danylyuk, and Nick Reynolds. "Preliminary Lessons in Conventional Warfighting from Russia's Invasion of Ukraine: February–July 2022." Royal United Services Institute, November 30, 2022. https://www.rusi.org/explore-our-research/publications/special-resources/preliminary-lessons-conventional-warfighting-russias-invasion-ukraine-february-july-2022.

Zhang, Ping. "China-Backed Hackers Target Biden Campaign in Early Sign of 2020 Election Interference." Voice of America, June 15, 2020. https://www.voanews.com/a/usa_us-politics_china-backed-hackers-target-biden-campaign-early-sign-2020-election-interference/6191166.html.

## Reports and Pamphlets

"Americans Split on Relationship with Russia." AP–NORC Center for Public Affairs Research, October 2, 2020. https://apnorc.org/projects/americans-split-on-relationship-with-russia.

Choi, Seong Hyeon. "North Korea's Provocative and Secret Interventions in South Korean Elections." Center for Strategic and International Studies, March 7, 2022. https://www.csis.org/blogs/new-perspectives-asia/north-koreas-provocative-and-secret-interventions-south-korean.

"Countering Disinformation in the United States: CSC White Paper #6." Cyber Solarium Commission, December 2021. https://www.solarium.gov/public-communications/disinformation-white-paper.

Cunningham, Michael. "Why State Legislatures Must Confront Chinese Infiltration." Heritage Foundation, July 27, 2022. https://www.heritage.org/asia/report/why-state-legislatures-must-confront-chinese-infiltration.

"Democracy Promotion: An Objective of US Foreign Assistance." Congressional Research Service, January 4, 2019. https://sgp.fas.org/crs/row/R44858.pdf.

"Democracy Promotion Programs Funded by the US Government: A Report to the Senate Foreign Relations Committee and the House Foreign Affairs Committee of the US Congress." U.S. Agency for International Development, n.d. https://pdf.usaid.gov/pdf_docs/Pcaaa756.pdf.

Ellehuus, Rachel. "Mind the Gaps: Assessing Russian Influence in the United Kingdom." Center for Strategic and International Studies, July 2020. https://csis-website-prod.s3.amazonaws.com/s3fs-public/publication/20720_Ellehuus_GEC_FullReport_FINAL.pdf.

"Examining the Clinton Record on Democracy Promotion." Carnegie Europe, September 12, 2000. https://carnegieeurope.eu/2000/09/12/examining-clinton-record-on-democracy-promotion-event-197..

Galeotti, Mark. "Controlling Chaos: How Russia Manages Its Political War in Europe." Policy brief. European Council on Foreign Relations, August 2017. https://ecfr.eu/wp-content/uploads/ECFR228_-_CONTROLLING_CHAOS1.pdf.

Garriaud-Maylam, Joëlle. "The Russian War on Truth: Defending Allied and Partner Democracies Against the Kremlin's Disinformation Campaigns." Draft general report. NATO Committee on Democracy and Security, July 13, 2023. https://www.nato-pa.int/download-file?filename=/sites/default/files/2023-09/014%20CDS%2023%20E%20rev.1%20-%20RUSSIA%20DISINFORMATION%20-%20GARRIAUD-MAYLAM%20REPORT_0.pdf.

Giles, Keir. "Russia's 'New' Tools for Confronting the West: Continuity and Innovation in Moscow's Exercise of Power." Chatham House, March 21, 2016. https://www.chathamhouse.org/2016/03/russias-new-tools-confronting-west-continuity-and-innovation-moscows-exercise-power.

"Investigation of Illegal or Improper Activities in Connection with 1996 Federal Election Campaigns." U.S. Senate Committee on Foreign Affairs, 105th

Congress, March 10, 1998. https://www.govinfo.gov/content/pkg/CRPT-105
srpt167/html/CRPT-105srpt167-pt1.htm.

Jones, Seth G. "Russian Meddling in the United States: The Historical Context
of the Mueller Report." CSIS Brief. Center for Strategic and International
Studies, March 27, 2019. https://www.csis.org/analysis/russian-meddling-uni
ted-states-historical-context-mueller-report.

Jones, Seth G., Emily Harding, Catrina Doxsee, Jake Harrington, and Riley
McCabe. "Competing Without Fighting: China's Strategy of Political
Warfare." Center for Strategic and International Studies, August 2, 2023.
https://www.csis.org/analysis/chinas-strategy-political-warfare.

Kramer, Mark. "The Soviet Roots of Meddling in U.S. Politics." PONARS
Eurasia Policy Memo No. 452, January 2017.

Kurlantzick, Joshua. "China's Growing Attempts to Influence U.S. Politics."
Council on Foreign Relations, October 31, 2022. https://www.cfr.org/article/
chinas-growing-attempts-influence-us-politics.

"Most Americans Think Russia Tried to Interfere in Presidential Election." CBS-
SSRS, January 18, 2017. https://www.cbsnews.com/news/most-americans-
think-russia-tried-to-interfere-in-presidential-election/.

Mueller, Robert. "Report on the Investigation into Russian Interference in the
2016 Presidential Election." U.S. Department of Justice, 2019.

"National Defense Strategy of the United States of America." U.S. Department
of Defense, October 2022. https://media.defense.gov/2022/Oct/27/2003103
845/-1/-1/1/2022-NATIONAL-DEFENSE-STRATEGY-NPR-MDR.PDF.

National Intelligence Council. "Foreign Threats to the 2020 US Federal
Elections." ICA 2020-000778D. March 10, 2021. https://www.dni.gov/files/
ODNI/documents/assessments/ICA-declass-16MAR21.pdf.

Nimmo, Ben. "Removing Coordinated Inauthentic Behavior from China and
Russia." Meta, September 27, 2022. https://about.fb.com/news/2022/09/
removing-coordinated-inauthentic-behavior-from-china-and-russia/.

"NIST Announces First Four Quantum-Resistant Cryptographic Algorithms."
National Institute of Standards and Technology, July 5, 2022. https://www.
nist.gov/news-events/news/2022/07/nist-announces-first-four-quantum-resist
ant-cryptographic-algorithms#:~:text=—%20The%20U.S.%20Departm
ent%20of%20Commerce%27s,we%20rely%20on%20every%20day.

Office of the Director of National Intelligence, Intelligence Community
Assessment. "Background to 'Assessing Russian Activities and Intentions in
Recent US Elections': The Analytic Process and Cyber Incident Attribution."
January 6, 2017. https://www.dni.gov/files/documents/ICA_2017_01.pdf.

Organization for Security and Co-operation in Europe. "Final Statement of the
OSCE/ODIHR Observer Mission." July 5, 1997. https://www.osce.org/files/f/
documents/a/9/16282.pdf.

"Preparing for 2020: How Illinois Is Securing Elections: Field Hearing Before
the Committee on Homeland Security, House of Representatives, October 15,
2019." U.S. Government Publishing Office, 2020. Accessed October 30, 2023.

https://www.govinfo.gov/content/pkg/CHRG-116hhrg40456/html/CHRG-116hhrg40456.htm.

"Public Confidence in Mueller's Investigation Remains Steady." Pew Research Center, March 15, 2018. https://www.pewresearch.org/politics/2018/03/15/public-confidence-in-muellers-investigation-remains-steady.

Radin, Andrew, Alyssa Demus, and Krystyna Marcinek. "Understanding Russian Subversion: Patterns, Threats, and Responses." RAND Corporation, 2020. https://www.rand.org/pubs/perspectives/PE331.html.

"Report of the Select Committee on Intelligence, United States Senate, on Russian Active Measures Campaigns and Interference in the 2016 U.S. Election, Volume 2: Russia's Use of Social Media with Additional Views." Select Committee on Intelligence, October 2019.

"Safeguarding Our Future: Protecting Government and Business Leaders at the U.S. State and Local Level from People's Republic of China (PRC) Influence Operations." National Counterintelligence and Security Center, July 2022. https://www.dni.gov/files/NCSC/documents/SafeguardingOurFuture/PRC_Subnational_Influence-06-July-2022.pdf.

Senate Select Committee on Intelligence. S. Rep. No. 116-290, 116th Cong., 2d Sess. (2020).

Soldatov, Andrei, and Irina Borogan. "Russian Cyberwarfare: Unpacking the Kremlin's Capabilities." Center for European Policy, September 8, 2022. https://cepa.org/comprehensive-reports/russian-cyberwarfare-unpacking-the-kremlins-capabilities.

United States of America v. Viktor Borisovich Netyksho, et al. United States District Court for the District of Columbia, July 13, 2018. https://nsarchive.gwu.edu/document/16702-indictment.

U.S. Information Agency. "Soviet Active Measures in the 'Post-Cold War' Era, 1988–1991. June 1992.

The White House. "The National Security Strategy of the United States of America." September 2002. https://georgewbush-whitehouse.archives.gov/nsc/nss/2002/.

The White House. "The National Security Strategy of the United States of America." October 2022. https://www.whitehouse.gov/wp-content/uploads/2022/10/Biden-Harris-Administrations-National-Security-Strategy-10.2022.pdf.

## Dissertations and Unpublished Manuscripts

Albanese, David C. S. "In Search of a Lesser Evil: Anti-Soviet Nationalism and the Cold War." PhD Diss., Northeastern University, 2015. https://doi.org/10.17760/D20194401.

Geoghegan, Kate. "The Specter of Anarchy, the Hope of Transformation: The Role of Non-State Actors in the U.S. Response to Soviet Reform and Disunion, 1981–1996." PhD Diss., University of Virginia, 2015.

Hale, Eric T. "A Quantitative and Qualitative Evaluation of the National Endowment for Democracy." PhD Diss., Louisiana State University, 2003.

Lane, Michael David. "'Of Whims and Fancies': A Study of English Recusants Under Elizabeth, 1570–1595." Master's Diss., Louisiana State University, 2015. https://repository.lsu.edu/gradschool_theses/4240.

Lubin, Matthew L. "International Aspects of the Ridolfi Plot." Undergraduate Diss., Dartmouth College, January 1, 1997.

Nutt, Cullen. "Sooner Is Better: Covert Action to Prevent Realignment." PhD Diss., Massachusetts Institute of Technology, 2019.

O'Rourke, Lindsey A. "Secrecy and Security: U.S.-Orchestrated Regime Change During the Cold War." PhD Diss., University of Chicago, 2018.

Savchenko, Pavlo. "The Insurgent Movement in Ukraine During the 1940s and 1950s: Lessons Learned from the Case Study of the Ukrainian Insurgent Army (OUN-UP)." Thesis presented to the faculty of the U.S. Army Command and General Staff College, Fort Leavenworth, Kansas, 2012.

Selvage, Douglas, and Christopher Nehring. "Operation 'Denver': KGB and Stasi Disinformation Regarding AIDS." Wilson Center, July 22, 2019. Accessed October 24, 2023. https://www.wilsoncenter.org/blog-post/operat ion-denver-kgb-and-stasi-disinformation-regarding-aids.

Stone, James. "Religion, Rivalry or Regime Change? Bismarck, Arnim and the Pastoral Letters Crisis of 1873/4." Unpublished manuscript, n.d.

Trachtenberg, Marc. "Soviet Policy in 1945: Some Research Notes. UCLA Department of Political Science, n.d.

## Lectures, Interviews, Testimony, and Archival Materials

Bismarck, Otto von, to William I. June 1873. Frankreich. 78/2. NFA. Vol. 1, 534–37. Politisches Archiv des Auswärtigen Amts, Berlin, Germany. Courtesy of Dr. James Stone.

Hayden, Michael. "Interview with Charlie Rose." *CBS Mornings*, January 17, 2017. https://www.youtube.com/watch?v=CwElxbmr2YU.

Kagan, Donald. "Philip of Macedon: Twilight of the Polis in Ancient Greece." Lecture, December 6, 2007, published on Brewminate, January 29, 2017. https://brewminate.com/philip-of-macedon-twilight-of-the-polis-in-ancient-greece/.

Nutt, Cullen. "When the Clever See Danger: U.S. Covert Action in Portugal." Draft working paper, Notre Dame Emerging Scholars Conference, n.d. https://ndisc.nd.edu/assets/320705/portugal_for_ndisc_nutt_fnl.pdf.

Report by Stolberg to the Foreign Office. August 4, 1877. No. 288. R6486. Frankreich 79. Stolberg. Politisches Archiv des Auswärtigen Amtes, Berlin, Germany. Courtesy of Dr. James Stone.

Rumer, Eugene. "Statement Prepared for the U.S. Senate Select Committee on Intelligence Hearing: 'Disinformation: A Primer in Russian Active Measures

and Influence Campaigns.'" March 30, 2017. https://www.govinfo.gov/cont
ent/pkg/CHRG-115shrg25362/html/CHRG-115shrg25362.htm.

Watts, Clint. "Statement Prepared for the U.S. Senate Select Committee on
Intelligence Hearing: 'Disinformation: A Primer in Russian Active Measures
and Influence Campaigns.'" March 30, 2017. https://www.intelligence.senate.
gov/sites/default/files/documents/os-cwatts-033017.pdf.

Wilde, Gavin. "Panic at the Info: The Limitations of Online Manipulation."
Unpublished manuscript, n.d.

# INDEX